The Revolution

Then I saw a new heaven and a new earth;
for the first heaven and the first earth had passed away,
and the sea was no more.
And I saw the holy city, the new Jerusalem,
coming down out of heaven from God,
prepared as a bride adorned for her husband.
(Revelation 21:1-2 NRSV)

The Revolution of the Candles

Christians in the Revolution of the German Democratic Republic

by Jörg Swoboda
edited by Richard V. Pierard
translated by Edwin P. Arnold

Mercer University Press

ISBN 0-86554-481-6   MUP/P125

The Revolution of the Candles.
Christians in the Revolution of the German Democratic Republic
Copyright ©1996
Mercer University Press, Macon, Georgia 31210-3960 USA
Abridged translation and revised edition of
Die Revolution der Kerzen.
Christen in den Umwälzungen der DDR
(Wuppertal und Kassel: Oncken Verlag, 1990)
All rights reserved
Produced in the United States of America
First edition June 1996

The paper used in this publication meets the minimum requirements
of American National Standard for Information Sciences—
Permanence of Paper for Printed Library Materials, ANSI Z39.48-1984.

Library of Congress Cataloging-in-Publication Data

Revolution der Kerzen. English.
The revolution of the candles : Christians in the revolution
of the German Democratic Republic / [compiled and edited]
by Jörg Swoboda ; [translation] edited by Richard V. Pierard ;
translated by Edwin P. Arnold.
xxxii+204pp. 6x9" (15x23cm.).
Includes bibliographical references.
ISBN 0-86554-481-6
1. Church and state—Germany (East)—History—20th century.
2. Germany (East)—Politics and government—1989–1990.
3. Germany (East)—Church history—20th century.
4. Baptists—Germany (East)—History—20th century.
I. Swoboda, Jörg.
BR856.35.R48   1996
261.7'09431'09048—dc20   96-21619
                                                    CIP

Contents

Foreword

by Jörg Swoboda

Ten years prior to the peaceful revolution in the former East Germany, the well-known evangelist Dr. Theo Lehmann and I wrote a song that contained an explicitly political statement:

> The mighty come and go,
> And every monument falls also.
> Only he remains who stands upon God's Word,
> The safest place on earth.

Within a few weeks the song captured the hearts of Christians in both halves of Germany. It was soon published in the West on an LP and found its way into many song books.

In 1988, one year before the *Wende*, the turning point, as the East German revolution was popularly called, a conference on youth missions took place in Nuremberg, West Germany. Dr. Lehmann and I were among the delegates from East Germany. At the concluding worship service we sat on the stage. Dr. Lehmann preached to the thirty thousand participants, and I led them in singing this song. The site of the meeting added to the intensity of this already tremendous experience. It took place on a large open field known as the Zeppelinwiese, the very spot where in the 1930s millions of people congregated for the annual conventions of the Nazi Party. After the war American soldiers destroyed the monumental colonnade that had been erected behind the thousand-foot-long platform where the Third Reich's leaders observed the celebrations. However, the platform remained as well as the tribune from which Hitler poured forth his diatribes, filled with insanity, hatred, and godlessness.

On the platform was erected the small stage where I sang this song. With outstretched arms I pointed to Hitler's dais, and cold chills ran up and down my spine because of the uniqueness of the moment. Only in the remotest corner of our hearts did we dare to believe that the mighty ones in East Germany would depart within our lifetime.

Just one year later we saw how the mighty would go. The atheistic "human-divinities" fell from their self-made, red-painted heavens, and their personal failings were exposed for all to see. The highest ranking official, Erich Honecker, was secretly spirited out of the country by the Russians but returned several months later to stand trial at the demand of the German authorities. After the trial was shamefully aborted, he went in exile to Chile and died shortly afterwards.

"We are the people!" That was the cry of the East German demonstrators during the year of the *Wende*, 1989. "*We* are the people!" This primal scream of a people throwing off the yoke of tyranny has always been the first cry of democracy. It thoroughly contradicted the groundless assertion of the leaders of the German Democratic Republic that *they* were the elected executors of the will of the majority, or, even more, the executors of the will of destiny.

This cry evolved through a three-step process: "We want out!" (to West Germany); "We'll stay here!"; and finally, "We are the people!" "We"—how marvelous that word sounded! It was a new word for us. The omnipotent Ministry of State Security, the *Stasi*, had made the people anxious, suspicious, and isolated. This expression *we* roared through the streets, first in Leipzig and Plauen, and then everywhere. At last our people proudly and self-confidently said no longer will we allow ourselves to be played off against one another. Abandoning our fears, we learned to stand tall. People who stand tall are beautiful.

I will never forget how we as parents in the GDR informed our children, under an oath of secrecy, about the true nature of communism. It was so hard for them to believe us because the truth was terribly dirty. However, during the *Wende* one could read it all in the papers. And then, we parents stood justified before our children. That was a key experience of the *Wende* period for our family, and it knit us together even more closely.

Those of us who were practicing Christians never defended our GDR citizenship on the basis that we liked the state, but rather that we had a task given to us by God. For the same reason, a few pastors had come over from the West in the 1950s in order to serve God among us.

Because I had been named one of the vice-chairs of the Youth Committee of the Baptist World Alliance, I was permitted from time to time to go to the West as a "business traveler on church business." Returning home by train was an unforgettable experience. As the train moved through the death strip in the divided city of Berlin, I prayed and looked out the window at the watchtowers and border guards, and I promised God to be faithful to my task and remain in the East. I thank God that he gave me and many other Christians the strength to perform our service without bitterness.

Soon another cry became intermingled with the slogan, "We are the people," and it grew stronger and stronger. During the Monday demonstrations it soon was the only phrase heard. "We are *one* people," exclaimed the marchers who thronged in the cities.

Still, at the time everyone was aware of one thing: this uprising could have cost us everything, including our lives. Only a few weeks earlier a bloodbath had taken place at Tiananmen Square, "the Square of Heavenly Peace," in Beijing, and one heard ugly rumors about a "Chinese solution." The authorities had formulated the orders to move against us and internment camps had been readied. A nurse in Leipzig, Raphaela Russ, whose account is included in this book, told us just how deadly serious the situation was on the night of October 9:

> The security forces stationed units of 100 men each about the city. . . . Parents were directed to pick up their children early from the kindergartens and daycare centers. . . . At the outskirts of the city . . . tanks were in readiness. The downtown area of the city looked like an armed camp. . . . Everyone was waiting for the order to the troops to move. At the blood-donor center thousands of units of blood were made ready.

That is the way it looked then. But thanks be to God that it turned out so differently!

Since 3 October 1990 we have been a united people. And we were the happiest people on the face of the earth, at least for the amount of time it takes to blink one's eye. Moreover, we East Germans had earned the right to enter into German unification with dignity because of our role in the peaceful revolution.

We are grateful that we as a people found a small window of peace in the midst of a world whose history has been filled with terror and war. God gave us the peaceful *Wende* and the unification of our divided country. That was, and remains, a miracle.

Not only did the church prove its worth as a place of refuge, but also it served as a place where persons could receive the proper orientation that would enable them to live with dignity in a totalitarian system. It offered a niche in the totalistic order where the state's hand did not reach. In a situation where the most important traditional social relationships had been cut off in the conscious, determined effort to build the new communist society, the church offered authentic human relationships.

Courageous pastors, youth workers, catechists, and countless lay people functioned at the grassroots of this church-centered effort, and they made an enormous contribution to the *Wende*. Many gained their first experience in practical democracy in the institutional church. In the midst of a totalitarian system they modeled democratic patters of behavior in their congregations. In so doing the elders transmitted to the young people an awareness of the God-given dignity of each individual. In a country characterized by silence, Christian gatherings served as training grounds for free expression of ideas. Still, one must not overlook the fact that many pastors did avoid making any specific references to the society or public order during their sermons.

In reality, every Christian congregation by its very existence publicly contradicted the state's doctrine that the church is a product of a society built on exploitation and, as such, was as good as dead. Many noted this contradiction and accordingly railed against the church. For example, a book *What Is Communism?* that was published by the GDR's Printing House for Youth asserted:

> The Christian faith poisons the human consciousness, hinders human intellectual and moral development, and disturbs societal involvement and frequently work activity. Even under conditions established by socialism, religion is a bulwark of ignorance which blocks the intellectual flourishing of the society.

The church did not always take such defamatory statements lying down. After all, thousands of church workers collaborated in the effort to shape the opinions and the conscience of the people. To be a voice for those who cannot speak is a vital part of the prophetic task of Christians in all parts of the world. Our faith in Jesus Christ is at its core a personal one, but it has practical consequences in life. It must carry out its prophetic dimension by preaching to the society.

Another important contribution of the churches was the principle of nonviolence. Monday after Monday thousands of demonstrators swarmed into the streets following the prayer services for peace. They went out to do battle with the giant Goliath, namely, the police, but unlike David they did not carry stones but candles in their hands.

Like a warm summer rain, the people motivated by reason and emotion streamed through the streets of the cities. Yet, there was not a single death to mourn. If the life of even one person had been lost, the consequences would have been inconceivable. The example of the peaceful Jesus, the principles of the Sermon on the Mount, and the restraining influence of the pastors all helped to produce nonviolence. In addition, the teachings and practical example of Martin Luther King, Jr. had a significant effect. Other factors included self-restraint on the part of the demonstrators and fear of the superior strength of the enemy.

Pastors of Protestant churches and in some cases Catholic figures as well were asked to assume the leadership of the round tables that began forming in November 1989, including the main one in Berlin. This happened because their upright lives had made them honorable and respected persons. The round table was the institution of the *Wende* that enabled face-to-face conversations between the old rulers and the representatives of the churches and the new political organizations. The round tables ceased after the elections on 18 March 1990, the first free elections in the history of the GDR, made them superfluous. Moreover, pastors often spoke at the public gatherings of the democratic movement, and when local Stasi headquarters were besieged by demonstrators and violence seemed imminent, pastors were called to help restore order. In some cases they even placed themselves like a shield in front of the beleaguered Stasi officials.

By virtue of their leadership roles in the various ecclesiastical institutions, pastors and church officials were the only dissidents who were skilled in the practice of administration. Thus, it was logical that many of them were elected to the new legislature or served as cabinet ministers, mayors, city managers, and presiding officers of the city councils. After reunification some were even elected to the federal parliament, the Bundestag. In our small town of Buckow, for example, the Baptist pastor became the mayor, while the director of the Baptist Theological Seminary was his deputy and later took over the office of mayor. I, a pastor and teacher at the seminary, was elected chair of the city council.

We are again *one* people, even if we—thank God—had always been one people in spite of the different standards of living, separate passports, and the Berlin Wall. What we now have to struggle with is the removal of the barriers that still separate us after forty years of having developed in totally different directions. Not only is this an intellectual, psychological, and economic challenge, but for Christians in particular it is also a spiritual challenge.

The current instability in the East results from several factors. Since the entire East German system of law was replaced by that of West Germany, we are virtually illiterate as far as legal matters are concerned. The violence that is so prevalent in the East, and according to experts even exceeds that in the much more populous West, had been nurtured over many years. The socialist system, whereby the state made up our minds for us, created a dangerous buildup of aggressive feelings. The orgies of violence that played year after year on West German television also helped pave the way and provided models for this kind of behavior. Then suddenly freedom came, and it was misunderstood as license. It caused the dams to break. What we had known for a long time about the West, we are now experiencing in the East: freedom without a purpose can only lead to moral self-destruction.

The repressed national consciousness emerged as brownshirted nationalism. It was enhanced by the normal tendency of youth to be rebellious and the single-minded agitation of West German neo-Nazis. The lukewarm response of the police and the courts to the violence against foreigners contributed false signals as well.

German reunification brought us the stable mark from the West, but economic growth has been much more elusive. People expected industries to flourish but instead industrial wastelands have arisen. Moreover, more than two million former owners of property in East German, most of whom had emigrated to the West, have filed application for the return of their possession. Because of the complicated legal question, investments are frozen and current residents are uncertain about their status of their homes.

Hopelessness is rampant. The suicide rate has soared while the birthrate has sunk to a third of what it had been. Unemployment is sky-high. To be sure, our West German brethren also suffer from this problem, but for workers in East Germany the loss of a job is a brand-new experience. The migration to the West continues. The mood is explosive in many areas. Some people here hold their heads in their hands and say: "We didn't go out onto the streets to demonstrate during the *Wende* just to be thrown out onto the streets now."

Many from the West tell us to just roll up our shirtsleeves and get to work. Actually, there are enough people who are willing and able to work here. But the factories are equipped with outdated machinery because the GDR government did not invest in modernizing its industrial plant. Investment capital is necessary for new production facilities but East Germany lacks this.

For us East Germans, the restrictions on speech and travel were our greatest annoyances, but reunification resolved this situation. Amazingly, hardly anyone speaks about these freedoms anymore, let alone expresses thankfulness for them.

For us as Christians this must not be the last word. Wherever our home may be, we should be living examples of thankfulness and contentedness. We "cannot forget what good things the Lord has done for us" (Psalm 103:2). At the same time, we will continue working together with others to insure that the miracle of German unification is not gambled away.

But as democratic and exemplary the society of the Federal Republic of Germany may be, it like the rest of this creation bears the stamp of the Fall of Man. To discern this and put aside all wild expectations is a difficult process. Change always produces uncertainty and fear. It is our task as Christians to point others to the "reasonable" faith in Christ the Apostle Paul commended to us. By so doing we encourage and help others, and thereby fulfill the will of God.

The bottom line for the church is the question of how it can recover that inner strength it possessed in centuries past and that will enable it to make a positive imprint on society. That requires changed men and women, individuals who have experienced a revolution of the heart brought about by the power of the Gospel of Christ.

Foreword

by Richard V. Pierard

My first encounter with East Germany was in February 1963 when I was a graduate student at Hamburg on a Fulbright scholarship doing research on my doctoral dissertation in German history. One part of the program was a week in Berlin, and here I had a chance to see the enormous contrasts between East and West. The wall had gone up only eighteen months earlier, and the bricked-up windows in the buildings on Bernauerstrasse and the border fortifications made a deep impression on me. In those days East Berlin was a dismal place, a dark and ruined city, except for a showpiece street from the Stalin era and a few restored buildings. The construction boom in the communist half of the city was just beginning.

Three months later I was given the rare opportunity to spend eighteen days in Potsdam working in the East German Central Archives. My research was on German colonial policy before World War I, a rather arcane topic, to say the least, and one so distantly removed in time as to present no ideological danger to the regime. In these weeks I learned firsthand what living in a communist dictatorship was like. I experienced the drab housing, simple food, inefficient transportation system, ubiquitous propaganda slogans, shops with poor quality goods, muzzled press, atmosphere of suspicion, and all-knowing police that for citizens of the German Democratic Republic was the way of life. The one exception was that I carried a passport with an exit visa and a fixed date when I had to leave the country. I also made a few acquaintances who, after they were convinced I really was an American and not a police spy, opened up and told me much about the realities of existence in the GDR.

Obviously I felt a huge sense of relief when my stay ended and I crossed over the border to the West, but my curiosity about this strange land had been whetted. After completing my doctorate, I began teaching at Indiana State University. In 1967 my wife and I spent several days in the GDR visiting historical sites, and this time I became acquainted with some active Christians. The experiences of believers in this officially atheistic land so impressed me that I published my first article about the church there in _Eternity_ magazine in August 1969. That same year I took an ISU student group to East Berlin, where I arranged for an official in the Ministry of Education to speak to them about life in his country. It was quite an experience for these young people from middle America to meet a real, live communist in the flesh.

In the 1970s I returned to East Germany several times with my lifelong friend and fellow historian Bob Linder from Kansas, and we made a point of visiting Christians, learning more about the church there, and sharing the insights we had gained in news articles for _Christianity Today_. In the following decade I took both of my children, David and Cindy, to the East so they could have some impression of what life was like there. As my list of contacts grew and experiences in the GDR multiplied, I even became sort of a minor authority on the country, and I occasionally gave lectures or slide presentations about it.

While serving as a Fulbright professor at the University of Frankfurt am Main in 1985, I witnessed the celebration of the fortieth anniversary of the end of World War II in Europe. Although the event was downplayed in West Germany, the GDR authorities pulled out all the stops to make it a festival of communist triumphalism. I obtained press credentials from the foreign ministry which enabled me to come to East Berlin and see the leaders of the state at close hand as they showcased the military and economic power of their socialist system. The following year I was back in Berlin to do some archival research on German colonialism, and I was even interviewed by the Christian Democratic Union's newspaper _Neue Zeit_ about the current religious and political situation in the United States.

Finally, in 1989 the opportunity of a lifetime came. As part of its effort to gain international respectability the GDR had recently agreed to take part in the Fulbright academic exchange program.

One of the positions scheduled to be filled that year was in U.S. history, and the person would have to be able to give lectures in German. I decided to apply and to my great surprise I was accepted. But then the GDR Ministry of Higher Education stalled on making the appointment. I was just about to give up the venture when word came through from East Berlin that I was to spend eight weeks at the country's flagship institution, Humboldt University in Berlin, and then transfer to the provincial Martin Luther University in Halle for the remainder of my stay.

This was indeed a strange arrangement, but I was positive that such a chance to live and work in a communist system like that of East Germany would not come my way again. It was now or never. Events would soon prove just how correct my decision was. Sometime after reunification had occurred, I learned from the person who was my sponsor at Humboldt University why this assignment had been made. A friend of his who was examining the files of the Ministry of Higher Education discovered that the secret police (the Stasi) had ordered this. I "had contacts with churches" and thus it was too risky to allow me to remain in a major city.

When I landed in Berlin on 18 September, I already possessed a good knowledge of the society and assumed that I would be under police surveillance, so I knew I had to be careful not to cause my friends unnecessary difficulties. What I did not realize was that I was about to find myself in the middle of a major revolution, and that I would be a "participant observer" in one of greatest human dramas of our times.

It was clear from the moment of my arrival that the GDR was in deep trouble. The rigidity and inadequacies of central planning had brought economic growth (which in the 1970s had been quite remarkable) to a standstill, and shortages plagued every sector of the economy. To be sure, in contrast to the other Soviet bloc countries, East Germany had relatively decent housing and food supplies for all; but in comparison with West Germany its citizens had little in the way of consumer goods. The lack of foreign exchange meant that many items people took for granted in the West were unavailable in the GDR except in the special "Intershops" where one could only spend Deutschmarks or other "hard" currencies.

The rising tide of discontent was particularly obvious in the numbers of people leaving for the West, both who applied through legal channels for permission to emigrate and who fled illegally. Thanks to the "shoot to kill" order given to the border guards, few made it across the minefields and fences demarking the 800 mile border between East and West Germany or over the Berlin Wall, but clever individuals could purchase false papers and escape through other Soviet bloc countries. Then during the summer of 1989 Hungary opened its border with Austria, and increasing numbers of East Germans fled through this new escape hatch. When the GDR authorities tried to stamp out the Buda "Pest" (a play on the German word for plague) by refusing visas for travel to Hungary, people who were fed up with the system thronged into the West German embassies in Prague and Warsaw seeking asylum. The nightly television news coverage in the outside world of these refugees became so embarrassing to the regime that it finally relented around the end of September and allowed them to go to the West.

Yet the tired and aged leaders of the GDR seemed incapable of realizing that this hemorrhage of people meant the socialist system was breaking down. The all-powerful secret police continued to maintain its rigid control over a populace that was becoming increasingly restive. Finally, the straw that broke the camel's back came on 7-8 October, the weekend of the fortieth anniversary of the GDR's founding. The head of state and party boss, Erich Honecker, had invited the leading lights of the socialist world to the grand birthday party in Berlin, including Soviet leader Mikhail Gorbachev. On the evening before, 100,000 young people paraded past the reviewing stand on Unter den Linden in a staged demonstration of support for Honecker's regime. The Free German Youth, the official youth organization, had brought them in by bus and train from all over the country. Standing a scant hundred yards from the reviewing stand, I noticed that some were shouting "Gorby, help us." On the next day, Saturday, 7 October, the customary military parade took place but it did not seem to me to have drawn a spectacular crowd. Most people gathered in the Alexanderplatz area to drink beer, listen to the many bands, browse in the craft stalls, and just enjoy a nice sunny day. Toward evening, some youths began a more or less spontaneous demonstration for democracy, and the police quickly moved in and broke it up with an inordinate expenditure of force.

On Sunday evening, three thousand people jammed into the Victorian brick Gethsemane Church in the Prenzlauer Berg district to pray and to protest the police brutality. It was a moving experience to see the dedication of these people. Upon leaving the church, they took to the street carrying lighted candles and were immediately confronted with another brutal police action. In response to this repression and the continuing exodus of GDR citizens, demonstrations erupted across the country after the Monday night prayer meetings for peace, a practice that had begun in Leipzig some months before and was spreading from town to town. The turning point in the rapidly rising crescendo of dissent may well have been in Leipzig the following evening, 9 October, when the police did not try to stop the demonstration.

From this point on, the GDR regime rapidly came unglued. Gorbachev had bluntly told the seventy-seven-year-old Honecker that East Germany's problems would have to be solved in East Berlin, and within ten days he had been ousted from power by his own party and replaced by the youthful Egon Krenz. The officials responsible for economic development and media policy also resigned. Most restrictions on the press were removed, and the newspapers and electronic media now reported the ongoing demonstrations and reform discussions in great detail. When I first came to East Berlin, I watched the West German television news to find out what was going on in the way of protests, demonstrations, illegal political meetings, and such, and then turned to the GDR network to see what was being covered up and what sort of ideological spins were being put on events. However, by late October I found the television (and newspaper as well) reports in the East to be so objective and interesting that I always tuned in here first to see what had happened in the GDR and then checked the Western news simply to see what interpretations were being put on the day's events. Intense discussions went on everywhere, especially in churches, and I remember going to one where the people pelted a local council leader for two hours with hard and often emotional questions about police actions, housing inadequacies, and ideological education in the public schools, which parents particularly resented.

The week of 4-11 November was surely the high point of this great adventure. On Saturday, 4 November, on Berlin's Alexanderplatz, I stood in the midst of a crowd of a half-million people (some estimates were even higher) who protested the Stalinist tactics of the Stasi, called for economic and educational reforms, and demanded the resignation of the Krenz government. It was the greatest mass rally in the history of the GDR, and the emotional impact of such a sea of humanity defies description. During the following days the Communist Party's Central Committee met in emergency session, and the situation had so deteriorated that even faithful party members were denouncing the leaders' policies and failures. My colleagues at Humboldt University invited me to join their demonstration in front of the party headquarters, an utterly unreal experience for an American who is a Baptist and Democratic Party member.

Then, as I sat watching the evening news on 9 November, the Berlin party chief announced during a press conference at 7:07 p.m. that the government had decided that all citizens would be free to travel. It took a while for the importance of this to sink in, but it meant that the Berlin Wall would no longer contain the populace. While East Berliners streamed through the crossings, crowds of West Berliners climbed on the wall in front of the Brandenburg Gate. During that remarkable weekend many hundreds of thousands thronged into West Berlin and untold numbers of others crossed over the borders into West Germany. On Saturday, one week after the Alexanderplatz demonstration, I stood on Bernauerstrasse (where I had been twenty-six years earlier) and watched the people pour through the opening the wall. It was such an emotional experience that I still cannot write about it without tears filling my eyes.

In fact, for me the meaning of all this was summed up in the service that Sunday at a small Baptist church in Berlin-Marzahn where I had been attending. After we all offered up our thanks to God during a special time of public prayer, we concluded by singing the seventeenth-century Lutheran hymn "Now Thank We All Our God." To this day, I cannot sing this hymn dry-eyed.

The pastor of the church also introduced me to Jörg Swoboda, who invited me to give some lectures at the Baptist seminary in Buckow on church-state relations, one of my research areas. While there, he asked me if I would contribute a piece to a book he was putting together on the East German revolution. He said that the perspective of an outsider who had experienced the events of the *annus mirabilis* would add something to the volume. There have been few assignments that I more gladly took on than this one, and my brief essay (in German, naturally) in *The Revolution of the Candles* was entitled, "The Reflections of an American on the *Wende*." For me it was a great honor to have been part of this symposium, and my sincere hope is that North American readers will find it just as inspiring as German ones have.

Many people have helped me to understand what life in the old East Germany was all about. I would like to thank four couples in particular: Dr. Rudolf and Angelika Treumann, who welcomed me into their home in spite of the personal and professional risk this entailed; Dr. Theo Lehmann and his wife Elke, with whom I share a common birthdate and whose witness for Christ has inspired me in more ways than they can imagine; Pastor Bruno and Ruth Schottstädt, who introduced me to their congregation and with whom I shared many of the events of the *Wende*; and Gottfried and Hilde Stenzel, pillars of the Baptist church in Halle who have been like a second family to us. Finally, I am grateful for the support and love of my wife Charlene, who allowed me to run off to East Germany so many times by myself but fortunately had the opportunity in 1989 to experience personally some of the events there.

Foreword

by Edwin P. Arnold

Although the events of 1989 lie some years in the past, their impact is still being felt throughout the world politically and economically. The Church of Jesus Christ as well can learn much from the courageous efforts of pastors, youth leaders, and ordinary Christians who took the Word of God seriously and, like David, went to do battle against Goliath.

Jörg Swoboda edited the original German version of this book out of a passion. Each of the contributors to this volume did so because of a passion. The story of the heroic efforts of the East German Protestant Church and the numerous groups that had rallied to produce this bloodless revolution simply had to be told. But what was it that compelled me to translate the book, which in its original was twice the length of this edited and abridged version, with no prospect of a publisher in sight?

It is amazing how a seemingly insignificant action can produce a chain of events that changes the course of one's life. In 1972, while teaching a class of advanced German students at Clemson University, the thought occurred to me that writing to young people in a German-speaking nation ought to provide a high degree of motivation for the students to learn the language. All the students agreed to write, and I sent off for names and addresses. Within a few days I received an envelope from the pen pal agency. Upon opening it, I was shocked to learn that more than half of the names provided, including the one intended for me, were of people in East Germany, known then as the German Democratic Republic.

Believing that contact with citizens in a communist state might somehow get them or us into difficulty, I was ready to return the names and request only ones from West Germany, Switzerland,

and Austria. But a call to the Federal Bureau of Investigation helped me to change my mind. An agency assured me that contacts like this were beneficial, and the students and I began writing.

In 1973–1974 I taught English at a *Gymnasium* (an academic high school) in Nabburg, Bavaria. During the spring break my family and I arranged to make a weekend trip to the home of my pen pal. It was an occasion that would change my life. I became convinced that I had to learn more about this mysterious country.

The opportunity came two years later. The GDR educational authorities regularly sponsored "Herder Institutes," summer sessions designed for German language teachers from all over the world, and I decided to enroll in one. But which of them would be best for me? Just then a brief news item in *Christianity Today* caught my attention. It mentioned an article by a Dr. Christoph Haufe regarding the activities of Christian young people outside of the established church at the state-run universities. He himself taught at the Protestant Seminary in Leipzig, a city that was not very far from my pen pal family. I applied for the Leipzig institute and was accepted. I was determined to meet this man and learn what I could about these activities. I was sure he could introduce me to others also.

The four and one-half weeks I spent in the German Democratic Republic opened my eyes. While sitting under the instruction of some of the country's foremost Germanists, I gained a hearty dose of socialist propaganda. But, during my free weekends, I not only visited my pen pals but I also met many Christians through Dr. Haufe's suggestions. Two of the most important were Dr. Hans Seidel, also at the Protestant Seminary, and Pastor Klaus Grabner of the St. Thomas Church in Leipzig. I cherish to this day the friendships I made then.

Prior to these two trips into East Germany, I assumed that only very few churches were open and that they were just small congregations comprised mainly of older women. I was surprised to see quite a different reality in virtually every service I attended. I experienced churches that were quite full and I heard sermons that could in no way be considered government propaganda. On the other hand, the dirty, drab, and dreary impression of the places in the country I visited contrasted sharply with what I had read in the GDR press and what I was being told at the Herder Institute. I was also enlightened by what I heard from many of the seminar participants from East Germany and other countries of the socialist bloc. I got quite an earful about the realities of life in these societies.

When I returned to my university in the fall I had a number of names and addresses that I had gotten while in Leipzig. My students were eager to write to them. But, pen and ink are one thing; personal encounters are of a much higher order. I was eager to go back and take students with me. In 1980 I led my first group of students to East Germany. Some professors went along as well. As was the case for all subsequent trips, all arrangements had to be made through *Jugendtourist*, the official agency that took care of all foreign youth groups desiring to travel in the GDR. We stayed for ten days and visited Weimar, Leipzig, Dresden, Berlin and Lommatzsch (my pen pal's town).

I followed a basic pattern, with some changes, for the next eight trips. The reactions of the students upon spending their first full day in the country were of shock, even though I thought I had prepared them in advance for what they would see. I will never forget the reaction of one coed, a well-balanced Christian, who was nearly hysterical on her first evening in the country. I honestly feared whether she would be able to cope with the remaining nine days. She did, and the reason was that she got to know a number of young people personally. (Unfortunately, she could not meet her own pen pal because he had been called up for service in the army.) She and most of the other students began to empathize with the people and the situations they had to put up with on a day-to-day basis.

Each trip provided me with more pen pals so that most participants had already corresponded with one or more East German young people before they left the U.S. In fact, this contact by mail led many students to decide to go on the next German Study Abroad Program. They wanted to meet their pen pals personally.

I could go on. The experiences with the students I would not exchange for any amount of money. We shared joys as well as terrible sadness, especially upon leaving our newfound friends.

One of my major objectives in taking students into the German Democratic Republic was to enable them to see firsthand what socialism was doing to a country. Much they could learn by simply looking. However, I wanted them to have opportunities to talk with people who were not afraid to tell the truth about the society. It is here that I am especially grateful to our Lord for the access we gained to Christian groups. In Leipzig, we regularly met with young people from the St. Thomas Church and/or the Leipzig Seminary. In Eisleben, Frau Margo Humbert and members of St. Ann's church were responsible for receptions that the students will long remember. Ironically, it was in 1989, shortly before the collapse of the whole system, that I received my first written warning from the director of *Jugendtourist*. This stated that any "privately arranged contacts" were forbidden. Yet, I can still vividly see Mrs. Humbert as she put her arm around our guide's shoulders and insisted that the group come to the church for a reception. We went.

When the borders were opened later that year and the government fell, I was delighted to learn of the role that the churches had played in the so-called "revolution of the candles." Then I became eligible for a sabbatical leave in the spring semester of 1993, and I chose as my research topic "The Role of the Church in the East German Revolution of the Candles." My plan was to go to Germany and interview leaders of the movement. Thanks to my friends who helped me with contacts, I was able to spend two weeks speaking with pastors and laypersons who had been on the front lines, so to speak. Included among these were Pastor Walter Schilling of Braunsdorf, and Pastors Christoph Wonneberger and Christian Führer in Leipzig. I was awestruck at the courage displayed by them and the millions of citizens who had had enough of the system.

Many thought I would write a book about these events, but by now more than three years had passed and a number of excellent books had already appeared. Besides, I really had never written a book before. However, one day as I was staying in a town near Bad Blankenburg, I noticed a poster announcing that a local church was serving as a satellite link for a Billy Graham crusade currently taking place in Europe. I went that evening and during the preliminaries saw Jörg Swoboda perform several Christian songs. I had never heard the name before. A week later, I was talking with an elder in a church in Leipzig and he mentioned a book called *Die*

Revolution der Kerzen (*The Revolution of the Candles*). The author was none other than Jörg Swoboda. After I began reading the book, I felt it ought to be translated into English. Here were statements made by Christians who had taken part in a revolution that had caused a regime to fall. And there were no known deaths!

For a long time I had been conscious that God was using my fluency in German and contacts I had made during my study-abroad trips and numerous other visits to the former East Germany for some higher purpose. At first, it seemed most important to me that American students got to see socialism first hand. With the passage of time, I came to realize that perhaps the most important thing these trips were producing was "the only real contact with freedom"—as my pen pal's wife Gudrun put it—that many of our East German friends had ever had.

God laid it upon my heart to translate this book in order to honor the courage and patience of the Christians in East Germany who had been instrumental in bringing about a miracle. However, I did not know how to go about getting a publisher. That is when Richard Pierard entered the picture. In the original edition, he contributed a chapter near the end giving the perspective of an American who had experienced the revolution while teaching in the country. When I reached that point, I immediately telephoned him in Indiana to tell him of my plan. He was delighted. He had wanted to do likewise, but since his field is history, not German, he didn't feel that he was the person for the job. He did give me a few suggestions, one of which was to contact a publisher called Smyth & Helwys.

Soon after this conversation, something I would regard as a "divine coincidence" occurred. In April 1994, Jörg Swoboda and his associate, the noted evangelist Dr. Theo Lehmann, came to North America for a speaking tour. I was able to arrange some meetings here in my area, including Furman University, a prestigious Baptist school. While at Furman they were asked to do a presentation in the chaplain's office. In introducing the two I mentioned that we were fairly sure the book would be published soon. At the end of the presentation, Dr. James Pitts, the chaplain, asked which publisher we had been talking with and I told him that Smyth & Helwys in Macon seemed interested. With an amused smile he said, "I'm the chairman of the board of Smyth & Helwys. I will do all I can to see that it is taken care of."

Eventually, Mercer University Press, with whom Smyth & Helwys is closely associated, was persuaded that *The Revolution of the Candles* should be issued by a university press, and Smyth & Helwys agreed.

This translation is dedicated to the memory of the hundreds of people who were killed or maimed in their attempt to escape to freedom. It is dedicated also to the leaders of the church and other groups who stood by their Christian principles, insisting upon love, forgiveness, and nonviolence. Last, but certainly not least, it is dedicated to the millions of "average citizens" who went onto the streets following these principles.

My desire is to make known to English-speaking Christians the causes behind one of the most significant events of the century. I have observed that most people in North America have only vague ideas about the revolution, and they are unaware that the churches played such an important role. As you will learn from the accounts that follow, Christians believed firmly that God was, in fact, honoring his Word. "The king's heart is in the hand of the Lord, like the rivers of water; he turneth it whithersoever He will. Every way of a man is right in his own eyes: but the Lord pondereth the hearts. To do justice and judgment is more acceptable to the Lord than sacrifice" (Proverbs 21:1-3 AV).

The Protestant churches did play a leading role in this unique revolution, but they were not the only organizations that contributed to the overthrow of communism in East Germany. And the church's record is not a spotless one, for large numbers of "collaborators" existed at the lowest as well as the highest levels.

Still, the record is one of courage and determination—from bishops down to grassroots Christians. As they stood for freedom and righteousness, they faced the possibility of humiliation, loss of jobs, imprisonment, beatings, and even death. Christians today can learn much from their experiences, and like them we too can praise the "God of history" for His faithfulness.

I wish to thank Reimar and Gudrun Zerm, my pen pals since 1972, for their friendship. Without their desire to have contact with the outside world, my career would have taken a different course and this book probably would never have seen the light of day in the English-speaking world. There are so many individuals who helped introduce me to the realities of life in East Germany, but four in particular stand out: Pastor Klaus Grabner and his wife Gisela, Dr. Hans Seidel, and Frau Margot Humbert.

Closer to home, I wish to thank Mrs. Ingrid Eisiminger and Dr. Andreas von Recum for their help with the translation of some difficult passages, and above all my wife Miriam, whose patience while I was away so many times in Germany and later was laboring on this translation exceeded all human expectations.

Note to the Reader

We have designed this book to communicate to you the flavor and passion of the East German Christians who laid their lives on the line during the revolution of 1989–1990 and participated in building a new and just social order. Thus, we have freely translated the passages from the German edition and added explanatory material in the text to make it easier to understand the events that took place. If you wish to pursue the topic in greater depth, you should consult the bibliography at the end of the book.

Bible verses quoted in the text with a few exceptions follow the wording of the New International Version.

Let Us Learn From Jesus

by Jörg Swoboda and Theo Lehmann

Let us learn from Jesus
    what he means by peace!
Even when it seems impossible for you,
    love your enemy.

This is when someone lays down his weapons
    and everyone thinks: he's crazy,
Because all of a sudden he's not winning the battle
    but rather winning over his enemy.

Hatred makes people nasty
    and turns their lives upside down.
Hatred undoes a life;
    only love builds it up.

Yes, this path is unworldly;
    it is foreign to our world.
This love is the power
    by which everything stands or falls.

Brother Judas

by Gerhard Schöne, 21 January 1990

Sit down next to me, Brother Judas.
take that rope off your neck.
Wipe the tears from your cheek.
enough has gone wrong already
that cannot be made right again.

You have spread mistrust among us
like weeds.
You have driven youths from the country,
Put many good people in prison,
and gotten rid of others.

You scribbled things in your school notebook
about every child.
You taught them to speak from both sides of their mouths,
To tell stories, to be hypocrites,
to walk softly and bend with the wind.

You drank the cup of friendship with me
as one of my brothers.
You read my mail,
listened to my telephone conversations,
were a guest in my home.

Then you wrote your reports,
you made a rope,
and out of it grew a network of nooses.
Many who were caught in them
had their necks broken.

And I too was your accomplice.
For a long time I gave you such a
sense of security.
By my silence and my tolerance,
I am partially to blame.

Treachery has consumed you.
Friendship is a mockery.
Your mind is corrupt
and your conscience almost dead
because of the thirty pieces of silver.

There you stand defenseless in the pillory.
People can spit on you.
Those who had never opened their mouths before,
who never stepped out of the shadows,
now are casting their stones.

Take a hot bath and scrub yourself!
You haven't been clean for a long time.
You must learn to repent and I to forgive.
Because we've got to live together,
    Judas, my little brother.

The East German State and the Churches

Richard V. Pierard

At the end of World War II Germany was in ruins. More than five million people had died on the battlefields or as a result of Allied air raids. The specter of starvation and disease threatened the lives of countless more. Twenty-five percent of the dwellings were uninhabitable. Millions of refugees from the eastern portions of Germany and displaced foreign laborers competed for the scarce housing and food. The transportation system had collapsed and industrial production was at a standstill. Local government and public services were virtually nonexistent. The German people were in a stupor due to twelve years of Nazi dictatorship and the devastating defeat, and they were paralyzed both morally and spiritually. Writers referred to this time in national life as "point zero."

The areas east of the Oder and Neisse Rivers, which included East Prussia and nearly all of Silesia and Pomerania, were detached from Germany and for all practical purposes annexed by Poland and the Soviet Union, while the victors (United States, Soviet Union, Great Britain, and France) divided the remainder of the country into military occupation zones. The capital city of Berlin also was partitioned into sectors, one for each occupying power. Because it lay inside the Soviet zone, the other three were guaranteed surface and air access from their zones in the West.

The Cold War and the Division of Germany

Although in their wartime conferences the Allies were unanimous in their determination to wipe out "militarism and Nazism," they could not agree on what to do with the defeated enemy other than to transfer sovereignty to an Allied Control Council, divide the country into occupation zones, hold war crimes trials, and engage in denazification. At the meeting in Potsdam in summer 1945 they did decide to set up essential administrative departments and to treat the economy as a whole, tasks which fell to the Allied Control Council, but in fact each power managed its zone as it pleased. The objective of the occupation was to enable Germany to get back on its feet while the Allied foreign ministers worked out a final peace treaty. But with the onset of the Cold War, all cooperation ceased and Germany's political and economic character came to mirror that of the two opposing sides. The Western powers merged the economic administrations of their zones, utilized Marshall Plan aid to assist recovery, and opened the way for self-government in the West. A key element of this effort was the introduction in their zones in spring 1948 of a new currency called the Deutschmark to replace the Reichsmark, whose value had been ruined by inflation.

For their part, the Soviets began restoring local government and even allowed several competing political parties to form. However, recognizing that the Communist Party did not enjoy widescale public support, they pressured the Social Democrats to merge with it to form the Socialist Unity Party (known by its initials as the SED) and the other parties to ally with the SED in an "antifascist democratic bloc." It soon became obvious that the SED was merely the Communist Party under a different name and the others existed only to rally public support for the official policies. The Soviets, who had suffered the greatest losses in the war, milked their zone for "reparations," even to the point of hauling away complete factories to Russia and forcing others to produce for the Soviet market.

The Soviets also wanted a unified Germany in which the Communists would play a decisive role, and they looked askance at the Western Allies' moves to establish genuine democracy in their zones and promote economic recovery. When the West in June 1948 introduced the new money in their sectors of Berlin, the Soviets denounced this as a violation of the postwar agreements on Germany and closed the surface routes to the capital city. Since an attempt to force their way into Berlin might trigger World War III, the Allies decided to try first to supply their half of the city by air.

The Berlin airlift frustrated the Russians' effort to force them out of the city and to halt the political consolidation of western Germany, and they ended the blockade ten months later.

Meanwhile, although Berlin was supposed to be under a common administration, Soviet actions prevented the non-Communist majority in the democratically elected city assembly from functioning. In September 1948 the Westerners walked out of the city hall, located in the Soviet sector, and set up a separate municipal government in their side of town. Thereupon, the Soviets recognized an SED-dominated regime in East Berlin.

Throughout occupied Germany the old *Land* (state) governments were reconstituted, and in the West they became the basis for a federal structure. They chose their own state parliaments and then their representatives, with Allied encouragement, adopted on 23 May 1949 a constitution known as the Basic Law for the Federal Republic of Germany. Chosen as the "provisional" capital was the university town of Bonn, south of Cologne. In the August elections for the parliament (the Bundestag) the Christian Democratic Party, a coalition of Catholics and conservative Protestants, gained the largest number of seats. When the CDU leader Konrad Adenauer formed a government the following month, the Western Allies granted the new West German regime limited sovereignty.

Although an Occupation Statute reserved certain rights to the Allies, the military authorities were replaced by civilian high commissioners. In 1951 the Western powers declared the state of war with Germany to be an end, although no peace treaty was in sight, and by 1955 all remaining restrictions on the Federal Republic had been removed and it became then a fully sovereign state. Only in Berlin did the Allies maintain their occupation rights.

Adenauer chose as his economics minister Ludwig Erhard, who put into place as system of welfare-state capitalism that stressed private ownership of productive assets and use of the market mechanism to set prices and wages. The government would not take engage in economic planning or own business enterprises but only intervene through welfare measures to assure that all members of the society benefited from the productivity generated by the pursuit of profit. The result of Erhard's measures and a vast infusion of capital from the United States through the Marshall Plan was a rapid and sweeping recovery that became known as the "economic miracle." Within a decade West Germany's level of productivity and standard of living were among the highest in the world. The devastated cities were rebuilt , democratic institutions were embraced by the populace, and cultural life flourished.

Adenauer aligned the Federal Republic with his Western neighbors in the efforts for European integration that led finally to the formation of the European Economic Community in 1957. He also utilized Cold War concerns in wake of the Korean War to bring about West German rearmament. First, he backed the European Defense Community scheme, which would have integrated West German troops into an international force along with those of other democratic countries. When it failed, he gained Allied permission to form a separate West German army, the Bundeswehr, and in 1955 his country joined the NATO alliance. Applicants for posts in the new army were screened to keep out militarists and convinced Nazis, and in order to forestall the dominance of professional military men, a conscription law was passed in 1956 obligating all able-bodied young men to a period of military or civilian alternative service. The Bundeswehr functioned under civilian control through the minister of defense and the parliament, rejected the German military tradition of unchallengeable authority and unquestioning obedience, and regarded itself as defense force in a democratic society comprised of civilians in uniform.

In the Soviet zone matters developed in a different direction. For one thing it had much less industrial and population resources that the three Western zones had. Its land area was slightly larger than the state of Ohio, ard population of 16 million was a quarter of that in the West. It was largely an agricultural region, with some heavy industry around Berlin and in Saxony and a few large chemical concerns. Brown coal or lignite, a low grade energy source, existed in substantial quantities and was recovered in large strip mines. Soviet demands for reparations put a heavy burden on an already weak economy.

From a political standpoint, during 1947–1948 a process of Stalinization took place in which the SED was transformed into an authoritarian party controlled by functionaries subservient to Moscow. Those members regarded as "unreliable" were purged, the Leninist principle of "democratic centralism" was introduced (authority exercised by the top leadership), and it was restructured along the lines of the Soviet Communist Party with a large Central Committee which nominally elected a Politburo, a small inner circle of self-selected officials. The zone was converted into a "people's democracy" on the order of the other Soviet satellites in 1947–1948, and ideological conformity was promoted through the teaching of Marxism-Leninism in the schools. The SED now dominated the civil bureaucracy, while strict censorship and police state methods kept the populace in line. To counter developments in the West, a "People's Congress" was convened which first demanded speedy reunification but then drafted a constitution which would be an alternative to the Basic Law. In a rigged election in May 1949 a new People's Congress was chosen which adopted this constitution. After the installation of the first cabinet of the Federal Republic, the Soviet authorities on 7 October 1949 reluctantly permitted the formation of a separate state called the German Democratic Republic.

Development of the East German System

The GDR became the new government of the Soviet occupation zone. A provisional legislature called the People's Chamber (*Volkskammer*) came into being which met with representatives of the various states (*Länder*) to choose longtime Communist functionary Wilhelm Pieck as president of the GDR, and the chamber elected as prime minister the former Socialist Otto Grotewohl. The constitution was on the surface a very democratic document and had much in common with the Federal Republic's Basic Law. However, the truly decisive political force in the GDR was the Socialist Unity Party and it would take things in a much different direction.

There were four other political parties—an (Eastern) Christian Democratic Union, a liberal party, a farmer's party, and a one that appealed to former army officers and others tainted by involvement with the Third Reich—and several "mass organizations"—the trade unions, farmers' mutual assistance league, women's association, youth league, cultural association, and a league of Nazism's victims. The parties were subservient to the SED and the mass organizations were satellites of it, and all of them belonged to a coalition known as the National Front. This body in turn drew up the unity lists of candidates that appeared on the ballots when elections were held in East Germany. A voter could choose only between approving a list in its entirety or rejecting it, and thus the outcome of an election was always a foregone conclusion. These were ritualistic shows of affirmation by the populace and emphasis was put on a maximum turnout. Voters were often marched from their places of employment to the polls, and public marking of ballots was encouraged. Seats in the People's Chamber were allocated among the SED, the non-Communist parties, and mass organizations according to a preset formula, and the country regularly went through the motions of parliamentary government, complete with the selection of a prime minister and his cabinet ministers and the passage of legislation.

The power, of course, lay with the SED. Its general secretary, Walter Ulbricht, was the key figure in the regime, although he shared power with the party's decisive organ, the Politburo. In the country's early years he had to contend with rivals but after a decade he came to wield virtually unchallenged authority. The SED was an elitist organization to which one had to candidate for membership, and it comprised about twelve percent of the adult population. Its members were expected to comply with the orders of the leadership, and advancement was according to obedience as well as ability. Party membership was a valuable asset in one's career development.

In matters of government, the Politburo made the important policy decisions and these were then carried out by the parliament and ministers. In 1954 the cabinet, now known as the Council of Ministers, gained the power to enact laws by decree without seeking the approval of the People's Chamber when it was not in session. Two years earlier, federalism was eliminated when the People's Chamber adopted a law replacing the five states (*Länder*) with fourteen administrative districts (*Bezirke*), and the GDR's political structure now was that of a unitary state, similar to Soviet Russia. That same year, the regime accepted the division of Germany as permanent by fortifying the demarcation line between the GDR and the Federal Republic and restricting travel to a small number of checkpoints. The only open border that remained was in Berlin.

Although the 1949 constitution contained far-reaching guarantees of civil rights, these were ignored. Since the GDR claimed to be "the first workers' and farmers' state on German soil," any criticism of the regime's policies or methods was denounced as an attack on these classes. Stalinist terror methods were utilized to squash all dissent, whether real or imagined. The mass media was rigidly controlled, and all literary, theatrical, and other forms of expression were tightly censored. In both the artistic and religious realms the heavy hand of repression was felt and demands for ideological conformity made. Propaganda posters and slogans adorned buildings and public places in the GDR. Children whose parents were classified as "bourgeois," that is, other than workers and farmers, were discriminated against in admission to institutions of higher education and in other aspects of life. Many who were dissatisfied with the situation left for the West, which in itself was a crime. Those charged with "flight from the Republic" could receive long prison sentences.

One of the most distinctive institutions of the GDR, the secret police, was created in 1950. Commonly known by its German initials MfS (*Ministerium für Staatssicherheit*) or the acronym Stasi, it grew to be one of the largest and most elaborate state security police organizations ever known. Although a separate ministry in the governmental structure, it was not subordinate to the Council of Ministers but rather answered directly to the SED leadership. At the national, regional, and district levels the Stasi was responsible only to itself and the SED. For all practical purposes, it functioned as a state within a state while it carried out its task of protecting the GDR from internal and external subversion, however broadly that was defined. It was a vast, labyrinthine bureaucracy whose fingers touched almost every aspect of life in the country—postal and telecommunications, economic and commercial endeavors, political education, espionage and counterespionage, surveillance of foreign visitors and diplomatic representations in the GDR, tourism, sports, and social and cultural life. It had its own internal police agency, armed force, interrogation and prison facilities, training schools, and financial institutions. The Stasi had more employees than the Nazi Gestapo, even though the latter had watched over a population nearly five times that of the GDR.

From the very outset, the most serious problem facing the GDR authorities was that of the economy. Soviet reparations had already stripped the area of machines and other productive facilities. Half of the total farmland was seized and distributed among small farmers or assigned to collective farms ("land production communities") similar to those in the Soviet Union. Most industries were confiscated and established as "people's firms." Small merchants, repairmen, craftsmen, and restauranteurs were pressured to merge their businesses into collectives. Through centralized planning the GDR became one gigantic monopolistic economic enterprise. In spite of the fact that outside investment capital was virtually unavailable and production had to be oriented to the needs of the Soviet Union and its bloc, considerable economic growth took place. However, this growth came at the expense of the wage-earning consumer, and their living standards lagged far behind their counterparts in the West. When the regime continued to push higher production quotas without corresponding increases in wages and consumer goods, the pent-up anger of the East German workers exploded in the famous uprising of 17 June 1953. The Ulbricht regime was saved by Red Army troops and tanks, but it now was morally discredited.

On the other hand, the Soviets relaxed their reparations policy and assisted the GDR's economic development. They decided to elevate the country's status so it would serve as a counterweight to the Federal Republic. In 1954 the USSR granted the GDR sovereignty and welcomed it as a charter member of the Warsaw Pact in 1955, the East Bloc alternative to NATO. A professional military force, the National People's Army, was created in 1956 out of the already existing police army. Unlike the Bundeswehr, it preserved some of the features of the old Prussian-German army, such as the goose step, jack boot, and requirement for unconditional obedience. In 1962 conscription was introduced, but in contrast to West Germany no alternative service opportunities were given. Conscientious objectors could either serve in militarized "construction battalions" (*Bausoldaten*) and suffer job and educational discrimination thereafter or go to prison.

Although economic conditions improved somewhat in the course of the 1950s, things were still wretched in comparison to the West, and the restrictions on personal freedom continued to mount. Meanwhile, Ulbricht's stature rose in the eyes of his Soviet masters when the uprisings of 1956 had no effect in East Germany, and in 1960 he was able to add to his power the chair of the newly created National Defense Council and the presidency of the State

Council, an executive committee which replaced the position of President Wilhelm Pieck, who had just died. From this point he held the top post in the party and the regime.

With Soviet backing, he was now in a position to deal with the continuing hemorrhage of GDR residents through the Berlin escape hatch. People could go to East Berlin, cross the sector boundary on foot or by public transportation, ask for and receive recognition as citizens of the Federal Republic, and fly out to the West to begin their new lives. This exodus was a costly drain on the Eastern economy because most who left were young people and skilled workers. It also placed limits on how much the regime could demand from those who remained. When Soviet leader Nikita Khrushchev began raising the stakes in the Cold War by threatening to sign a unilateral peace treaty with the GDR and converting West Berlin into a demilitarized "free city," the numbers of refugees mounted. Ulbricht finally received permission from his masters in Moscow take action, and on 13 August 1961 an ugly concrete block wall was hastily erected a few feet behind the Soviet sector boundary. In the subsequent months and years it was reinforced and enhanced and border guards were ordered to shoot at those seeking to scale the barrier.

The result was a stabilization of the GDR's political system. Dissidents were brought into line, the country was militarized, and sustained economic growth took place. Before long East Germany had the highest standard of living of any Soviet bloc country, although it lagged far behind that of West Germany. Ulbricht confidently revised the GDR constitution in 1968, giving legal recognition to the many changes in the political system and elimination of personal freedom. Although he enthusiastically backed (and apparently urged) the Soviet intervention in Czecho-slovakia in 1968 and even contributed East German troops, for a variety of reasons (one being his opposition to detente with West Germany) he lost favor in Moscow. Thus in 1971 the aging leader (he was now 78) was forced to retire as party chief and died quietly two years later. His successor was fifty-nine-year-old Erich Honecker, a loyal SED functionary, and architect of the Berlin Wall. Then followed a period of hard-line retrenchment, the virtually complete takeover of all remaining private business enterprises, and the establishment of what Honecker called "real, existing socialism."

The Rapprochement between East and West Germany

Adenauer had steadfastly refused to accept the loss of the territories east of the Oder-Neisse line, and in fact for some years publishing a map in West Germany that did not recognize the 1937 boundaries or acknowledged the existence of the German Democratic Republic was forbidden. In an effort to prevent international recognition of the GDR, the Hallstein Doctrine (named after a top foreign policy aide) was set forth in 1955. It provided that West Germany would not maintain diplomatic relations with any country (except the USSR) that recognized the Eastern regime.

After his retirement in 1963 the West Germans gradually relaxed the policy. When Social Democrat Willy Brandt became chancellor in 1969, he inaugurated an *Ostpolitik* (Eastern policy) that aimed at the normalization of relations both with the Soviet Union and Poland and between the two Germanies. Treaties with Moscow and Warsaw declared the eastern border as inviolable, the Hallstein Doctrine was discarded, and a four-power accord on the status of Berlin guaranteed Western access to the city. Then direct negotiations between East and West Germany took place concerning implementation of the Berlin agreement, and in the Basic Treaty (signed 1972) the two states agreed to accept the border between them, acknowledge each other's authority and independence, and respect human rights as spelled out in the UN charter. The GDR would also allow more of its people to visit the West in cases of urgent family needs. In 1973 both countries were admitted to UN membership, and two years later the GDR participated in the Helsinki conference on security and cooperation in Europe.

The Federal Republic now recognized the GDR as another sovereign state within the German nation, but not as a foreign country. Bonn's ultimate goal remained that of national unity, but this would be an interim step. Eventual reunification could only achieved by increasing contacts between the people in the two German states and improving the day-to-day lot of those in the GDR. Brandt's successor, Helmut Schmidt, continued the process of easing the lot of Germans in the East by paying ransom money for political prisoners, allowing the GDR to exile prominent dissenters to the West, and granting loans to facilitate trade.

Honecker, on the other hand, was less than enthusiastic about this new era of detente, and like with Ulbricht the Soviets had to pressure him into taking a more conciliatory stance. He continued the policy of "delimitation" (*Abgrenzung*), inaugurated by his predecessor in the 1960s, which stressed the uniqueness of the GDR and its differences from the Federal Republic, and he sought to limit the contacts which East Germans had with people from the outside. Honecker also deemphasized the national cultural ties that linked all Germans and began referring to the GDR as a separate nation. A constitutional revision in 1974 replaced the 1968 statement that the GDR was a "socialist state of the German nation" with the phrase "a socialist state of workers and farmers," and references to the "German people" and reunification were dropped. Even the words to the national anthem were no longer sung because they contained the phrase "Germany, one fatherland."

The Stasi dealt harshly with those who dissented from the new course, including peace activists. GDR propagandists talked so much about peace that the word no longer had any meaning, but the regime looked with a jaundiced eye on any kind of individual initiative in this. Peacemaking was a state monopoly. Also Honecker placed considerable importance on closer political and cultural ties with the Soviet Union, but the populace was allowed to have no contact with the 300,000 Russian troops stationed on his country's soil.

Prosperity rose during the 1970s, and people now had decent housing, adequate food, a modicum of consumer goods, and in many cases their own automobiles. Then the world oil crisis, an unfavorable trade balance, and rising indebtedness put a damper on growth, and at the beginning of the 1980s the economy began to turn downward. Because so many able-bodied workers had fled to the West before 1961, the percentage of retirees to those in the productive age range in the population was skewed all out of proportion. The regime countered the problem by allowing, even encouraging, pensioners to emigrate to the West and bringing more women into the labor force. By 1983 more than 86 percent of women were employed outside of the home, and an extensive system of daycare centers and kindergartens existed to accommodate their needs. To help prop up the lagging economy, the regime utilized various measures to obtain more foreign exchange, such as lump-sum payments from the Federal Republic to cover transit fees to West Berlin, requiring visitors to exchange a certain amount of money at an officially set, nonconvertible rate, and operating "Intershops" where visitors and even GDR residents (who had received money from West German relatives) could purchase consumer goods with Deutschmarks.

By the mid-1980s an ideological and economic malaise had settled over the GDR. West German radio and television, which reached almost everywhere, was a constant reminder to the populace of how bad off they were. The ugly barrier in Berlin was now defended by the regime as "the antifascist protective wall," but this phrase fooled nobody. Thanks to a liberalized emigration policy that was implemented to secure large loans from the West, thousands applied to leave. Others withdrew into an inner emigration whereby they disengaged themselves from the Marxist-Leninist system and sought just to be left alone. About the only new avenue for gaining identity and legitimacy that the regime found was in international sports competition.

Even as Honecker was gaining more recognition for the GDR abroad and even made a state visit to West Germany in 1987, the country's geriatric leadership (Honecker and many of the Politburo figures were now in their seventies) seemed unaware of just how much change was in the wind. The accession of Mikhail Gorbachev to power in the Soviet Union in 1985, with his program of *perestroika* (economic restructuring), *glasnost* (openness), and democratic reforms, and the rise of the Solidarity movement in Poland were greeted with a jaundiced eye by those at the helm in the GDR, and they welcomed the Chinese regime's suppression of the student-led uprising in June 1989. They were living in a twilight zone of unreality, convinced that Communism would prosper in the GDR for the foreseeable future and confident that the Stasi could handle whatever dissent might arise.

Then in late summer and early fall the dam broke and the whole system came unglued. What transpired was one of the most remarkable nonviolent revolutions in history. Events moved so quickly that within a year the GDR had disappeared from the face of the map and the country was reunited, albeit on terms dictated by the Federal Republic. The conservative Chancellor Helmut Kohl, with whom Honecker so proudly posed three years earlier, now governed all of Germany. Also the last vestiges of the occupation were eliminated with the removal of Western troops from Berlin and the withdrawal of the Soviet army from East Germany. Forty-five years after the end of the European conflict the victors concluded their final treaty with the new Germany. With the formal reunification on 3 October 1990, it could be said that World War II had officially come to an end.

The Church in East Germany

Since the churches played such a crucial role in the revolution of 1989, some discussion of the place of Christianity in this Marxist-Leninist country, one that espoused atheistic humanism as its official ideology, is necessary. In 1946 around eighty percent of the inhabitants of the area comprising East Germany were identified as Protestants. The Roman Catholic proportion, twelve percent, was much smaller because most of the prewar Catholic population in Germany lived in the area included in the Western occupation zones and the regions given to Poland. Only a minuscule number, one percent, adhered to the "free churches," such as the Baptists, Methodists, New Apostolic Christians, Seventh-day Adventists, Moravians, and Pentecostals of various types, and they tended to keep a very low profile. The Protestant or Evangelical (*evangelisch*) churches, as they are commonly labeled, were the heirs of the Reformation and were organized on the territorial principle. Originally the ruler of a German principality or state determined the faith of his subject, and this territorial church (*Landeskirche*) was under his oversight in some way or another. In the nineteenth century the rubric "Evangelical" came to include both Lutheran and United churches. The latter referred mainly to the Old Prussian Union Church of 1817, a merger of the Lutherans and Reformed into one evangelical church which King Frederick William III brought about, but some United churches were formed elsewhere.

The strength of the Protestant churches eroded as Germany became more and more secularized, and after World War I church and state were separated. The *Landeskirchen* continued as autonomous "regional churches," and the various state governments accommodated them in many ways—giving them legal status as corporations, maintaining theological faculties in the universities, collecting church taxes from their members, subsidizing church-run schools, and authorizing religious instruction in the public schools by church-accredited teachers. After World War II these practices were continued in West Germany. Also in 1948 the Protestants created an umbrella organization, the Evangelical Church in Germany (*Evangelische Kirche in Deutschland*, or EKD), which linked the regional churches in all parts of the occupied country.

In the Soviet zone the authorities recognized the anti-Nazi record of the Protestants and permitted the churches to remain open for worship, to carry on their social service ministries, and to rebuild their shattered infrastructures. This included restoring the *Landeskirchen* (there were five Union and three purely Lutheran ones), allowing the publication of religious literature and theological faculties in six state universities, and, as mentioned above, authorizing a political party that was religiously oriented, the Christian Democratic Union. When the German Democratic Republic was founded in 1949, its constitution contained far-reaching guarantees of religious liberty, including individual freedom of conscience and belief, parental authority over the religious training of their children, and for churches the right to form as corporate entities, give religious instruction in the schools, and hold services and provide pastoral care in hospitals and prisons.

As the governing party, the SED had to come to terms with fairly well-organized Christian communities, although being a Marxist body it had little use for religion. In order to draw people away from the churches, the SED utilized the stick of persecution—mainly discrimination against committed Christians and harassment of pastors and church leaders—and the carrot of ideology—a vision of building socialism in the "first workers' and farmers' state on German soil." The regime sponsored various functions which had a patently religious character, and through this met the religious needs of the populace under other rubrics. The ideology even had its own eschatology—the perfection of the true and human, of righteousness and peace. In place of the divine and transcendent, it posited "humanity" as the highest entity. Socialism and humanism were so closely linked that socialism came to signify the deepest fulfillment of the humanistic ideal. The party insisted that the churches integrate themselves into the new society and contribute to the building of socialism and the better common future.

In the early days of the GDR the attack on the churches began with actions aimed at eliminating their role in public life, most notably education, and restricting their activities to the purely "religious," that which would take place within the walls of the churches. The separation of church and school was the first struggle between the Protestant church and the Communist state. The introduction of Marxist-Leninist ideological instruction in the schools and the attempts of the SED-related youth organizations, the Free German Youth and the Pioneers, to lure the young away from Christianity were vigorously resisted by church leaders. The state response was banning the Protestant youth newspaper, police searches of church institutions, and harassment of youth groups and rallies. Some even compared the situation with the Church Struggle of the Nazi era

After the shock of the June 1953 workers' uprising, the Ulbricht regime recognized that the Protestant church was a formidable rival, since it possessed an ideology and effective organizational structure of its own, exercised influence throughout all levels of the population, and was the only remaining organization that still could function on an all-German basis. Thus, the authorities eased off on direct persecution and adopted a different approach. One aspect of this was the initiation of an emphasis on "scientific atheistic propaganda." This curricular modification involved the complete elimination of the remnants of "capitalistic thinking" from the minds of the people, including religious "prejudices" and "superstitions." Then, a new family law in 1955 placed marriage and family matters under state control.

But the most spectacular aspect of this new ideological campaign was the introduction in 1954–1955 of the Youth Dedication, a formal ceremony after the end of several weeks of special instruction in which boys and girls who completed the eighth grade in school were asked to pledge their lives and energy to the building of a socialistic order in the GDR. This was little more than a Communist confirmation service, and the significance of it as a substitute for the Christian rite was not lost on the church leaders. Although at first they strongly resisted the Youth Dedication, the churches eventually acquiesced. By the 1970s, around 97 to 98 percent of the fourteen-year-olds went through this annual rite of passage, and for all practical purposes it held hardly any deeper meaning for its participants than the Pledge of Allegiance recited by Americans does.

By the later 1950s the state was once again putting pressure on the churches. Although this was clearly guaranteed in the constitution, the revenue office in 1956 discontinued allowing the churches to use state tax lists in order to levy contributions from their members. In 1958 the Ministry of Education severely curtailed religious instruction. To subvert the church's place in social life, the SED introduced other *ersatz* rites in addition to the Youth Dedication, such as the socialist baby dedication ("name giving"), marriage, and burial ceremonies, and in 1958 adopted the "Ten Commandments of Socialist Morality" as the basic moral law for the new socialist man. They included a commitment to the international solidarity of the working class, defense of the fatherland, protection of the people's property, and work and discipline. As the financial screws were tightened, West German churches sent money to help support the Eastern ones and several pastors from the Federal Republic moved to the GDR to help alleviate the growing shortage of clergy there. In November 1956 the SED Politburo recommended the creation of a special Ministry for Church Questions (*Kirchenfragen*), which would function as a liaison between the state and the churches. The four men who held the ministerial post were all Communists—Werner Eggerath (1957–1960), Hans Seigewasser (1960–1979), Klaus Gysi (1979–1988), and Kurt Löffler (1988–1989)—and the agency's task was clearly that of keeping the churches in line with the Marxist state.

The most divisive issue of the period was the Evangelical Church in Germany's agreement in 1957 to provide chaplains for the Federal Republic's Bundeswehr. (Catholic actions in doing likewise were not a matter of dispute; the Vatican assigned chaplains on the basis of the 1933 concordat with Germany which was still in effect.) Since the Protestant churches in the GDR were members of the all-German organization, they were seriously compromised. The regime bitterly denounced this as Protestant support for NATO and West German "imperialism" and used it to undermine the EKD. At an important meeting in July 1958 the East German churchmen dissociated themselves from the chaplaincy agreement, endorsed their state's foreign policy as a quest for peace, and proclaimed their respect for and willingness to assist in the development of socialism.

As mentioned above, after the erection of the Berlin Wall the regime was now in a position to implement the *Abgrenzung* policy. Thus it put increasing pressure on the churches to separate from the EKD and emphasized the "common humanistic responsibility of Christians and Marxists" to build socialism and foster peace and understanding. Church figures were deeply divided over both matters. However, after several years of intense discussions about what their relationship to the EKD should be, the leaders of the GDR's eight regional churches finally voted on 10 June 1969 to form a separate organization known as the Federation of Evangelical Churches in the GDR (*Bund der Evangelischen Kirchen in der DDR*). The East German Baptists took a similar action in response to state pressure in 1964, and the Methodists and other free churches did likewise.

The Church in Socialism

In some ways, this ushered in a new era in church-state relations. Many church figures in East Germany believed the Marxist-Leninist state was here to stay and that they must come to terms with it. Increasingly they used the phrase "the church in socialism" to support their contention that coexistence was possible. The idea was articulated by Bishop Albrecht Schönherr in 1971 at the Church Federation synod: "A witness and service community of churches in the GDR will have to consider carefully its place: in this given society, not separated from it, nor in opposition to it." The interpretation of this was a matter of considerable controversy, as the Marxist-Leninist state did not want to see the church become involved in ideological formulation or shaping public understanding of the meaning of socialism.

There were ways in which the regime could use the church. It was encouraged to participate in Soviet-sponsored peace initiatives such as the World Congress of Peace Forces in 1973, but of course it was not permitted to pursue its own peace policy. The CDU was a dutiful servant of the state, even though only about four percent of the pastors actually were members of the party, and the material in its publications and statements at its congresses seldom gave the authorities any cause for concern. Only in the controversy over the legalization of abortion in 1972 did some CDU members break ranks, oppose a policy espoused by the SED, and vote against the law in the parliament. Since this was an issue of minor political significance, the state evidently recognized that certain of its occasionally contradictory interests could be best served by tolerating carefully circumscribed dissent.

Another way the church could be a useful instrument was in helping the GDR to gain international recognition and acceptance. By granting visas for church leaders to attend ecumenical gatherings and denominational conferences abroad, the identity and prestige of the state could be enhanced. Because much of the funding for such endeavors could be secured from sources in the West, the travel would not constitute much of a drain on the country's limited reserves of foreign exchange. When political issues arose at these meetings—such as combating racism in southern Africa, human rights concerns, the nuclear arms race, or the stationing of U.S. missiles in West Germany—the GDR representatives were expected to hew to the line emanating from East Berlin. At the same time, the threat of refusing visas was a practical way of putting pressure on independent-minded clergy to toe the mark.

The most important demonstration of the improving relationship was the "summit conference" between Honecker and the executive board of the Church Federation on 6 March 1978. At the heart of the carefully prepared meeting were several concrete agreements. Access was to be given to television four time per year for general informational programs. A limited ministry to those in prison would be allowed. The program of building new churches with money from West Germany begun in 1976 would be continued. Church charitable enterprises would be recognized as an integral part of the nation's general health care program. Clergy and other career church employees would be integrated into the state's pension system. The press release of the summit stated that "the relations of the church to the state have been increasingly marked by objectivity, trust, and forthrightness." The meeting reflected that the regime had come to accept the church's "social presence" and would use it to meet some of the state's goals.

Continuing Repression

Although some improvement in relations had occurred during the 1970s, the church was still only a "tolerated" institution and Marxist-Leninists believed that in the working out of the dialectic of history it would eventually pass away. Secret police surveillance of churches and their activities actually increased, because they remained organizationally and financially independent from the state and carried on their work without the approval of officials or with public funds. With their growing level of social engagement, the party and state authorities came to view churches as a gathering point for oppositional forces and strove to bring them under their control. The objective was to restrict them to "purely religious activity," hold them to the course of cooperation with the state adopted in 1978, and to prevent the "enemy" from using them as bases of operations. The churches were honeycombed with Stasi agents and informers, whose task was to disrupt the activities of an institution labeled as "hostile and negative" and to help bring about the emergence of "progressive and loyal" leaders. When the Stasi files were opened after reunification, the full magnitude of this penetration was exposed.

It was common knowledge that Christians were targets of discrimination, especially in the educational system. If a teenager had not gone through the Youth Dedication and participated in the SED's Free German Youth organization, he or she had little chance of attending a college preparatory secondary school and none at all of being admitted to the university. Those who studied theology at the universities had to take part in annual military training exercises like all other students. In fact, theological education became so politicized that the churches started their own seminaries, and by the mid-1970s these had higher enrollments than the university faculties.

The 1970 Ordinance on Public Functions required the securing of police permission for all functions except those "with exclusively religious character," that is, conducted by persons in the full-time service of the churches and occurring in the rooms normally used by the churches. The intent was to enable the banning of any public function such as a parade, rally, lecture, or concert where criticism of social and political developments in the GDR might take place. This severely hampered such public ministries of the church as evangelistic efforts, open air and tent meetings, and regional or national congresses. Approval would have to be sought for these and it was not easily obtained. The ordinance was modified somewhat by the 1978 agreement.

Since the authorities saw the youth as the hope of the future, they were particularly concerned about efforts to reach young people. Marxist-Leninist ideological indoctrination was a central feature of education at all levels, Free German Youth activities were consciously scheduled to coincide with the times of church services, and participation in church youth organizations like the "Evangelical Student Parishes" was discouraged. Dr. Theo Lehmann of Chemnitz (known in the GDR days as Karl-Marx-Stadt), East Germany's foremost youth evangelist, was a particular thorn in the side of the authorities. His meetings drew such large crowds that the Stasi spied on him constantly and the local SED central committee became upset. The authorities even offered him and his family the opportunity to emigrate to West Germany but he refused to do so.

The frustration with state policies restricting church youth activities culminated in a dramatic action in August 1976. Pastor Oskar Brüsewitz of Zeitz committed suicide in the town square by setting himself on fire. His protest against the ruination of East German youth and the church's institutional accommodation with the state was widely reported in the Western media, and it sullied the GDR's human rights record and the integrity of the church leadership who tried to minimize his deed.

In 1979 "premilitary" training was introduced into the schools at the 9th and 10th grade levels, and in spite of vehement protests by church officials the state would not back down. This was simply one more illustration of how the GDR had become the most militarized state in the world. The church responded by starting its own program of "education for peace," the Peace Decade, a ten-day program of prayer, religious services, and peace workshop that was held every November. Meanwhile, young people launched an independent peace movement called "Swords to Plowshares," using as their symbol the sculpture of the blacksmith beating a sword into a plowshare (the vision of Micah 4) which the Soviet Union had donated to the United Nations in 1957 and now stands before UN headquarters in New York. The churches had employed this in the 1981 Peace Decade materials and youths sewed patches on their jackets that carried the emblem. The police proceeded to tear them off and arrested some for antistate activity, while the Free German Youth responded with a campaign slogan: "Peace must be defended; it must be an armed peace." Caught between the state and grassroots activism the church leaders distanced themselves from the movement.

But new issues kept coming to the fore, particularly the environmental problem which the regime tried to sweep under the carpet. More and more grassroots antinuclear arms, human rights, and environmental groups were springing up, and many of them looked to sympathetic pastors for help. Since the churches offered "free space" where technically the police would not bother them, they naturally became places where activists could meet and plan their strategies. A revolution was about to begin, and the churches, whether they wanted to or not, would find themselves at the center.

A Chronicle of the Revolution

Günter und Hartmut Lorenz

We have learned afresh in these months what political results the spiritual mission of the church of Jesus Christ has.

When delegates from the Protestant church federations in both German states met in mid-January 1990 at Loccum in Hanover and drew up a joint statement containing these words, they were making an interim assessment of the developments that had transpired since the fall of 1989 and looking into the future. In the dramatic events of October which completely altered the GDR, Christians not only took part but also were a moving force.

Reflecting on the change that had occurred, the Protestant churchmen in Loccum formulated what would prove to be a controversial description of the path they needed to follow. Its key points were:

> We desire the two German states to grow together. This will occur in a series of steps within the framework of an all-European process of understanding. . . . The special community of Protestant Christians in Germany has remained alive in spite of the division of the country and the organizational split within the church. Regardless of what the future political development will be, we want to give this special community of the entire body of Protestant believers in Germany an appropriate organizational form in one church. We desire to deal carefully with the experiences and differences that have arisen during this time of separation.

Shortly afterwards, Dr. Werner Leich, bishop of the Thuringian regional church and president of the Federation of Protestant Churches in the GDR, was asked by his church newspaper what experiences the East German Christians would be able to contribute to shaping the future. He answered:

> Our experience has shown that we are the people of God. Whatever happens within our church, we must do ourselves. To be sure, the sacrifice of time and money to renovate churches, the simple day-to-day witness in the workplace, the readiness to help one another are not to be found everywhere, but their presence has significantly grown. In the GDR every Christian knew that he belonged to a minority. He had to have a reason to be a believer and to remain one. We have discovered something special in the last months. Our service in the areas of prayer and preaching can change the political structure when God knows that the time is ripe. I would like to see this sense of certainty preserved.

Preserving this should be the reason for reflection upon the revolution. It is impossible to describe fully all that took place—the process of change, dramatic events, and personal experiences. We can only highlight points that are parts of the whole picture. We cannot recount everything in strict chronological order either, for the events and experiences and the evaluation of them are closely interrelated. However, the picture that does result is one in which the participation and commitment of Christians contributed decisively to the growing opposition to the rule of the SED, and from this developed the nonviolent and peaceful grassroots movement in the autumn of 1989.

18 December 1989. Tonight was the last Monday prayer service for peace in Leipzig. These intercessory worship services began in the Nikolai (St. Nicholas) Church and then spread to the other downtown churches. As the waves of people fleeing East Germany via Hungary swelled and the internal political situation worsened during August and September, they became the focal points of protest for thousands of citizens against the excessive incursions of state power. From October on, the size of the demonstrations following the church services swelled from ten thousand to hundreds of thousands. With the cry "We are the people" they had become a mighty force. Now, Superintendent Johannes Richter, speaking to a packed congregation at the St. Thomas Church, took stock of the Leipzig events in October:

We look back on 9 October. We gathered together for the first time in a prayer service here in our church. We can remember that day vividly. The blood in our veins froze. What we knew was so frightening that it almost took away our ability to speak, but we sang and listened to the words of Scripture. We prayed and then went outside into a situation fraught with uncertainty, one in which anything could happen. We had taken to heart the admonition of our bishop and heard the last minute appeal of the "Leipzig Six." And then the miracle of Leipzig took place. The overwhelmingly massive demonstration moved completely around the center of the city unmolested. The shadow cast by the Square of Heavenly Peace in Beijing had been driven away.

We look back to the weeks lying between that memorable Monday and today. We have witnessed breathtaking events. Unimaginable, indeed, inconceivable things have happened since then. But mixed with the great hopes and expectations of those days are concerns. There are concerns about the movement's calm, peaceful, and nonviolent continuation. There are concerns that decisions about our future will once again be made by others. There are concerns whether we have sufficient competence and altruism to meet the demands placed upon us. There are concerns whether we have the staying power after so many years of humiliation, those times when we were treated like children, to pursue our own way patience, clarity, and decisiveness. There are concerns whether we will be able to structure a society of reconciliation, one in which all people, regardless of their world view or political persuasion—as long as it is not a neo-Nazi one—are able to feel safe and secure.

He went on to say that the churches and representatives of the democratic opposition groups have asked the citizens of Leipzig on this day, 18 December, to form a human chain along the streets through which hundreds of thousands walked during the previous ten Mondays. The lights of countless candles will remind us of those who suffered under the violence and oppression of the Stalinist power structures, of the events during this autumn in our country, of the imprisonments, of the nonviolent resistance, and of the beginning of democratic renewal. This quiet rally will reflect a spirit of determination and at the same time demonstrate a spirit of peaceableness, in spite of the discordant voices that are being heard on the fringes of our society.

How the Crisis Developed

The 1987 Background. In the GDR the churches were the only organizations that were not managed and controlled by the state, in spite of the many ups and downs in relations between the Protestant Church and the Communist state. Peace, environmental, and human rights groups that were working for societal change at the grassroots level found meeting space available in church buildings. The church, in turn, found itself drawn into questions and conflict situations at odds with its own views. Such access to meeting areas was denied them everywhere else. To be sure, the relationship between the church and these groups was certainly not always harmonious, for example, when the groups *demanded* the space. Or when the church, realizing that to carry out its obligation to seek the welfare of all, must walk a fine line between conformity and resistance to the government, was not about either to cover up or defend the spirit of opposition found in the groups.

At the turn of 1987–1988 an open confrontation between the state and the church occurred. This came as a surprise because the year saw a signifcant relaxation of tensions. Honecker visited the Federal Republic, while a paper issued jointly by the West German Social Democratic Party and the SED entitled "The Conflict of Ideologies and Our Common Need for Security" seemed to signal a desire for dialogue. Live telecasts between East and West Germany became possible. The church and its associated groups were allowed to take part in the international Olof Palme Peace March through the GDR on its own initiative and with its own slogans. Church participants reported enthusiastically at the Church Federation synod in Görlitz about the common ground they felt between themselves and Marxists, even though initially there were some anxieties.

But soon after the Honecker trip to West Germany a chill set in. The "thaw" proved to have been a political maneuver. The brusque response of the government to the synodical paper "Bearing Witness in the Matter of Peace" and to the widely discussed church document "A Rejection of the Spirit and Logic of Political Separation (*Abgrenzung*)" made this clear. The confrontational course became quite obvious in November 1987 when the State Security police stormed the "Environmental Library" maintained by an opposition group in Berlin's Zion Church and confiscated materials it deemed "dangerous." The situation intensified in January 1988 with the arrest of participants in a demonstration during the annual party commemoration of the deaths of Karl Liebknecht and Rosa Luxemburg. The actions by the state authorities were against members of groups whom the church had no real obligation to defend; however, it did so because of its own deep sense of responsibility.

24 November 1987. "Toward midnight a prosecuting attorney accompanied by several State Security officials appeared with a search warrant naming the Environmental Library located in the manse of the Zion Church, where pastor Hans Simon lives," according to a bulletin of the Federation of Protestant Churches. "The library was searched. Several duplicating machines as well as paper were confiscated. The prosecutor's office stated that they were not concerned with the materials found in the Environmental Library but rather with some hectographed sheets called *Grenzfall* (Borderline Case) Authored by some independent activists, the publication dealt with peace, environmental, and human rights matters. Seven young people who were in the Library were taken into custody. Five of them, among them a fourteen-year-old and a seventeen-year-old, were released on the following day."

25 November 1987. The official church communique continued: "Other members of action groups in Berlin were arrested, but they have been set free again. As a result of the raid, members of various groups set up a vigil at the Zion Church. They demanded the release of the two who were still in jail, Wolfgang Rüddenklau and Bert Schlegel; an end to the investigation; the restoration of the Environmental Library; and the cessation of all repressive measures against political activists."

28 November 1987. The arrest warrants against the two individuals were quashed, and they were released from custody. However, the investigation continued.

29 November 1987. "At a worship service in the Elias Church in Berlin attended by approximately 600 young people from Berlin and elsewhere in the GDR, it was agreed to suspend the prayer vigil for the time being because the two had been set free."

Yet, in spite of the release of the prisoners, the situation remained tense. The young people decided to continue the vigil—as a symbol of solidarity with those who remain under the close scrutiny of the State Security and as a symbol of protest—but also as a demonstration of their peaceableness. They were unmoved by conflicts inside the church governing bodies and the local church councils over the value of such action and whether they should be continued on church premises in Prenzlauer Berg, a densely populated working-class district in Berlin. At the same time the prayer vigils indicated that they had overcome the fear of the all-powerful and omnipresent State Security and that self-confidence was growing.

10 December 1987. A worship service was held at the Gethsemane Church on the fortieth anniversary of the UN Declaration of Human Rights. A group favoring the right to give up one's citizenship and leave the country made a public statement. The possibility that some alternative societal engagement could take place here seemed hardly discernible. Thus, solidarity among the peace, environmental, and human rights' groups was difficult to achieve, but contacts were being made, prompted mainly by human rights concerns.

9 January 1988. The possibility of participation by outside groups in the traditional SED Liebknecht-Luxemburg demonstration was discussed at a meeting. No decisions were made but cooperation appeared out of the question. However, gaps in information and issuing statements to the Western media that had not been coordinated with the other groups were sources of irritation

17 January 1988. Groups assembled this Sunday morning at Frankfurter Tor, the starting point of the parade, which advocated a variety of causes. The quotation of Rosa Luxemburg, "Freedom is always the freedom of the individual to dissent" was used as a protest slogan against this government of nonfreedom. It also gave the State Security an excuse to take action against them. More than a hundred people were arrested, mainly ones seeking to emigrate or hoping that because of this action they would be expelled to the West. But in addition to these, members of other groups were arrested and preliminary proceedings started.

19 January 1988. Representatives of the various groups drafted a protest at the Zion Church calling for the immediate release of all those taken into custody and cessation of preliminary proceedings and repressive measures (such as surveillance) against political activists seeking social change. The governing body of the church in Berlin-Brandenburg tried to mediate the issue. To cope with problems associated with emigration—a source of increasing social tensions—and the forced exile to the West of several peace activists following the events of 17 January, a "Contact Office" was established in the administrative building of the Berlin church.

28 January 1988. The following appeared in the main SED newspaper, *Neues Deutschland,* eleven days after the Liebknecht-Luxemburg parade protest:

> The march commemorating our country's murdered heroes was intentionally disrupted; the memorial service for the martyrs of the Communist Party was willfully desecrated. They did not join the procession out of reverence but rather to draw attention to themselves. What took place was reprehensible, like an act of blasphemy. No church would accept the degradation of a procession honoring a Catholic cardinal or a Protestant bishop. In the same way, how can we be expected to remain silent when someone deliberately disrupts and violates the remembrance of Rosa Luxemburg and Karl Liebknecht. To make a more secular comparison, imagine that a procession on the way to the final resting place of Olof Palme were to be besmirched by protests. Moreover, in every civilized country laws exist that deal with situations where the memory of deceased persons is dishonored.

With its pseudoreligious understanding of this commemoration of the dead, the SED said the dissidents had committed a sacrilege by calling attention to their problems in such a manner.

10 February 1988. In Dresden the Ecumenical Assembly of Christians and Churches in the GDR for Justice, Peace, and the Preservation of the Creation opened. Close to 150 delegates from nineteen churches, free churches, and religious communities were seeking to bring their experience and insight to the worldwide Christian dialogue on the vital issues of humanity. Discussed was the statement "Nine Reasons for Outrage," a frank and shocking report of the depressing reality of everyday life in the GDR. The authorities were incensed because it portrayed the true picture of the situation here rather than their propagandistic one.

19 February 1988. The regime responded with an unmistakable threat. The SED Politburo member responsible for church affairs, Werner Jarowinsky, summoned Bishop Leich, chair of the Protestant Church Leaders Council, and harshly reprimanded the church's actions. As no reply was permitted, the encounter could hardly be called a dialogue. Here are some quotes:

> That which causes concern is the open and increasing misuse of church facilities for purposes that have nothing to do with the church or the exercise of religion but that, on the contrary, hinder and even endanger the right of believers to the free exercise of their religion. . . . According to information we received about the gathering in Dresden, the main issues were dropped from the agenda and replaced with other matters. And this occurred at a time when the possibility is within reach to reduce by one-half the world's most dangerous weapons systems, intercontinental nuclear ballistic missiles. The common responsibility to deal with such matters was pushed into the background by raising questions which, to be blunt, can only lead to confrontation.
>
> One cannot overlook the fact that certain elements reject the movement for a "church in socialism," that is, the integration of Christian citizens and church institutions into the society. They would like to resurrect the model of the church as political opposition to socialism, the church as Trojan horse, even though that had failed long ago. . . . In these days, when even in the GDR atomic missiles are being dismantled for the first time, they would have the council focus on side issues which have nothing to do with the church's mission. This must be the case, if the major questions of disarmament are pushed aside or relativized, matters are discussed in a dozen working sessions that belong exclusively to the domain of the state, and public statements are made that receive damaging repetition in the Western media.

More original quotes from Jarowinsky:

> The happenings in several Berlin churches are matters of justifiable concern; they have become an unreasonable and dangerous burden. Purely political events have been staged, and antigovernment slogans and appeals for street brawls and confrontations are permitted. . . . The boundary of reasonable behavior has been overstepped, the bow has been pulled too tight. . . . There is even the suggestion that current church structures and rules should be replaced by others.
>
> When representatives of the church openly talk about the formation of new substructures, and that there is logistical control from without and collaboration with them, then it is time for reconsideration of just what is going on. The bodies that are responsible for the management of the church must provide clarification and bring about a change of its ways. After all, churches are being transformed into tribunals, into offices for lawyers, and people answer the telephone with "Contact Office," "Solidarity Office," or "Coordination Center."
>
> They are playing with fire. They are projecting distorted images and developing new concepts of who the enemy is. The path extends from the notorious events at the Zion Church to the Rosa Luxemburg—Karl Liebknecht demonstration and what happened at the commemoration of the bombing of Dresden last week. . . . It is high time that the church do something about this and sees to it that everywhere the church will once again be the church.

3 March 1988. The head of state, Erich Honecker, surprisingly met with Bishop Leich. The church-state conversation between Honecker and the Church Federation's executive board headed by Bishop Albrecht Schönherr took place ten years ago today. That meeting dealt with equality and respect for all citizens, and even the bishop's statement was entered into the official report, namely, that the relationship between church and state is only as good as that which the individual Christian citizen experiences in his home community. The talks resulted in a relaxation of tensions and many new points of agreement between the two sides. Honecker now conjured up this "historical meeting" and the "policies aimed at future collaboration in these new relationships." But regardless of how much he emphasized "the joint responsibility of the socialist society and the churches" and the "overall favorable development" of these relations, the phrases were worn out. The Jarowinsky statement still remained in the background, and Bishop Leich frankly, albeit cautiously, formulated the issues that were of concern to the church.

After ten years we still needed to give considerable thought to dealing with these matters "in light of developments in the society and the church and what may yet transpire." The problems arising from different communities living together in one society could be dealt with by means of frank discussions. He then named problems which did not originate in the church but still it must act on them, albeit unwillingly, in order to give those affected a hearing. These included: the increasing number of requests by people not only to leave the country but also at the same time to surrender their GDR citizenship; travel restrictions and the refusal to give reasons for rejecting applications for trips abroad; the refusal of the state to engage in substantive discussions with the church and state on the urgent matters of education, military service, and conscientious objection; the high-handed manner in which state offices and departments deal with citizens and their concerns; and equality of opportunity for all in elementary education, technical schools, and higher education. "We are asking for decisions and concrete actions that will signal a better future for all."

But those signals were not forthcoming. The tensions increased. In the course of 1988 a vicious campaign was waged against the church newspapers in the GDR. They were the only ones that attempted to deal with the matters in the society which caused so much dissatisfaction and that reported the activities of those groups trying to do something about them. The government forbade the publication or heavily censored the reports of the regional churches' annual conferences because of the critical discussions that occured in these meetings. In October opposition groups launched a "reader protest" because of the heavily censored and watered-down articles that appeared in the *Berliner Kirchenzeitung* and the lack of press freedom in general. The demonstration was quickly dispersed by the security forces, but the incident exposed the increasing intellectual impotence and decline of state authority and the growing fearlessness and readiness to act on the part of the dissidents.

7 May 1989. Local elections took place in the GDR or "the communal folding of the slips of paper" as it was sarcastically labeled. The opposition within the church was no longer prepared to remain silent about the farces known as elections. Among the populace the antielection mood was also growing. Significantly more people than before used a voting booth instead of marking their ballots publicly, and then they wrote *NO* on the preselected list of candidates and remained at the precinct until the official count was taken. By comparing results at the individual polling stations with the official published tallies, they discovered that the numbers were without a doubt manipulated; the figures simply didn't agree. They initiated legal actions but the prosecuting attorneys either rejected them outright or did nothing at all. The Protestant Church Leaders issued a statement demanding an investigation but it went unanswered. In the following months public protests against the fraudulent election took place around the country. People would gather on the seventh day of the month at a specified place and give a loud "concert of catcalls."

Summer 1989. The suppression of the democratic reform movement on Tiananmen Square in Beijing aroused the entire world. The internal political atmosphere within the GDR was becoming more tense. Applications to leave surged because many feared that the "Peking conditions" might develop within their own country. Weeks full of drama followed. Many GDR citizens virtually took over Federal Republic's embassies in Budapest, Prague, and Warsaw as a way of forcing their government to allow them to emigrate to the West. Finally in September the Hungarians opened their border with Austria and a mass exodus to the Federal Republic followed. On the eve of the elaborately planned fortieth anniversary of the Republic, the GDR regime appeared helpless. In a desperate effort to save its image, it made concessions, one small slice after another, but in vain. The church again raised its voice to proclaim the bitter truth that the state tried to dispel or suppress.

2 September 1989. The Protestant Church Leaders expressed concern about the continuing flood of emigrants. In a letter to the local congregations they urged people to remain in the GDR, but yet they recognized the problem at hand. The "essential cause for the exit visa applications is the denial of anticipated and long overdue changes in the society." It is "indispensable and urgent that a process be set in motion to secure the responsible participation of the citizenry in the building of our society and that a productive public discussion of the tasks before us take place that will restore confidence in the work of our state agencies."

The church insisted on an open and realistic discussion of the reasons for dissatisfaction and the mistakes that have been made and consideration of specific criticisms that would be efffectual in bringing about changes. Needed was accurate information about political and economic matters and realistic reports in the meda "that does not conflict with that which one sees and experiences day after day." The opportunity to travel to other countries, regardless of the reason, and the right of all former GDR citizens to return to their homeland were absolutely necessary.

17 September 1989. The bishop of Magdeburg, Dr. Christoph Demke, sent a letter to the church workers in the *Landeskirche* of Saxony-Anhalt and it was published in the church press. He pointed out that the irrational contradiction between what one experienced in everyday life and what appeared in the newspapers was becoming unbearable. He called for "open, courageous dialogue regarding the reality that exists in our country. For without this knowledge we will not find answers to the questions of how we ought to proceed in the coming years. . . . To see both the good and the bad, to distinguish between that which ought to remain and that which must not continue, is necessary as we approach our fortieth anniversary."

The bishop said that the following should remain: safeguarding the basic needs of life, such as work, housing, and medical care, but done in a different way than merely by state subsidies; the responsibility to seek and maintain peace; the nation's antifascist commitment; and the socialist concern for sharing the burdens and the fruits of one's labor with one another, but this should include individual responsibility strengthened by a market economy. What ought not to continue were: the contradiction between what the regime calls reality and the experiences of daily living; the idea that rights are given to the people as rewards and presents; the inclination to mistrust all initiatives that have not been planned by the state and the use of the state security organs to meet any perceived threat; and the state's claim that it is always right, thus making the admission of errors almost a catastrophe and corrections as a sign of weakness.

Bishop Demke summed up his views in the slogan, "Our faith gets involved." He added:

> Faith itself is a struggle with reality. For the reality that we confess at the beginning of every worship service is controversial and becomes involved in the reality of this world: "Our help is in the name of the Lord, who made the heavens and the earth," that is, the path that our church follows stands under the reality of His lordship, so also the path that our country is treading. Often we don't see traces of His lordship. We pray for it: "Your kingdom come!" We are waiting for the time when the truth of this reality will light up the world, as it is promised, "that at the name of Jesus every knee shall bow, of everyone that is in heaven, and on earth and under the earth, and that every tongue shall confess that Jesus Christ is Lord, to the glory of God the Father." We can only expect this if we ourselves bow down before this Lord.
>
> How good it is that this Lord of whom this has been said is named Jesus. Under His eyes we must fight for the reality of our country. There is no cause for smugness or a know-it-all attitude. It is also time that the uncomfortable truth that causes pain be turned into good deeds that bring healing. One need not play "hide and seek" with one's own wretchedness, the wretchedness of our church. But there is also freedom here to distinguish in a concrete way between the good and the bad. Everything can take a turn for the better and we play our part in making it so.

19 September 1989. The annual synod of the GDR Church Federation held in Eisenach just ended. The main topic was supposed to have been an evaluation of the conclusions (contained in thirteen weighty texts) of the Ecumenical Assembly of Christians and Churches in the GDR for Justice, Peace, and the Preservation of the Creation. But the increasingly more explosive political situation occupied center stage. Bishop Leich, chair of the Protestant Federation, declared: "After forty years we in the GDR find ourselves in a situation that necessitates a change in the way we do things. . . . We want to contribute to making life in our society more attractive."

A general debate followed, in which example after example of societal evils were mentioned, together with wishes, demands, and hopes for the future. After lengthy discussion, the synod adopted a comprehensive position paper on the current situation and the church's role in it:

> Placed before us today is the challenge of preserving that which is worthwhile while at the same time seeking new ways to make this a more just and participatory society. We want to help make our country a desirable place in which to live and encourage people to stay here. Therefore, we ask them to remain and contribute to making a better future for all their fellow citizens.

Continuing in this same vein, the paper expressed the desire for reforms in the country, an open and public examination of the societal problems, the responsible collaboration of everyone in the process, and truthfulness as a prerequisite for an atmosphere of mutual trust. It specifically demanded a responsible pluralistic media policy, a democratic multiparty system, freedom of travel for all, economic reforms, responsible treatment of public and private property, the right to hold peaceful demonstrations, and an election procedure that allowed genuine choice among programs and candidates.

The synod testified to the fact that fifty years after the outbreak of World War II we still needed to keep the memory of it alive. For us Germans, coming to terms with the terror and guilt of the past can never cease. We were warned of newly emerging nationalistic and neo-Nazi voices and opinions and told we must oppose these with everything we as a church have at our disposal. It further reminded us "that the future development in our country depends largely on the ability and readiness for dialogue within the church and in the society." There was no reasonable alternative to the continuation and expansion of dialogue at all levels. This was the only way to achieve a just and democratic society, one that would be at peace within and without, and also at peace with the environment.

4 September 1989. The Leipzig "Prayers for Peace" resumed after the summer break. These weekly prayer services have gone on since the beginning of the 1980s. But now an increasing number of those wanting to leave the country articulated their concerns here under the church's protective hand. The cry "We want out!" was frequently heard. Three weeks later on 25 September news reports indicated that following the prayers for peace a full-blown demonstration of 5,000 people took place on the square outside the Nikolai Church. The police and security forces used massive force against them.

2 October 1989. At the Gethsemane Church in Berlin, young people of the church-affiliated peace, ecology, and human rights groups began a vigil that was supposed to continue without interruption until 10 October. Their desire was to express solidarity with the ones arrested and fined for their part in the Leipzig demonstration the week before, and they called for their release from confinement and exemption from punishment. The daily intercessory prayers offered at the Gethsemane Church articulated their rage, complaints, and accusations, but also their hope and desire for changes in the country. Nonviolence was also preached; because the peace of Christ determines our life, we must remain nonviolent. But we must also be uncompromising in our pursuit of change.

6 October 1989. Today the official media of the land celebrated the fortieth anniversary of the founding of the GDR. Pictures of the arrival of foreign guests were seen on TV screens, Mikhail Gorbachev on his trip through Berlin to his lodging was enthusiastically greeted by tens of thousands of citizens with the cry "Gorbi, Gorbi," and a pompous state occasion once again conjured up glory and honor for the socialist German Democratic Republic. That evening there was a torchlight spectacle with the Free German Youth parading through the city center designed to demonstrate enthusiasm and devotion for this state, the Socialist Unity Party, and their leaders.

While all of this was going on, a workshop with the theme "Where Do We Go From Here, GDR?" was held at the Church of the Redeemer in the Lichtenberg district of Berlin, far removed from the festive atmosphere. It was organized by the Protestant Youth Department of Berlin. A joint declaration was read that was prepared two days earlier by representatives of various opposition groups who saw the church as the only available forum they could use to reach the public. It stated: "We greet the many initiatives now taking shape as indications of a genuine awakening and of the growing courage to express one's political positions publicly." Among the signatories were representatives of the emerging "citizens' movements": New Forum, Democracy Now, Initiative Peace and Human Rights, New Democratic Departure, Initiative Group Social Democratic Party, and several local peace groups. The sixteen signers pledged to work for a democratic transformation. They saw as of prime importance the need to engage the country in discussions that would enable a democratic election. They challenged everyone to become involved and to demand political changes.

More than two thousand people, mainly youths, crowded into the church. From two podiums people of various ideological and religious persuasions spoke about their hopes and dreams for the future and the reforms they felt were urgently needed. With regard to the future they agreed that the vision of socialism should not be relinquished. They talked about a democratic form of socialism and the GDR as an alternative to the Federal Republic. Being at the forefront of such a quest for new values meant we had a chance to start over.

6 October 1989. Leipzig. The mass gatherings following the peace prayers on the previous Mondays and the attacks by the "forces to preserve order" have heated up the atmosphere in the city known mainly for its industrial fairs. In today's *Leipziger Volkszeitung* appeared a letter under the headline, "Hostility to the State Will No Longer Be Tolerated":

> The members of the [one hundred man] combat unit "Hans Geifert" condemn the unconscionable actions that have been going on for some time in the city of Leipzig. We are for the citizens of the Christian faith who conduct their worship services and prayers in the Nikolai Church. The constitution and government of our socialist GDR guarantee them this freedom. What we oppose is the misuse of these church functions to carry out provocations against the GDR. We are deeply disturbed when we are confronted with such things after a day's labor.

Therefore we expect that everything will be done to guarantee public order and safety, in order to protect those values and achievements of socialism that we have attained in forty years of hard work. We desire the continuation of what has built so far for the well-being of the people. We are ready and willing to protect what we have created through the labor of our own hands by putting a stop to these counterrevolutionary actions, once and for all, even if it must be with our weapons in hand! We deny these elements the right to use songs and slogans of the worker class for their purposes. In the final analysis, they are only trying to hide their true motives.

This letter was signed by a "Commander Günter Lutz on behalf of the combat group 'Hans Geifert'." When people from the peace groups went to talk with Lutz about the piece, they learned that he had not written it. The forgery, however, indicated how serious the situation was becoming, and the threat of armed force was no idle gesture, as one would soon see.

4 October 1989. The dramatic events in Dresden fueled agitation throughout the country during the week prior to the fortieth anniversary celebration. Thousands of people besieged the main railway station. Sealed trains of the East German Railroad transporting refugees from Prague to the Federal Republic would roll through here tonight. Many planned to jump onto the trains in a desperate attempt to escape with the others. They stormed the train station. The police and security forces were armed with nightsticks and water cannons and had orders to use as much force as necessary. Many innocent people were caught up in the street battles, arrested and led away in a brutal fashion, and taken to police stations and jails within a thirty-five-mile radius.

The Revolution Forges Ahead Peacefully

8 October 1989. The state festivities in Berlin have ended and things in the capital were now going in an different direction. In the center of Dresden a huge demonstration took place in reaction to the events of the previous four days. The march ended peacefully in the evening on Prager Strasse near the railroad station. The following report is from the Protestant News Service:

During this time the demonstrators sought to make contact with the police. They collected the demands and chose twenty people from their midst to present them to the authorities. Meanwhile, Bishop Hempel and the Protestant Superintendent of Dresden Ziemer had gone to the city hall to confer with Mayor Berghofer. They arranged for the delegation to be received by the mayor on the next morning, Monday, 9 October. Four representatives of the Protestant and Catholic churches would accompany them, with the full understanding that they would not be considered as partners in the dialogue. In the evening, the people who had assembled in four Dresden churches were informed of these developments. The buildings were so full that the meetings had to be repeated in three of them.

On 10 October the Dresden newspaper, *Die Union*, carried this account of the previous day's events:

On Sunday evening something happened on Prager Strasse that opened up a new way. Thousands of people, among them many youths, gathered in a peaceful, nonviolent way to express their opinions about the problems currently burdening our country.

The security forces stood facing them. Several Dresdners, among them the Catholic curate Frank Richter, went directly toward the uniformed officers and requested the opportunity to talk with the person in charge. The conversation took place, and nonviolence and the readiness to dialogue, both on the part of security forces as well as those assembled, made this possible. The demonstrators delegated twenty "speakers" to formulate their desires and questions. They included: a nonviolent dialogue, information about those who had been arrested in the previous days, problems of media reporting, travel opportunities, the election system, a civilian alternative to military service, and recognition of the New Forum

Those present greeted the first opportunity for talks with Mayor Wolfgang Berghofer of Dresden with gratitude and joy. That this dialogue in fact was possible was due to the efforts of Bishop Dr. Hempel and Superintendent Christof Ziemer, efforts which deserve our respect. The police patrols laid their shields down, the canine units were withdrawn, and the demonstration dissipated, peacefully and without incident.

The following paragraph, also taken from the newspaper of the Dresden Christian Democratic Union, indicates that a genuine turning (*Wende*) had occurred there:

> On Monday afternoon, the conversation took place between the delegated speakers and church officials with the mayor of Dresden in the city hall. All were thankful for this dialogue, which was open, objective, and friendly. Some of the dialogue participants went to the Nikolai Church in Leipzig to inform those gathered there of the encouraging and cheering news that it is possible to talk with one another. Others from the group reported about their experiences on Prager Strasse and the meeting with mayor that evening in the Dresden Cathedral, the Church of the Cross, the Church of the Atonement, and Christ Church. Since a neutral public meeting hall was not available, the churches welcomed the citizens of Dresden.

In the meantime, demonstrations and rallies occurred in other cities and even smaller towns. The actions began in Saxony and Thuringia, and then spread to the center of the GDR and finally but rapidly into the North. The starting points always were the prayer services for peace in the churches, and from these the people took the admonition for nonviolence and peaceableness into the streets and public squares. Within a few days most of the several hundred persons arrested in Dresden were set free. Superintendent Ziemer stated that the conversation in the city hall marked a new beginning and sent an important signal that people could move from confrontation to dialogue.

7 October 1989. In the late morning, the military parade droned on past the party and state leadership and foreign guests of state seated on the reviewing stand on Berlin's Karl Marx Allee. The state celebration then was transformed into a public festival, which like everything else, was carefully planned. However, the desired spirit of the occasion never came through. Some people who gathered in the late afternoon on the Alexanderplatz understood the seventh of the month as a signal for something else. Once again, with a chorus of catcalls they started to protest against the fraudulent election of 7 May. But this time the police and security forces did not let it go very far. Arriving immediately, they plunged into the mob and tried to disperse it. In so doing they seized individuals indiscriminately and made many arrests. Soon the crowd swelled into thousands, and the police forced them from the square. Then they moved north toward the Gethsemane Church where others were engaged in a prayer vigil that evening.

The procession did not reach its objective. The authorities labeled the action a "counterrevolution," and the police forces were directed to suppress it at all costs. They beat people at random, chased and captured many who were fleeing, and hauled away those who were arrested. In such a manner the fortieth anniversary celebration of the GDR ended, even as the world was watching. TV coverage, albeit brief, was provided by teams from the West at great personal risk. Everyone sensed that the government was tottering, but the *Wende* had not come yet.

On the same day, far removed from these activities, the gathering to found a new Social Democratic Party of the GDR (the original one had been absorbed into the SED in 1946) took place in Schwante, a village north of Berlin—in a room of the church parish house.

8 October 1989. The occurrences of the previous day and week stirred the hearts and emotions of people everywhere in the GDR. Because clashes with law enforcement personnel had occurred during the week at the Gethsemane Church after the evening intercessory worship services, the area in front of the church had been cordoned off. This Sunday the events that had transpired the evening before were the topics of discussion, protest, admonition, and prayer. The church was completely full and lighted candles were in the windows of the surrounding houses.

When the service concluded, the people left the house of God only to find themselves facing a human chain of police and State Security officials. Even the side streets were blocked off. Police cars arrived on the scene. They were ready to stop any demonstration in front of the church. People were ordered to pass single file through openings in the police lines so their identities could be checked and then they were to go on their way home. The protest became noisy, scuffles and jostling ensued, and the mass of people surged toward the nearby Schönhäuser Allee. There the crowd found itself literally encircled. From both sides police vehicles with large shields mounted in front of the radiators moved in and shoved the screaming people, whom the police were beating with clubs, into a concentrated area in the street. Many were running about frantically and tried to flee. Those who ran on to the sidewalks were pursued into hallways and even apartments where they were seeking refuge. Large numbers of people, including innocent bystanders, were apprehended, beaten, and carried away on trucks to special detention centers where they were psychologically and physically mistreated.

Later it was learned that 1,083 persons were victims of such "detentions" on 7 and 8 October in Berlin, that is, they were taken in and held for police interrogation. Only weeks later would an independent investigating commission (which included church members) begin clarifying the events. It would help those affected to assert their rights, and, by confirming their peaceful intentions, see to it that they were vindicated. But to completely expose the power structures and to identify and charge those who were suspected of criminal behavior was not possible even after months of work. The tightly woven network of relationships between the SED, Stasi, police, and judiciary proved to be absolutely impenetrable.

9 October 1989. In Leipzig it was as if the air were burning. On 7 October the police had chased down demonstrators on the Georgi-Ring. On 8 October, at the same time as the police action in Berlin, another small demonstration occurred in the Leipzig city center and the police quickly halted it. People now were fearful what the consequences might be of the next confrontation with the state authorities.

Anxiety was to be found everywhere in the city. What will happen after this Monday's prayer service? Rumors were flying about troop movements and especially the orders for their deployment. Will Leipzig, like Beijing, experience its own Tiananmen Square? But a strong sense of determination was also in the air. We want no confrontation, but we will demonstrate! We insist, "no violence," but we will not back down!

For the people of Leipzig, this was the day of the peaceful rising and the *Wende*, the turning point. Realizing how perilous the situation was, people on all sides were working to forestall further escalation of tensions, to counter the assertion of power with levelheadedness, and to find areas for dialogue and agreement. "The Nikolai Church open for everyone" was slogan posted at the doorways to the church since the prayer services for peace began in 1982. But on this Monday other churches in the city center were open as well—St. Thomas, St. Michael's, and the Reformed Church. By two o'clock the main floor of the Nikolai Church was already full. Many of these early arrivals were undoubtedly members of the police and the Stasi. The pastor usually roped off the balconies and then just before the service at five o'clock opened them to accommodate those who had really come to pray. In the meantime Professor Kurt Masur, music director of the world-renowned Gewandhaus Orchestra, read an appeal over Leipzig Radio for peace and calm. It was directed not only at the populace but also at the power structure.

This was the "Appeal of the Six," one of the most crucial actions of the revolution. Recognizing the seriousness of the hour, Maser had invited several prominent figures in Leipzig to his home to discuss how they could bring the situation under control and get a dialogue started. In the group were three important local SED functionaries, a cabaret performer, and a university professor of theology. Their appeal urged the people of Leipzig to avoid violence and provocative actions "in order not to jeopardize a dialogue concerning the development of socialism in our country and the initiatives for resolving the difficult situation." The statement was also read in the packed churches where it was warmly received. In addition, Bishop Hempel rushed from Dresden and went to all four churches to admonish the people to keep calm and let reason prevail.

The situation in the Nikolai Church was a strange one. In a deliberate action whose intent was not clear at first, hundreds of SED party members had taken seats long before the start of the service. One of them, a student, wrote about it two days later in the newspaper of the Free German Youth, *Junge Welt*:

> Something truly worth thinking about and pondering hap-
> pened to everyone who experienced it this Monday in Leipzig;
> indeed, it was astounding. In the St. Nicholas Church several
> hundred SED members were among those seated there. The deci-
> sion to do so was a controversial one, but its success justifies the
> unusual means used to attain it. The objective was not to intimi-

date those Christians who wanted to pray, but rather to demonstrate by actions our willingness to dialogue with representatives of the church and the groups now associated with it.

That the church leadership understood and accepted this offer was demonstrated in the ensuing service of prayers for peace. Within the church was an astonishing atmosphere of common agreement about current problems of our society. I was not the only one who noticed this. Without glossing over the various ways of looking at the problems, the need for urgent dialogue with one another about the important questions was stressed. In addition, the church representatives opposed violent protest actions and called for clearheadedness.

Nikolai Church Pastor Christian Führer remembered the event like this:

> In spite of the long hours of waiting, the atmosphere in the church was amazingly good. The worship service proceeded as we had planned it. Isaiah 45 was the text for the sermon. We kept our minds focused on the service in spite of the tensions that day and noise being made by the thousands milling around outside.

Following the worship services, a huge demonstration of seventy thousand formed, a truly amazing number of people who gathered voluntarily. This evening will remain in their memory as the "miracle of Leipzig," the real beginning of the *Wende*, the decisive point of the peaceful revolution with its rallying cry, "We are the people." The armed forces of the state were in readiness; later we heard that hospitals and infirmaries were preparing to take in the wounded. But they didn't intervene. They laid aside their helmets, protective shields, and nightsticks and engaged in conversations with demonstrators. They were busy only in regulating traffic.

In the days following, the source of the command to show restraint was a topic of much discussion and speculation, but so far no clear explanation has emerged. Many factors seem to have converged—particularly the example of Dresden and the resolve and levelheadedness of the Leipzigers. When they passed by the Gewandhaus Orchestra Hall that evening, the marchers expressed their thanks to Professor Masur for the appeal he initiated with cheers and applause. On the next day, the *Leipziger Volkszeitung*, the local SED newspaper, printed the comments that the Gewand-haus staff made supporting their conductor in a West German television interview:

> Let us have a meaningful dialogue in our country among all members of the society. It certainly makes sense if people of other persuasions have the opportunity to express themselves publicly. We have to face the facts regarding our problems. We must not pretend that there aren't any. We must not lose any more time.

9 October 1989. The *Wende* has also begun in Berlin, although it will be some days before the SED starts appropriating the term to characterize its own hesitant, gradual involvement in the country's transformation. Nearly three thousand gathered at the Gethsemane Church to reflect on the events of the previous two days. This time they were completely unmolested, and following the service they dispersed peaceably and without demonstrating. In the worship service, however, concern was expressed about the ones who had been arrested the evening before and were still in custody. Speakers also condemned the demeaning humiliation that the demonstrators reportedly were suffering at the detention and interrogation centers.

Bishop Gottfried Forck of the Protestant Church in Berlin-Brandenburg presented four "requests" (not demands) that he and some colleagues had formulated in response to the events:

> 1. We urge all citizens to exercise their freedom of speech immediately, without fear, so that dialogue about our future will start.
> 2. We urge the government of the GDR to take clear and credible actions to enable the development of a democratic, socialist state based on the rule of law.
> 3. We urge the police and security forces to use the utmost restraint in dealing with impatient and critical citizens who have taken to the streets so that irreparable damage is not done.
> 4. We urge that the unhappy people in our land not conduct public demonstrations without police permits so that those who are in charge politically will not be able to say later that they were unduly pressured into making changes.

11 October 1989. For the first time the SED Politburo publicly mentioned the recent developments in the country. It admitted problems and omissions and hinted at concessions. It announced that "on the foundation of the socialist order" efforts at improvements will be made and a dialogue started. At the same time, however: "The socialist system on German soil is not up for discussion." Nothing was said about changes in personnel. The TV news reports continued in the same old way, within the same type of language, to tell how Erich Honecker, Günter Mittag, and Joachim Herrmann would inform the chairmen of the "bloc parties" (the non-Communist groups linked with the SED) about the Politburo statement.

Meanwhile, on the same day, more than 220 workers at the diaconal institution "Queen Elizabeth" (a medical and social service agency and the only Protestant hospital in East Berlin) signed an open letter to the Politburo, People's Chamber, and Minister of Health which pointed out the damaging consequences of the country's misguided course and pleaded for help. The agency had lost eight percent of its total staff because of emigration. It stated further:

> We cannot fill the gaps; we are at the limit of our capabilities. We fear that we can no longer adequately provide for the needs of our patients and will have to close down part of our work. We are not the only agency in this situation. Thus, we find it incomprehensible that the government has failed to face the facts and to honestly look for the causes.

The social workers did not want to be "guilty of any harm, injustice, or further disastrous developments by remaining silent." Instead they asked for the kind of honest reporting in the media that would reflect the existing diversity of opinion, openly explain the problems and difficulties, and at the same time question them. The signatories were incensed by the "use of brutal force against people who carried nothing in their hands except a candle as a symbol of hope." They insisted on the immediate release of all demonstrators and called for the legalization of groups that were promoting dialogue and democracy. Moreover, they went on to state: "In addition, we expect the groups that are now in the process of organizing for the purpose of speaking up for dialogue, openness, and an active democracy in our society will be legalized." The letter concluded with an affirmation of hope and confidence in the country and that change will occur.

13 October 1989. Bishop Forck informed a packed congregation at the Gethsemane Church about the conversation he and other church leaders had the day before with Berlin Mayor Erhard Krack. They discussed the events of the previous weekend, the tasks lying before them, and the possibilities for dialogue. He also communicated a message from the State Secretary for Church Quesions that most of those arrested during the weekend demonstrations had been released. One unresolved matter was the continuing imprisonment of persons charged with being "violent criminals." In his opinion, defending oneself against arrest was not an act of violence. Finally, he said he was drafting a formal complaint to the Berlin chief of police and the Council of Ministers about the mistreatment of those taken into custody.

Then the bishop delivered a moving sermon. He recounted the experiences of prisoners and their understandable anger about what was being done to them. Then he cited the words of Psalm 119:106: "I swear and will keep my word. All the laws of your righteousness I will preserve," and suggested that those who treated us in this way may have often been fatigued and under orders from their superiors. They need people to overwhelm them with patience and love.

> We cannot create conflicts. We cannot take a stand for righteousness if we exclude people from the People's Police and other organs of the state from being touched by the love of God. This love can give them a new sense of purpose in life, and they will no longer deal harshly and unjustly with others.

Forck added that a long and difficult path still lies ahead before we can achieve the conditions which will be satisfactory to all. "My wish is that we will be able to walk this path with the patience Christ exhibited by his life and that people can be won by this means. Then we will build the kind of society within our state where people can be happy."

On the same day, Bishop Forck expressed the hope in an interview in the Berlin weekly *Die Kirche* that the church-state accord of 6 March 1978, to which the state has again and again referred, can continue in effect. A number of important matters have not been resolved, such as differences in educational policy and alternatives to military service. Likewise, he would like a response to the church inquiry about the vote counts in the May elections. He expected at least an apology for the irregularities that occurred and the issuance of clear guidelines for an honest election next time. Also the practice of casting one's vote in public must be discontinued, and it should be possible for groups outside the circle of the bloc parties to place candidates on the ballot.

15 October 1989. Probably in all worship services this Sunday the events of the previous week were mentioned in the sermons, announcements, and intercessory prayers. In many places bishops, church leaders, and other groups expressed their opinions in pastoral statements and circular letters. In Thuringia Bishop Leich called for a "Renewal in the Truth" in his pastoral letter. The first prerequisite for it would be an open and public discussion encompassing all areas of our relationships with the country, and then an honest media policy. He then called for free and secret elections and total freedom of travel. He condemned the use of excessive force by the security organs against peaceful demonstrators and said that church members and ordinary citizens alike should stand firm on the basic principle of nonviolence. Pointing to the task of building the future, he urged people to speak out unambiguously and stop using a double language—one for public life and one for the private sphere. By so doing, one prepares the way for a "renewal in the truth."

Letters making similar points were sent out by Bishop Hempel in Saxony and the Greifswald church leadership. Even the theology students at the GDR's leading university, Humboldt University in Berlin, issued an open letter demanding an immediate public dialogue on current problems and democratic restructuring. They were concerned about the unhealthy social situation that resulted in a mass exodus and widespread resignation, and lamented that those in the government responsible for this have chosen to blame the problems on forces outside our borders, criminalize nonconformist activities, and use excessive violence and arrests against the protesters. In a similar fashion, theology students at Rostock University affirmed the legal and political maturity of the citizenry as a human right and endorsed an open and constructive public dialogue. Solutions to current problems will be only found when we stop following the prescribed government guidelines and seriously consider other arguments.

Another open letter carrying two thousand signatures was released that day by the New Democratic Departure. Directed to the Berlin mayor, it called for an independent commission that would investigate the charges of police brutality on the previous weekend and prevent the reoccurrence of similar situations. Members of the Leipzig Association of Fine Arts held a benefit auction of art works in the city's St. Luke Church, and raised around 50 thousand marks to assist prisoners in their fines. Two of East Germany's leading painters, Wolfgang Mattheuer and Werner Tübke, even contributed works to the auction.

And still more happened this Sunday. The Berlin Protestant Youth Office staged a concert in the Church of the Redeemer that included twenty songwriters, singers, and popular rock groups from around the GDR. In line with concert's theme, "Rock against Violence," they dedicated their performance to those demonstrators who had been arrested and fined. Three thousand young people crowded into the church to hear popular songs and reports about the week's events. One speaker, Dietmar Halbhuber, said they were singing and playing to insure that the people did not have to pay the fines themselves, to vindicate those who were detained, and to secure an investigation commission that would determine what offenses truly were punishable ones.

Among the performers was Kurt Demmler, who utilized eyewitness accounts from Leipzig in one song. He told his hearers not to be satisfied with "a little bit of dialoguing, a little bit of reform." An artist who had been arrested described his experiences. A teacher who had just been fired because he had joined the New Forum urged fundamental changes in the educational system and freeing the schools from ideology. Also, a declaration signed by the cast of the prestigious German Theater in Berlin was read to the crowd. It demanded the creation of an investigation commission and an explanation of the incidents by the Interior and State Security ministries.

16 October 1989. This evening demonstrations and prayer services occurred throughout the country. In the Stralsund Nikolai Church more than a thousand prayed for a peaceful renewal of their society. They consciously viewed these services as the spiritual center of a movement for renewal in which Christians would contribute to solving the problems at hand. The Greifswald student congregation invited the local university's Free German Youth leaders to a conversation, and the seriousness of purpose was very evident. The spectrum of issues discussed ranged from the problems faced by the student organizations to paramilitary sports, discrimination against students who refuse to become reserve officers, and books that required special permission to be read.

At an evening press conference in the Dresden city hall Mayor Berghofer reported on the second round of talks which he had that day with the twenty delegates of 8 October and the Lutheran and Catholic church representatives. He proposed the creation of task forces from within the city council to deal with the specific problems cited by the demonstrators. The Group of Twenty could work with them, and the public would be kept informed through panel discussions and other means of publicity. Berghofer also said all those who had been arrested were now free except seventeen individuals who have been charged with violent crimes.

At the press conference Superintendent Ziemer underscored the role of the church in this dialogue as both that of companion and intermediary. He said the recent events must be dealt with, since people had been treated in a degrading manner and suffered deep emotional wounds. He and the other superintendents in the Dresden church urged the formation of an independent commission to investigate the use of violence in their city and throughout the country. It should be comprised of people from various levels of government as well as churchmen and its report should be made public. This would insure the continuing dialogue was nonthreatening.

Once again, people assembled in the downtown churches, and the Group of Twenty and the church representatives reported on the talks at the city hall. Because the city officials could not—or did not want to—provide space for a meeting, the Twenty accepted the invitation of the churches. Many of those present expressed dissatisfaction with the dialogue process and skepticism about continuing the talks. Some said the dialogue was merely a tactic of the regime.

If the government really wanted dialogue, it should reopen the border with Czechoslovakia and remove the special privileges which members of the military, State Security, and the party elite have. Other changes needed were civilian alternative service, economic reforms, an end to military parades and torchlight processions, term limitations for elected officials, and cancellation of the tasteless propaganda television program "Der Schwarze Kanal." After the informational meetings ended, thirty thousand people peacefully marched through the downtown area.

In Leipzig, 150,000 took part in today's Monday demonstration. Several positive steps had occurred during the week, most notably more open reporting in the media, and it was clear that far-reaching changes were on the way. This induced more people than ever to join these manifestations of public concern. Churches in the city center were filled long before the beginning of the prayer services, and thousands more crowded around outside them.

Those at the St. Thomas Church were told of the various talks that had taken place during the previous week, but many Leipzig citizens felt they fell short of a full-blown dialogue. In his sermon Provost Günther Hanisch characterized the situation as a loss of confidence between those governing and the governed. He hoped that the promised dialogue would not deteriorate into a meaningless slogan. He said that truthfulness is absolutely necessary for dialogue, as it allows confidence to grow again, but he still sees too little truthfulness. This also requires admitting past mistakes and not blaming others, and it can only take place between partners, not victors and vanquished.

After the services ended, the people converged on Karl Marx Platz (after the *Wende* it took back its old name of Augustusplatz), the vast square by the university, shouting the name of Mikhail Gorbachev and just as loudly demanding freedom to travel, democratic elections, and official recognition of the New Forum. A huge procession formed here and the people moved out carrying banners and placards proclaiming their desire to remain in the GDR and welcoming dialogue, so long as it would lead to fundamental reforms.

17 October 1989. The critical situation in the country produced intensive debates within the SED Politburo and Central Committee. As a result, Erich Honecker was forced to step down as the SED General Secretary and the GDR's head of State, while two other Politburo members, Günter Mittag (economic matters) and Joachim Herrmann (media and propaganda) were also ousted. Egon Krenz was then chosen as General Secretary of the party. Shortly afterwards he addressed the nation on television and appealed to the various segments of the population for unity. Referring to "the representatives of the churches and all those affiliated with religious bodies," he said:

> The socialist society needs and wants your cooperation. There is more that unites us than separates us. I want to emphasize strongly that, in mutual respect, we intend to make greater use of these ties and develop them further for the welfare of our state, in which we all live.

18 October 1989. Less than twenty-four hours after his election as General Secretary, Egon Krenz met with the top leadership of the Protestant church. Honecker had already scheduled this meeting before his sudden retirement, and his successor felt it was of the utmost importance to honor the commitment. Present at the discussion, which lasted almost two hours, were Bishop Werner Leich, chair of the Church Federation; his two deputies, Bishop Christoph Demke and Manfred Stolpe, president of the consistory (the administrative head) of the Church of Berlin-Brandenburg; and the leader of the Church Federation's secretariat, Martin Ziegler. According to the official press release, an "open, frank dialogue took place on their mutual responsibility for constructive collaboration between state and church." They agreed "that the German Democratic Republic, whose history is also part of the history of the Protestant churches of our country and the societal engagement of Christian citizens, must be preserved." This requires mutual respect for each other's convictions and mission and will lead to a new chapter in constructive cooperation between the state and the church:

> The dialogue partners underscored their firm desire to create confidence and act on it. In this way each can take seriously that which they have achieved and an atmosphere will develop in

which answers to pressing questions of importance to everyone can be found. The conviction was expressed that, as we look toward shaping the present and the future, more binds us together than separates us.

The specific topics on the agenda were the need for changes in the society, beginning a frank dialogue while at the same time avoiding "rash actions" that might make the situation worse, the continuing development of socialist democracy, and a new media policy that would be distinguished by openness, practicality, and realism.

Reporting later to the their fellow church leaders, they said that the main issue was regaining hope and confidence. The denial of open and public discussions, a media policy out of touch with reality, and the use of violence at demonstrations have seriously damaged confidence, as the massive emigration so painfully indicates. They pressed for fast action on these and other matters, including open dialogue with the new groups that have formed, passports for all citizens, an unambiguous election procedure, the creation of a government subject to law, democratic law-making processes, and a clear delineation between the responsibilities of party and government. They also saw the need for dialogue about the educational system and alternative service for draftees in health care and other civilian areas.

19 October 1989. Although the Protestant churches have given the process of change great momentum, we must not overlook the active involvement of other Christians. Prayer services also were held in Catholic churches, Catholics participated in the citizens' group discussions and negotiations with local government officials, they were numbered among the demonstrators, and in an ecumenical spirit they supported Protestant initiatives and activities. Likewise, the "quiet ones in the land" were there, the pietistic *Gemeinschafts*-Christians and members of the free churches, who traditionally were not involved in public activities. Their chapels and meeting houses were also centers of prayer for peace and intercession for the country during the October weeks. They too marched in the demonstrations and spoke up for the sovereignty of the people, democracy, nonviolence, and renewal of the society. But they also wanted spiritual renewal and contributed many of the "religious" slogans carried in the processions: "The root of the problem—God's honor has been taken away"; "Without a return to God, our people become bankrupt"; "Instead of many NDs—more NTs." (ND = *Neues Deutschland*, the SED newspaper; NT = New Testament).

The Council of the Association of Protestant Free Churches, the umbrella organization whose members included the Methodists, Baptists, Evangelical Free Church, and (with observer status) the Moravians (*Brüder-Unität* or Herrnhut Brethren) passed a resolution today about the situation in the GDR. It declared its consternation and sorrow because so many young people were fleeing the country and have left such "painful gaps" in their congregations and social service agencies. At the same time the council was "alarmed and indignant that violence was used against people who want to stay here but have engaged in peaceful demonstrations aimed at bringing about changes." To counter the "deep moral poverty" requires fundamental societal changes:

> The daily contradiction between the "reality" as depicted in the official media and the actual reality experienced by the people will no longer be uncritically accepted. More and more citizens are articulating their objections, making proposals for change, and boldly demanding their rights.

Since the free churches have always supported personal as well as religious freedom, they wanted to be involved like the rest of the citizenry in shaping the society. But as their statement put it: "This heritage places us under a great obligation. We confess that out of pragmatic considerations and a piety that encourages withdrawal from the world, we too often yield to the temptation to conform." The congregations had mixed reactions to this section. Some regarded it as an inappropriate self-accusation, but others viewed it as an important insight. The document then spoke of the mission of free church Christians and encouraged them to prepare for unhindered talks that will get to the root of our problems. The Free Church Council underlined the point that it was in full accord with the demands being made by other church bodies—changes in information and media policy, fair elections, and reforms in the legal system, travel, military service, and environmental policy. The concluding paragraph was especially important:

Our involvement in societal matters does not stand in contradiction to our personal witness and obligation to preach the Gospel. We realize the temporal nature of everything on earth. We know God's kingdom is not of this world. But it is precisely this knowledge that God will bring about the final salvation that gives us courage and hope to live in the world and at the same time places a great responsibility upon us

20 October 1989. At a meeting in Neustrelitz of the leaders of the Greifswald and Mecklenburg churches, the host, Superintendent Winkelmann, stated that the patient but persistent calls for change and well-attended prayer services were the situation in the churches of the northern GDR as well. They shared information about the prayers for peace in Rostock, Neubrandenburg, Neustrelitz, Greifswald, and Stralsund, an open forum in Schwerin's St. Paul's Church, and demonstrations in Greifswald and Neubrandenburg. The leaders stressed that the political groups like the New Forum must receive official recognition soon. Both *Landeskirchen* will provide space for them and work to enable a direct dialogue between the citizenry and the government.

21 October 1989. While the situation in the country is still unstable, the "voice of the people" has become a force to be reckoned with. Now a process of reappraisal is beginning in church circles. At the synod of the Lutheran Church of Saxony Bishop Hempel applauded the "hesitant beginnings of a new dialogue, the first indications that the government will listen to the people," but he questioned whether skepticism should be put aside. He was concerned whether the critical voices would be heard, significant change occur, and meaningful public dialogue take place. He insisted that "those in power must for their own sakes get close to the ones they govern, and even to their critics. They need criticism and self-criticism, not merely within their inner circle but within full view of the public.

Hempel underscored that the church's task was to urge both sides to refrain from the use of violence. "Our Lord has shown us clearly that violence always destroys more than it preserves. Let us be obedient to Him." The problems of the day are really between the government and the common people; what those "nameless ones" think should be important to the regime. So many are leaving, especially young people, because they have lost any hope of being able to change things from the grassroots to the top and achieve more pluralism and freedom, without being labeled as "enemies of socialism." Exacerbating the situation is the ideological pressure brought to bear on the children which forces them to wear two faces, one at school and the other at home. This mass exodus from the GDR is a human, economic, cultural, and emotional bloodletting of the first rank.

22 October 1989. During an open forum led by Kurt Masur at the Leipzig Gewandhaus, Superintendent Friedrich Magirius of the Nikolai Church took the podium and said he regarded Krenz's meeting with the church leadership as an important sign. He then suggested some points for the dialogue on renewal, including an "open, honest education of our children and young people." He was loudly applauded when he added: "We consider it necessary not to have to raise people who have two faces, one for school and one for home." Magirius also urged the formation of a commission to investigate the police violence and the creation of independent courts. Theology professor Peter Zimmermann, one of the "Leipzig Six" then proposed a law to create a national alternative civilian service. He linked his suggestion (which still bordered on the taboo) to the desperate personnel situation in the health care and social service field, certainly one of the country's most pressing problems. Similar public forums took place this Sunday for the first time in Berlin, Halle, Dresden, and Frankfurt.

23 October 1989. An international press conference was held at the new Fennpfuhl Protestant church center in Berlin-Lichtenberg. Representatives of various opposition groups recounted their experiences two weeks earlier, insisted the deployment of the police and security forces was carefully coordinated, and called for a full investigation, the release of all political prisoners, the dismissal of charges against the demonstrators, and restitution for those affected.

Among the evidence presented at the press conference was a hundred-page document collection compiled by a Berlin Protestant youth pastor, Wolfram Hülsemann, entitled "Personal Accounts—

Days and Nights after the Seventh of October, 1989, in Berlin." He said that the shocking reports by those who were arrested and beaten was being made available to the public because it was the only way that this abuse of state power could be exposed and dealt with.

Administrator Manfred Stolpe and the General Superintendent of Berlin, Günter Krusche, both declared that the courage needed to deal with the truth would be painful for all parties. However, the church saw as its task to be a kind of "wailing wall," an outlet for the disclosure of unpleasant truths, and the leadership fully supported the release of this material and holding the press conference itself. It was necessary that the reports be transmitted to the responsible authorities so they could act on these matters. All charges must be resolved as soon as possible, persons who suffered injuries must receive compensation, and guarantees must be made that all differences of opinion will be settled by political means and without the threat of violence.

Here is one quote from Hülsemann's book:

> Sunday, 8 October 1989, at 22:15, I saw the following with my own eyes: At the back entrance of the Schönhäuser Allee elevated train station, a woman in the advanced stages of pregnancy was waiting for her husband. She called out: "Peter, are you coming?" At that moment, a policeman swinging a type of whip containing a spike-covered ball hit her squarely across the face. The woman immediately collapsed and cried for help. The policeman left right away. The train dispatcher observed the incident and she too screamed. The officer replied: "Keep your trap shut!" I couldn't see anything else because the train on which I was riding pulled out of the station.

Various witnesses told the press that the security forces continued to inflict unnecessary physical and psychological violence on the people taken into custody. Many were held for longer than twenty-four hours and had to obtain medical treatment after their release. Little was done about this even after the city established an investigating committee. The hearings dragged on for months and the commission came up against a wall of silence, excuses, deception, and "lost" documents. Although a full investigation was never possible, it did expose the incidents and forced the resignation of several important police officials and prosecuting attorneys.

In Leipzig this Monday six Protestant and Catholic churches in the downtown area served as departure points for the demonstrations. More and more people were taking part, and tonight around 300,000 marched around the city center in a completely closed ring, without beginning and without end. Additional thousands stood in front of the opera at Karl Marx Platz since there was hardly any room left in the procession. Countless candles gave the event a pleasant, peaceful light.

The demands written on the banners and chanted by various groups have become increasingly varied. Last week they were mainly for the freedom to travel, but today they called for restructuring of the society, democratization, free elections, freedom of the press, official recognition of the New Forum, civilian alternative service, reformation of the educational system, and making ecology a vital part of the economy. They railed against the State Security Service and the hated GDR television commentator, Karl Eduard von Schnitzler. The crowd chanted slogans like: "We are the people," "Put the Stasi to work," "Schnitzler, off to the mines," "Egon, open up the borders," "We'll be back on Monday," "Too much power in one hand, is not healthy for this land," "Go away, Egon—it's no use," and "Gorbi, Gorbi." On the thousands of placards and banners were such phrases as: "Stay in the country and stand up for your rights," "Free elections, true results," "Now or never—Democracy," "No privileged class," "Egon, stop talking, just give us perestroika," "Believe the Gospel," "Jesus Christ says: I am the Way, the Truth and the Life," "This country needs new men," "Independent parents' councils," "Civilian alternative service is a human right," "For forty years we were nice, but now wake up from your sleep," and "The state and party are two different things." In German many of these were catchy rhymes.

At the St. Thomas Church service, Professor Ulrich Kühn preached on the topic of power. Citing the relationship between Jesus and Pilate, he explained that power is a "commodity loaned to us" for the welfare and protection of the people. We do not appropriate it for ourselves; rather it is given to us by God. Intrinsic to it is accountability. Political power must be protected from misuse, and in our country it must be controlled by the public. Power must be shared and the people must have a say. This requires the separation of state and party because dialogue and a monopoly of power are incompatible. Free elections that include a choice among party programs are imperative. A separation of powers among the executive, legislative, and the judicial branches of the government is also needed. Kühn now had introduced a new idea into the public discussion—revision of the GDR's constitution.

24 October 1989. The People's Chamber chose SED General Secretary Egon Krenz as head of state. He also became the chairman of the National Defense Council. That evening twelve thousand Berliners peacefully marched in protest of this action. Once again all the state powers were in the hands of one person and the demand for the separation of party and state had been ignored. The day before, two thousand people had walked to the Council of State building following the Monday prayers in the Gethsemane Church. They placed candles on the steps and delivered a petition asking that several candidates be considered in the election of the head of state.

26 October 1989. The weekly Protestant News Service bulletin contained an overview of the events of the week, which opened with this concise paragraph:

> From one end of the country to the other church congregations, buildings, and functions are serving as gathering points and occasionally even places of refuge. They have also become the centers for public declarations and dialogue about our society. Christians, Protestant as well as Catholic, ordinary members, church workers, synod members, and bishops are becoming involved in the public dialogue and struggle to reform the society of the GDR as partners, mediators, and givers of admonition. Reports about these activities from churches and parishes have been flowing into our editorial offices.

One of these came from a rural area in Saxony, and it is exemplary of what was happening across the country. In the town of Markneukirchen (Vogtland) on 8 October the congregation made a silent procession around the parish church carrying candles after a prayer vigil. These were repeated during the next few days, each time with several hundred taking part. After one of these services the city council acceded to the request to talk about necessary changes. On 17 October the first conversation took place, and the following evening three thousand people came to the worship service and silent procession. In Klingenthal, a spontaneous demonstration with an estimated one thousand participants occurred on 13 October. The people then went to the church where a prayer service and informational session were held. They demanded to talk with the local SED leaders, who agreed to do so. An even larger procession occurred a week later and it too ended at the church where a brief service took place.

29 October 1989. The Lutheran Synod of Saxony drafted a declaration at its fall conference which was read today in all worship services of its churches. These were clear words concerning the situation in the country:

> Behind us lie weeks and months in which a deep crisis of confidence developed between the people and the government, and this was reflected in the continuing exodus, demonstrations, and violence. Under the pressure of these events the leadership of the Socialist Unity Party, after so long a time of silence and inactivity, has announced a change in its policies and declared its willingness to enter into dialogue with the population. The success of this depends on whether it is possible to regain hope for our country and confidence in the leadership.

The synodical letter continued: "According to God's Word, truthfulness must be a foundational principle of our society." This applies not only to the media and the one-sided educational system, but also to every individual. "According to God's Word, power must be used within limits." That means it must under independent control. This can be achieved by separating the government and the party, allowing criticism of offcial policies, and guaranteeing free elections with a secret ballot and honest choices between parties and candidates. "According to God's Word, a community will stand or fall depending on the extent to which it guarantees legal rights." This requires equality before the law and an independent judiciary, and it is urgently necessary to revise the penal code and repeal those laws that restrict people's constitutional rights. "According to God's Word, every person has the same individual dignity." A society is judged by the value it places on its weakest members. It must guarantee equal rights to those people who cannot look after their own interests. One way to do this is to introduce civilian alternative service. That could lead to improvement in the health care services where the personnel shortage is at a crisis level.

In the meantime, the report which the Saxon church office prepared about the events in early October in Dresden was released. It contained over one hundred first person accounts of the incidents at the main train station. One example was the statement of a fifteen-year-old:

> I watched as a civilian and an armed policeman started to attack my dad. At that moment, 9:30 p.m. on 6 October, I was suddenly grabbed by two policemen, each with a shield, helmet, and club, and dragged along. I did not offer any resistance so they wouldn't use the clubs on me, but they beat me on the legs anyway. Then we were forced to climb into the police trucks. Whoever didn't move fast enough or wasn't able to do so was beaten or shoved around in a very rough manner. We had to place our hands behind our heads. . . . They brought more and more people to the truck. While they were pushing others into ours, I remember quite vividly a somewhat heavyset individual whose entire face was covered with blood. . . . After a rather long time we were divided into groups and loaded into other vehicles. While they were doing this, I saw a young man, who was well groomed and had a plaster cast on his arm, pulled down from the truck and beaten.

Here was an experience at the local jail:

> During a full body search, the person next to me did not spread his legs wide enough or stand far enough away from the wall while leaning against it to suit the officer. He also was in his stockings since they had checked the soles of our feet. "Move! Farther away from the wall!" The officer kicked him with his boot and he fell and hit his forehead on a heating pipe. Then he sat down to put on his shoes. "Nothing doing, no chair!" He said he couldn't get around because he had stood so long in the police garage and needed to sit. The policeman snatched the chair away and the man fell down again.

Particularly moving is the letter a young man serving in the riot police sent to his pastor:

I am writing to you because of what happened here in Dresden. I am a Christian but because of my weak faith I allowed myself to be drafted into the army. [He had been assigned to a militarized security police unit.] Believe me, none of us recruits wanted the situation to develop as it has. We were merely the ones who had to stick our necks out. There were only two choices for us: Either we carried out our orders or were sent for a long—for a very long—time to the army prison in Schwedt.

On Wednesday and Thursday [4-5 October] the situation was simply incredible. We were facing people who were throwing rocks, as well as Molotov cocktails and bottles of acid. Our platoon was there on Wednesday when the train station was besieged. On Thursday we were at Prager Strasse. They brought us in after the situation had gotten of hand and positioned us at the place where it was most dangerous. We were gripped by fear. Rocks smashed against our shields, and Molotov cocktails and bottles filled with acid smashed on the pavement in front of us. Two of our men fell to the ground because stones had broken their visors. Then we were pulled back from the front rank and put down our shields. We were divided into groups of five and ordered to plunge into the mob and capture those who had thrown the stones.

Our officers, the city policemen, and the Stasi remained at a safe distance behind the chain separating the people from the security forces. During these moments I experienced for the first and only time in my life the feeling of mortal agony. Before us was a raging mass of humanity and behind us, our officers, the Stasi, and the ultimate prospect of a court-martial. What we did there in the midst of the throng of people was out of fear and the desire for self-preservation.

What took place in those days (and what certain units of the police and security organs have been doing from the very beginning) is both repulsive and shocking to any thinking human being. Innocent bystanders and peaceful demonstrators were given the same "reception" by "people" at the police in the barracks as those who threw the fire bombs. Especially disgusting is the fact that these "people" (they cannot really be human beings) beat women, girls, and older people.

I am not the only one who has lost his fear of and respect for the public prosecutor because of these actions. This is why I am writing you. I am asking for only one thing: Pray for me and forgive me if you can. Please read this letter in the young people's group at your church and show it to everyone who would be interested in knowing what it is like for us draftees who are compelled to perform deeds that are unworthy of a socialist state.

In various cities today "Sunday talks" took place between citizens and civic officials. In Berlin, twenty thousand people came to the city hall to talk with the mayor, the head of the SED district leadership, and representatives of other agencies. Among the participants was Humboldt University theology professor Heinrich Fink, who raised questions about the incidents of 7 and 8 October since he himself was one of those involved. He suggested an investigation to resolve the matter and reminded those present that in the Bible conversion is always bound together with repentance. This is something that is still lacking in the GDR. In Leipzig, Kurt Masur hosted the second "Sunday Conversation" at the Gewandhaus Orchestra Hall, and Christians were once again among the dialogue participants. Superintendent Richter of the West Leipzig church district declared: "Up to now we have had a totalistic society, one that was organized through and through. I want a society that has only as much organization as necessary but as much freedom as possible."

Also today, at the Berlin Protestant social service center "Queen Elizabeth" two hundred delegates from around the country who belong to the New Democratic Departure convened and decided to constitute their movement as a political party. Several pastors, theologians, and church workers were among the group, the best known being Rainer Eppelmann of Berlin. For some time he has been an open critic of the regime and a leader of those pastors who have joined the opposition. The party desires to cooperate closely with all democratic organizations and the environmental groups. Other groups which met today were the Initiative Peace and Human Rights, the first independent organization in the country, and the citizen movement Democracy Now.

30 October 1989. Numerous demonstrations occurred following prayer meetings around the country. In Leipzig 300,000 marched after the services and tens of thousands more jammed the inner city streets. In the Nikolai Church, Superintendent Magirius discussed the church-state conversations during the previous week in Leipzig and pointed out that it was not really a matter of talks between the state and the church but rather between the state and the people. Various individuals grew impatient about meaningful results from the dialogue and insisted that the time was past for formalized and evasive answers. The feelings of dissatisfaction were reflected in a placard at the demonstration referring to the SED: "The vanguard is behind us."

In nearby Halle fifty thousand demonstrators took to the streets after prayer services in three churches. They too demanded concrete reforms, including freedom of the press and expression, the democratic right to a say in the government, the rule of law, and changes in the educational system. In Schwerin, forty thousand paraded through the downtown area after the prayers for peace in three churches. Among other things, they called for placing all political parties be placed on an equal footing and abolishing privileges for the select few. Even in the little town of Pössneck five thousand marched silently from the parish church through the center of town to the city hall.

At the weekly prayer service in Berlin's Gethsemane Church the congregation was informed that the vigil, which began on 2 October as an expression of solidarity with those arrested during the Leipzig demonstrations, now has ended because the GDR government granted amnesty to those arrested in the various actions around the country during the first week of October. Although the vigil candles have been extinguished, they will remain in readiness near the altar.

On the Long Road to Renewal

1 November 1989. The state offered the churches the opportunity to talk about matters that have long concerned them. The Conference of Church Leaders met to consider the offer and accepted it in principle. Durning the month of November talks will be held on health care, welfare, the educational system, environmental and energy concerns, and military matters, including the possibility of civilian alternative service. Other topics the churches want to talk about in the future are human rights matters linked to the Helsinki accords, economic and social policies, and increasing the level of new church construction, for a long time an especially acute problem.

2 November 1989. The Protestant News Service publicized the address that Superintendent Christoph Ziemer had delivered to a special session of the Dresden city council a few days earlier when he presented the Saxon church's report on the mistreatment of demonstrators. He stressed that the eyewitness accounts made "shockingly clear that basic rights have been violated and that people suffered physical and emotional harm, due to a planned, aggressive, undifferentiated, and reckless deployment of police and security forces." He then called for a thorough investigation by an independent committee drawn from various elements of Saxon society including "representatives from the churches of our city."

Ziemer acknowledged that a dialogue has begun but warned that talking itself must not become an excuse for the necessary changes. The prophet Jeremiah says (regarding false prophets): "Peace, peace, and yet there is no peace. . . . They heal the injuries of my people merely superficially." A thoroughgoing renewal is required, and this will not happen until there is a recognition and a verbalizing of guilt and errors. As renewal is a very painful process, it only becomes credible when we assume responsibility for inappropriate behavior and for wrong developments. Also each of you has to change yourself and deal with the burden of the past so that it does not block the path before us.

At synods of the Protestant Union chuch in Erfurt and the Lutheran church in Eisenach, Bishops Demke and Leich criticized the failures of SED rule in East Germany and urged Christians to stay in their country and work for meaningful change. The synods praised those church members who were contributing to the renewal process. Leich called particular attention to the task which Christians would have in the process of reconciliation. In this:

> We must bear witness to the truth, and we dare not spare
> ourselves in the process. For too long we have lived with two
> different languages and have raised our children in them. We
> developed one language of conformity to the state and party that
> we used publicly and another one of complaining and criticism
> for use in the private realm. If we really want renewal, then we
> must learn to speak with one language.

3 November 1989. At the gatherings for prayer in the four churches of Görlitz in the southeast of the GDR the pressing problems of the city were discussed. One was the ruinous condition of the old part of the city, which had survived the Second World War virtually unscathed. At the conclusion, the eight thousand people picked up their candles and banners calling for reforms and moved quietly through the streets. Many placards called for a halt to tearing down old decrepit buildings. Slips of paper were passed out to the marchers that read: "No violence."

On GDR television that evening, SED General Secretary Egon Krenz announced the resignations of more prominent Politburo members.

4 November 1989. Church people have been a vital part of the ever-growing "citizen's movement" which included people from all walks of life and with many different societal interests and concerns. Thus it was only natural that countless church members and church workers, from the bishop to the custodian, from the church training institute to the local women's circle, would be standing in the crowd at the protest demonstration on Berlin's Alexanderplatz. Initiated by artists and theatrical personnel in the capital, this was the largest mass rally of any kind in the history of the GDR, and it was totally voluntary. More than a half million people registered their support for safeguarding fully the constitutional right to the freedom of expression, press, and assembly.

Among the twenty-five speakers who mounted the platform at the rally were some from the church. Marianne Birthler of the Protestant City Youth Office was involved with the telephone "hot line" operation the Gethsemane Church and played a key role in looking after those who were victims of police brutality. In her speech she renewed the demand for a complete investigation and resolution of all such incidents. Professor Konrad Elmer of the Paulinum Seminary in Berlin presented the concerns of the political group called the Initiative SPD, the recently reconstituted Social Democratic organization in the GDR.

Of particular note was the address of Friedrich Schorlemmer, a pastor and teacher at the Protestant Church of the Union's seminary in Wittenberg. He had been involved for some years with the peace, human rights, and environmental groups that opposed the official policies of the GDR regime in these areas, and to the authorities he was very much a *persona non grata*. Through his theological thinking and writings he had a direct impact on these groups. Schorlemmer gained considerable notoriety in 1983 at the time of the 500th anniversary celebration of Martin Luther's birth, an event which the GDR regime had hijacked for its own political purposes. During a large Church Congress which occurred in conjunction with this at Wittenberg, he had a blacksmith make a sword into a plowshare on an anvil in the courtyard in front of the Luther Seminary. Hundreds witnessed the incident and pictures of it were shown widely on television abroad .

Schorlemmer warned his hearers not to limit the dialogue that has begun to 'letting off steam" and so allow it to degenerate into "popular rubbish."

> Dialogue must become the norm in the relationship between the people and the government. It must not be an emergency measure in a crisis. The one who displayed the sharp claw of power yesterday and today holds out the soft furry paw of dialogue need not wonder why many still fear the claw beneath. Those who considered the "Chinese solution" to be the correct one yesterday, must clearly state that such an idea is totally out of the question today. Otherwise people will continue to have anxiety.

At the same time he cautioned against any thoughts of revenge:

> Let us not set up any new battlelines. Let us believe that everyone is capable of a new beginning! Let us not tolerate voices or opinions expressing revenge. Let us not set a new intolerance in the place of the old intolerance. Tolerance grows out of the understanding that we also make mistakes and that we will add new errors to old ones. But to make sure that no one goes unchallenged who would again claim errors to be truths, we need a genuine democracy, one that will tolerate no predetermined claim to absolute truth and leadership. Therefore, it is democracy, now or never!

Schorlemmer called for an alert solidarity of all democratic forces. "When democratically minded people become fragmented, that is always the hour of opportunity for dictators." At the conclusion, the Wittenberg pastor reminded the crowd of the words of another Wittenberg pastor, Martin Luther: "Let your minds bang up against one another, but hold your fists still!"

5 November 1989. There was relief in Dresden. The people had just learned that the plans to construct a silicon plant in Dresden-Gittersee had been shelved. In the spring of the year environmental activists found out about the project which the authorities were keeping secret. With the support of the church, they publicized how the plant was a grave danger to the environment and refuted official disinformation intended to make the venture appear harmless. The news outraged the population, especially the residents of Gittersee. Pure silicon was needed for the production of computer chips (Dresden was the center of the GDR's computer industry), and highly toxic and explosive raw materials were to be brought to the factory for processing along heavily used transportation routes. In addition, the very stability of the terrain on which the plant would be built was uncertain since the state uranium mining firm had extensively tunneled the area.

A center of opposition was the church congregation in Gittersee, whose weekly intercessory services aimed at averting this danger had taken on the character of a protest. Now people from all over Dresden gathered in the Church of the Cross to share the relief, joy, and thankfulness of the residents of Gittersee. People carried flowers, candles, colored cloths, and banners and celebrated this triumph over the old centralized power and economic structure.

6 November 1989. Once again thousands were in the Leipzig churches to hear words of reconciliation. On Karl Marx Platz a dialogue among between representatives of the state, the Leipzig populace, and the New Forum took place before three hundred thousand people. Then, in spite of the pouring rain, the crowd formed into a demonstration and marched around the city center. Their chief demand now was a law guaranteeing the unlimited right to travel. Earlier that day in Berlin the interior minister had presented the draft of a new travel statute that would allow every person to abroad for thirty days each year, but it had some restrictions.

7 November 1989. Prime Minster Willi Stoph and the entire Council of Ministers resigned as a body. Ten thousand SED members demonstrated in front of the party headquarters building in Berlin where the Central Committee was meeting in an emergency session. Meanwhile, the Constitutional and Legal Committee of the People's Chamber rejected the draft travel law.

8 November 1989. The entire Politburo of the SED stepped down. The Central Committee elected a new one, but several of the old faces were still to be seen. Hans Modrow, district leader of the SED in Dresden, was taken in the Politburo and nominated to the post of Prime Minister in a new caretaker government that would be formed. He was seen as one who had worked for reform.

9 November 1989. At first the message was received with utter astonishment and a feeling of incomprehension, but then with exuberant joy. Politiburo speaker Günther Schabowski announced in a televised press conference in the evening, almost in passing it seemed, that "one may apply for travel to foreign countries without the need to show special reasons [such as travel to conferences or to visit close relatives]. Permission will be granted without delay." How and in which office this totally unexpected decision was made has still not been clearly determined. During the evening tens of thousands streamed through the checkpoints at the Berlin Wall and other borders of the GDR. Two hours before midnight the border guards capitulated in the face of the onslaught and simply allowed the people to pass over unchecked. Thanks to television, the whole world was watching as people from East and West Germany, almost numb with the joy and incomprehensibility of the moment, hugged one another with tears in their eyes.

10 November 1989. The regular session of the church leadership took place against the backdrop of the abruptly altered situation, but the statement they issued was moderate and reserved and reflected the new dimension in the process of change since 9 November.

> Our society is changing from hour to hour. The opening of the borders, for which we all have waited, created a situation for which nobody was prepared. Today the Conference of Protestant

Church Leaders cannot give an evaluation of the present or predictions for the future. But prayers and intercessory worship services are the most important things which we as Christians can do to fulfill our commitments to our society. No one else can do this for us. We will continue in prayer for peace, justice, and the preservation of the creation.

The leaders then directed a word of thanks to everyone "who contributed to the nonviolent nature of the demonstrations since 9 October," and requested that they keep doing so and take a stand for nonviolence wherever they may be.

Only without violence do we achieve peace and justice; only without violence do we preserve the life that has been entrusted to us. Our prayers are based on the promise that God hears the one who is praying. We desire that His will be done. From this we gain the strength to tackle the immediate tasks lying before us in this time of rapidly changing and confusing developments.

15 November 1989. Protestant church representatives met in Berlin with officials from the Ministry of Education and the Academy of Pedagogical Sciences to discuss problems in the educational system. During these talks, State Secretary for Church Questions Löffler, who next day would be out of a job, confessed quite frankly that he "had been given firm orders to decline all requests of the churches in the GDR for conversations on educational policy matters, especially those with the Ministry of Education and the Academy of Pedagogical Sciences." As he explained it, his office had become an enforcement agency for the arbitrary policy decision that "educational matters do not concern the churches." His department was supposed to facilitate communication between church and state and coordinate matters of mutual interest, but increasingly its task had become "to explain why talks were rejected and to formulate warnings." In educational matters all it did was handle some concrete cases of discrimination and, in a few instances, infringement of the laws guaranteeing freedom of religion and freedom of conscience.

Now he was asking the church to collaborate in carrying out the reformation of public education. The government finally had acknowledged the long-ignored suggestions and urgings of the church in this area, and they would be used in the restructuring.

17 November 1989. Prime Minister Modrow delivered his inaugural speech in the People's Chamber. He specifically invited the churches and the various "interest groups" to share their views and their advice for the realization of his program of "democratic renewal and economic stabilization." Quite revealing was his remark: "That which has taken place here after 7 October 1989 in the way of democratic and, in the best sense of the word, popular changes, is irrevocable. The people would sweep aside anyone who dares to try to restore the old order."

In the new government, the lawyer Lothar de Maizière was appointed Deputy Prime Minister for Church Questions. He was heavily involved in church affairs, since he belonged to the Church Federation's synod (and served as acting president at its Eisenach meeting in September) and a week before he had been named chair of the East German Christian Democratic Union, replacing its longtime leader Gerald Götting, who was ousted because of his cozy relationship with the Communist rulers of the GDR. He commented in the parliamentary debate about the active role of the church in the process of change:

> We had a choice either to fall passively into economic collapse or actively look the reality of our crisis straight in the face. We have stood up to the crisis and the problems that remain to be solved. We confronted the questions: "What shall remain? What must not continue?" The CDU is thankful that church representatives have given thoughtful answers to both questions at a time when our government leaders remained silent. By such statements the churches have accepted their political responsibility to grapple with the basic questions that concern all citizens. With the formulation of the government's new program, we who are the political force of our country are finally assuming responsibility for shaping the policies that are needed today.

20 November 1989. In a pilot project at the hospital at Dresden-Friedrichstadt, forty young men have voluntarily started civilian alternative service. Most of them were "total conscientious objectors," men who would not perform any kind of military service. Another group doing community service was made up of construction soldiers who sent their draft notices back. These models revealed how strong the support for such an idea is and why a law establishing this was so badly needed. The Saxon Protestant Youth Office originated the project and secured the support of healthcare and welfare agencies and the local military command.

24 November 1989. In Dessau, where people gathered regularly in the churches on Fridays to pray for peace and renewal and then marched to the city hall and engaged in dialogue, an important breakthrough occurred in police relations. The local police chief said that the police force belonged to the people and there had not been any problems with disorderly conduct, and so he ordered the barbed wire at the county building removed. At a dialogue at St. John's Church a number of reform demands were made and the senior district pastor, who was active in the local citizen's movement, conveyed them to the authorities in an open letter.

2 December 1989. Senior Church Counselor Volker Kress of the Protestant-Lutheran Church Office in Saxony and Catholic Suffragan Bishop Weinold received permission to meet with the prisoners at the Bautzen penitentiary who had started a hunger stike and receive their demands.

3 December 1989. On this day, the first Sunday in Advent, at precisely twelve noon, people fored a human chain that stretched from one end of the country to the other, from the island of Rügen to the Erzgebirge, along highway 96—and from Schwedt to Eisenach, along highway 2. "Renewal and Democratization of Our Society—A Light for Our country" was the motto of this campaign, and it was sponsored by the Protestant Youth Work, Aktion Sühnezeichen (Operation—Signs of Atonement), and other church organizations, along with the many citizens' groups. Tens of thousands of people joined in, even those in small towns, and in several cases entire church congregations following the worship went to be a part of the human chain. So it was that this effort brought into the rural areas the spirit of peaceableness expressed during the urban demonstrations.

It was announced in Berlin that General Secretary Egon Krenz and the entire Politburo and Central Committee of the SED have resigned. Before this the Central Committee had expelled Erich

Honecker and eleven other top functionaries from the party. A provisional "working committee" was now leading the party.

4 December 1989. The people would not slacken their commitment. In Leipzig 150,000 people take to the streets following the services for peace in the downtown churches. Thousands marched in Halle and other cities as well.

6 December 1989. Krenz resigned as head of state and as chair of the National Defense Council of the GDR. Instability marked the country's internal affairs.

7 December 1989. In these worsening circumstances, the national Round Table met for the first time. The Berlin church invited the members to utilize the spacious quarters of its Dietrich Bonhoeffer House, and three respected clerics served as comoderators. They were Martin Ziegler from the Protestant Church Federation; Dr. Karl-Heinz Ducke, Director of the Studies Office of the Catholic Bishops' Conference in Berlin, and Methodist pastor Martin Lange, chair of the ecumenical cooperative group, the Association of Christian Churches in the GDR. Individuals from the old, established parties as well as the new political groups and organizations came to the Round Table, and so the leading forces of the country's society were represented here.

In his welcoming remarks Ziegler spoke about the "square problems" that the Round Table had to solve. The host churches viewed their task as that of offering a platform for dialogue and serving as a mediator in the discussion, but when they saw that it was in their best interests, they would intorduce their own points of view. The talks at the Round Table could not be, and did not claim to be, a substitute for the government and parliament. From these talks, however, could come ideas and suggestions that the elected bodies could use in their decisions making.

It required considerable effort simply for the Round Table to define its purpose. It would seek to carry on a discussion with one another and the public about how to overcome the crisis facing the GDR and preserve its independence as a nation. It also wanted to be informed of all important political decisions and to be included in the deliberations leading to these. Other things it wished to see done were: setting a date for parliamentary elections, writing a new constitution, immediate measures to create a state founded upon the rule of law and preservation of the people's interests, and above all, a carefully supervised dismantlement of the Ministry for State Security.

8 December 1989. During these times no church committee, from the smallest group to the top management level, could blithely ignore the situation in the country and the expectations that people were still bringing before the church for its consideration. How perilous and fragile the situation was could be seen in a message that the Conference of Protestant Church Leaders directed not only to our "Brother Christians" but to all "fellow citizens" following a special session today. It contained the urgent plea to protect that which has been achieved in a "peaceful revolution" from the dangers that beset it, and to continue allowing ourselves to be controlled by the "spirit of reconciliation." The laws necessary for daily living must not break down, the land must not fall prey to anarchy, and the provision of the necessities of life must continue. "Peace in the society must be strengthened." They admonished people not "to fall into the trap of hate-filled, revengeful thinking," in spite of their anger about the acts of violence, lying, and misappropriation of funds that were being uncovered. "Clearheadedness and rational thinking alone will help us."

The leaders indicated that the Round Table, moderated by representatives of the church, has an important task to fulfill:

> It is attempting to serve as a bridge from this transitional period until free elections take place. It intends to pull together the political forces in our society so they can assume responsibility for the steps that are needed now. It will prepare the way for those that the people will determine for themselves in free elections and referenda.

13 December 1989. This evening Prime Minister Modrow invited the two top church leaders, Bishop Leich of the Church Federation and Bishop Sterzinsky, Chairman of the Berlin Catholic Bishops' Conference, to a conversation the details of which were made known to the public. The topic for consideration was the problem of safeguarding the welfare of the public in the face of rising emotions, social unrest, and violence by radicals. All agreed that the churches have a heavy obligation because of their commitment to protecting basic human values and the healthy functioning of the community. The churches are also backing the commendable efforts of those involved in the Round Table to obtain workable agreements and to prepare the next steps in the lawmaking process. Further, the dialogue partners stressed the need to deal with the injustice of the past by exposing their structural roots and by the use of the law. However, they must assume responsibility for tackling the day-to-day work in the economy, public administration, and the cities and towns. Never had the rulers of this country given a clearer call to the churches for help.

17 December 1989. At the traditional Advent choral festival in Potsdam's Nikolai Church today the Federal Republic's president, Richard von Weizsäcker, was present. He had come to West Berlin for a private visit, and Manfred Stolpe, the Berlin-Brandenburg Church's administrative head, a resident of Potsdam himself, arranged for a conversation between him and the provisional leadership of the GDR. They included the new head of state, Liberal Party secretary Manfred Gerlach; Prime Minister President Hans Modrow; and the Deputy Prime Minister, Lothar de Maizière. The large audience greeted the four statesmen with hearty applause. Following the performance, they went to Cecilienhof Palace for talks among themselves.

Meanwhile, at an emergency convention in Berlin the SED tried to determine what the *Wende* meant to their party. The delegates decided to expand its name with the addition "Party of Democratic Socialism;" a few weeks later the party simply adopted it as its sole name. The new PDS chairman, lawyer Gregor Gysi, suggested that the party carry on discussions with all churches and religious communities to develop a new law on religious groups that would "more precisely define and guarantee" their position in the GDR. This suggestion did not have much impact. Many considered the PDS to be the same old SED in spite of the apparent efforts at renewal.

18 December 1989. We have now reached the point mentioned at the beginning of this look back at the events of this fall, the day of the last Leipzig demonstration of 1989. In Berlin the Round Table, still meeting at the Dietrich Bonhoeffer House (it would be here until relocated in a state conference center three weeks later), unanimously requested the churches to continue providing its leadership. The three churchmen served as moderators until after a total of sixteen sessions the Round Table completed its work on 12 March 1990, the Monday prior to the election of a new parliament.

19 December 1989. Federal Republic Chancellor Helmut Kohl came to Dresden for talks with Prime Minister Modrow. At this time he also met with Bishop Leich, Bishop Hempel, and other Protestant churchmen. He paid tribute to the mediating role of the churches in the political changes and said "A great deal of credit" goes to them for the peaceful manner in which the discussions were carried on. He expressed similar sentiments when he met with high officials of the Roman Catholic Church on the next day .

The chancellor told the church representatives that his objective was German unity as soon as possible. A month earlier Modrow had suggested a policy of rapprochement between the two German states by means of a "community by agreement," which would go beyond the Basic Law of the Federal Republic. For his part, Kohl had proposed a plan that called for "confederative structures between both states in Germany," which went further than Modrow's offer. Both were still on the table for discussion in Dresden. But at the rally where the chancellor stood in front of the ruins of the Church of Our Lady and people were waving the black-red-gold flag of the Federal Republic, it was clear that what most East Germans wanted was speedy reunification. Those voices that still urged their fellows not to give up their peacefully attained self-determination, not to place one's hopes on prosperity by means of a quick annexation to the Federal Republic, and not to permit a "sellout" of the GDR were hardly heard any more.

24 December 1989. Christmas masses and worship services in the churches of all confessions were especially well attended. Sermons associated the all-important historical date of Christ's birth with the present historical moment of the *Wende* and the altered relationship. The dramatic and highly politicized happenings that occurred day after day in the last weeks had come to a halt, and during the holidays the people could express thankfulness and joy for the changes that have come to their land. People in both parts of Germany could enjoy the renewed relationships with their friends and relatives.

It remains to be seen whether people paid more attention to the message of the Christmas Gospel in their churches than they usually have, and whether they really heard the proclamation of salvation and the call to faith. The churches are highly regarded now because of their engagement in the recent struggles and their mediatorial role, and these were decisive factors in the peaceful revolution. It also was acknowledged that spiritual power, not ideology, was the effective moving force. But the real question is: how many have opened themselves to the mystery of faith because of the events and experiences of this rremarkable point in time?

Looking to the Future

The years following the fall of 1989 see a Germany situated in the middle of a changing Europe shaping itself, and the prospect is one of new possibilities and new goals. What seemed to be developing into an historical era, now turned out to be a forty-year epoch that has been overcome and is fading from memory, like a bad dream. But shadows of the past still remain and they are casting themselves on the pathway leading to the future. As difficult times break in on us again, Christians will, because of their credibility and public-spiritedness, once more be expected to help bring about changes, to walk the pathway out of the shadows without fear and resignation. As the winter and spring of 1990 progressed, pastors and church workers sat with citizens' committees at countless Round Tables in city halls and public buildings, where they labored to dismantle the firmly established command, management, and administrative structures of the old leadership and break up the formerly all-powerful Stalinist State Security apparatus.

Looking to the months ahead, when two separate states would no longer exist, new tasks would fall to the German churches as the people learned to live with one another. But we ought not to conclude our chronicle on this topic. Two quotations will show that the same insights that were present when the church helped to shape the revolutionary process were now to be applied to the building of the new united Germany.

On 25 February 1990 the new synod of the Federation of Protestant Churches made the following declaration:

> The processes in both German states, but especially those in the GDR, have accelerated and intensified to a degree that no one could have foreseen. On the one hand, citizens of our country are gaining opportunities to take part in politics, the economy, and public affairs in areas that previously were off limits. On the other hand, the full extent of the economic, legal, and moral deterioration is coming to light, piece by piece, in an alarming way. It is clear that a large majority of the population wants to see a unified Germany. The economic and political unity of both German states seems attainable within a short period of time. Only a few still strive for a renewed socialism.

In an interview that same day, the newly elected chair of the Church Federation, the bishop of Magdeburg, Christoph Demke, replied to a question about the relationship between the mission of the church and those political obligations taken on by Protestant clergy in the fall revolution:

> We view the present time as one of special challenge, as an unusual time, and therefore, we as church leaders have completely promoted and affirmed the political activity by many of our colleagues. . . . However, I would like to stress that the political engagement with spiritual consequences arises from one's intercessory involvement for a renewal of our society. When we, during our times of intercession, place this topic of renewal on God's agenda, then it must have an impact upon our own thoughts and feelings. To this extent, the political involvement of church workers is a matter that has spiritual consequences. But I hope that as democratic independence develops in our society, it will be possible to cut back some on this sort of service, which many of my colleagues see as only temporary, where they, so to speak, are jumping into the breach. Then direct service to a congregation once again will become the central focus for all church workers.

The Mass Exodus from the GDR

From the time of its founding the German Democratic Republic had difficulty keeping its population. The oppressive hand of the Communist dictatorship was more than many people could stand, while the Soviet exploitation of its client state and the inefficiencies of state-directed monopoly socialism retarded economic development. With its political freedom and economic prosperity West Germany was a magnet that attracted thousands of East German settlers each year. Particularly inclined to leave were skilled workers and young people, and the result was continuing instability and sluggish economic growth. The Federal Republic gave them generous subsidies and instant citizenship since it regarded them as fellow Germans. In the view of most historians, the Berlin Wall was thrown up almost as an act of desperation to save the GDR from total collapse.

This transformed the country into virtually a prison, but a modicum of prosperity did result. Because of the tight restrictions on foreign travel, that is, to the West, there was bitter resentment in the country, particularly among younger people. Once persons reached retirement age—sixty-five for men, sixty for women—they were free to leave, but the others had to apply for exit visas that could be very difficult to obtain. Most East Germans were simply curious about the West and probably would have come back after a holiday there, but the regime was almost paranoid in its refusal to let people go. As the international stature of the GDR grew, it had to ease travel restrictions somewhat, particularly for certain selected groups, and this only heightened resentments. Thanks to the agreements with the Federal Republic the GDR did allow a few people to emigrate, often after years of waiting for approval of their applications to do so. But when the economy began slowing down in the mid-1980s, the pressures to leave increased dramatically and the visa offices were swamped with applications. Since

East Germans were free to travel in the Soviet bloc countries, some used this as an escape route. They would go to Hungary or Czechoslovakia and then find some way out to the West. By 1989 the emigration requests had reached a new high and then the Hungarians opened their border with Austria. The result was a hemorrhage of people which destabilized the tottering Honecker regime and fueled the protests that led to its downfall.

The emigration problem presented those East German Christians who were trying to carry on an effective witness with an enormous dilemma. Being a Christian in a Communist country was a costly proposition. The ideological education their children received in school undermined the faith they learned at home, and they suffered serious discrimination as well. The youth activities of the churches were sharply circumscribed, and the Stasi particularly targeted harassed youth ministers and evangelists. At the same time, congregations lost some of their most valuable members by emigration. Yet someone had to maintain the institutional activities of the church and present to the Gospel to their neighbors. Leaving one's fellow believers behind produced bitterness and resentment, while the ones who left were tormented by anxiety and guilt.

The following accounts illustrate the difficulties and ambiguities of the emigration issue for Christians. The first two are by people who left "legally," the third by one who fled "illegally." The next two pieces reflect the positions of those who stayed. It is worth noting that two of the families who emigrated were members of these congregations. The last two are a pastor's prayer for those who chose to stay in East Germany and a statement drawn up by the Baptist Study Group for Peace.

"If We Were to Face the Same Question Today . . . "

On 9 November 1989 Manuela (27) and Manfred (30) Hödtke received permission to emigrate with their two children. Manfred described the circumstances surrounding the move.

There was a great deal that concerned us and still does. I hope that I can express it with the right words, as we would like for these lines to be a basis for reflection about the pro's and con's of applying to leave the country and not just reasons to condemn people.

The thought of leaving had been simmering in the backs of our minds for a long while. We are both very critical people and we had become aware very early in our lives to what extent one may be critical in a socialist state and just where the boundaries for such criticism lie.

I was employed in an electronics business and was confronted almost daily with the bottlenecks of the GDR economy.

For thirteen years I played in a band named "Light" which was supported by our Baptist congregation. We had engagements all over the GDR in youth evangelistic campaigns other church occasions, and we were always watched and followed by members of the State Security Service.

Many desires in our hearts remained unfulfilled. A brother in our congregation once said: "Christians have desires too. They ought to fulfill them in a responsible way before God." As young people we naturally wanted to visit the West, but our applications were always rejected. There was no freedom to travel; the prospects were hopeless.

The year 1989 was a decisive one for us. The fact that the Chinese government acted against its own people, the shocking statement of the GDR leadership in support of the massacre in Beijing, and the Warsaw Pact meeting in Bucharest where it was agreed that "every socialist country can make its own pot of soup" were all actions that made it clear to us that we should apply to leave.

As a couple we sat down and prayed for clear direction, and on 30 August 1989 we submitted an application to resettle in West Berlin so we could still be near our family and friends. It is difficult for me to describe this decision because there was such great confusion in our minds. What will the congregation say about this? How will they react? What reprisals will we have to endure for having applied?

Actually, the response of the authorities and my coworkers was quite courteous and proper. Pangs of conscience only appeared when we learned about the negative comments by some members of the congregation. We had to listen to them and in many respects their charges taxed the limits of our strength. We were very disappointed about this. It was hard to take because we had not expected such a negative reaction from the congregation, but at least some members were understanding.

We received the approval to emigrate on 9 November 1989 at 8:00 o'clock in the morning, the day the borders we opened. Our minds were topsy-turvy, but we still decided to go. The Lord had given us a clear "yes" to the path we had chosen, and I quickly found a job, an apartment, and an open and receiving congregation.

If we were to face the same question today as in the summer of 1989, we would not have applied for a visa to emigrate since the reasons that had led to it no longer exist. Now we have contacts with brothers and sisters in both parts of the city and can take advantages of these at any time. For this we are thankful to God.

Are We "Outside"?

The young Uszkoreit family left East Germany "legally" after a two-year waiting period. They describe the tensions they faced.

In January 1989 we learned that we would be permitted to leave sometime during the year. The two-year waiting period was not very pleasant? Waiting period? Can one wait for a whole new life? Or just for the day on which it will begin?

Why did we decide to leave? There were so many reasons, important and unimportant, small and large. But all totaled they were enough for us. What were the main reasons? One was the stubborn refusal of our applications to travel "for family reasons" to visit close relatives, such a father and a brother. They had left fourteen years ago without permission, and one time we were told "off the record" when we were called in for a discussion about the matter that this would be a hindrance to us for the rest of our lives.

Also we thought, "so that's the way it's going to be?" We had satisfactory employment and a decent apartment, albeit in a terrible neighborhood in Berlin. We had lots of friends and a church congregation in which we felt comfortable. But where do we go from here? We would have had exactly the same thing in ten, twenty, or thirty years—without any changes or development that would bring something really new into our lives.

To be honest, thoughts of material goods also moved us. In spite of, and because of, the gifts which our relatives brought us, we weren't satisfied. How can one be satisfied when, in spite of a good education and a forty-eight-hour work week, he or she can have many things only thanks to considerate "relatives in the West." And we must be constantly thankful to them for our entire lifetime, even though we certainly don't work less than they do?

We would be less than honest, if we failed to mention the feeling of oppression and even fear of the all-powerful socialist (?) system along with the negative developments in the society as further reasons for wanting to leave. We were well-behaved fellow travelers who marched along with the rest when we were outside but who griped when we were at home

It was not until these two years of waiting after filing our application to leave the country that we experienced both the petty and significant examples of a frightening political apparatus. At the time we began "courageously" to attend the meetings of groups in the churches that wanted to expose wrongs and change things. We really went there more for the purpose of being seen by the "professional attenders" [police informers] in order to be considered as troublemakers. We had heard that doing so could speed up the process of obtaining an exit visa. Who knows how many others were there for the same reason?

The shocking information about environmental pollution, the deterioration of our cities, the poor state of our (un)healthcare system, and much more that we learned through these activist groups could only solidify our decision to go. We often thought that something must be done, but it was no longer a reason for us to remain. The only thing we wanted was to get out. And the many experiences of being hassled in government offices made it easier and easier to detach ourselves internally from this society.

When the long awaited moment came, it was not nearly so easy as we had imagined it would be. Somehow we didn't think, "Now something new is starting," but rather, "Now everything is over." And so the final goodbye to our friends and "our" congregation was rather dismal. Even the day of our departure, which we had imagined for two years would be one of joy and excitement, turned out to be more like jumping off a cliff.

The feelings of this day consisted of perhaps ninety percent fear of the unknown and the finality of the trip. Of course, there was the joy of seeing relatives again and looking through our apartment, which was already waiting for us. But on this evening as we sat in the apartment, we had the feeling that we had been abandoned.

After a lengthy period of adjustment the Uszkoreit family settled into life in the Federal Republic and the new Germany, but there was always the attraction of returning to visit their "home" even though they had no desire to live in the East again.

Three Plane Tickets to Budapest
Gabriele Zilz

The reasons for leaving our own homeland were quite different for the two us. My husband Rüdiger played the principal role in our decision to leave. He did not have any sense of fulfillment in his job. Work time was often wasted because no materials were available, or the managers made decisions that seemed so illogical as to raise questions about the purpose of the work. As a Christian he did not wish to bear arms so he refused the serve in the military. Although he repeatedly filed repeated petitions and appeals to avoid service and he got to know firsthand the methods of the State Security Service, eventually at the age of 26 he was drafted into a construction battalion. He spent a year and a half at a large air base near Berlin

After his fifth application to make a trip to the West was denied, he didn't need to tell me once again how sad this made him. I could tell by simply looking at him. He had wanted to do it so he would not always have to put up with hearing about such trips from friends and colleagues. He didn't talk about the topic of "emigrating" anymore, although we had had discussions about it for eight years. Rüdiger waited until I reached the point where he was.

That would not be long. I was not permitted to take the *Abitur* [the high school test that allowed one to enter the university] because male students with lower grade point averages were given preferences. They had committed themselves to serve as professional soldiers for twenty-five years. At first it didn't bother me that much. But then when I had started a four-and-a-half-year course at a trade school because I had not finished my secondary education, I became quite conscious of this injustice. On top of that

I would have to continue working, and then just one week after the birth of our daughter Rüdiger was called up to the army.

Although the constant discussions about applying for an exit visa disrupted our marriage, I just couldn't say yes to the idea. I knew he did not feel comfortable at all in our home anymore and that he really would rather leave.

We also had pangs of conscience in the matter. What would our Baptist congregation have to say about it. After all, the help of every man was needed in the construction of our new building in Berlin-Oberschöneweide.

During a holiday on the Baltic both my daughter and I were healed of our eczema problem. But after only fourteen days back home we had open lesions again. She was treated with the same useless medications that I had received as a child twenty-five years earlier. As her mother I almost fell into despair, and we finally decided to move to the West.

Of course, we did not want to make this decision on our own, and we asked God for guidance as to whether this was really the right thing for us to do. After reading the daily Bible verse on our calendar, we had a prompt answer to our prayer: "Stop brooding about it and go!"

Following this, we applied for a tourist visa to Hungary and purchased three plane tickets to Budapest. We then went to a refugee camp, spent some time waiting there, and finally traveled to West Germany, where we were welcomed into a fine congregation and made many new friends. Now even the eczema is gone.

The Zilz family found a new home in Hamburg.

"Dwell in the Land and You Will Be Fed"

Sören Schmidtmann, Berlin

What is our position as a Free Church congregation on the matter of the mass exodus? Basically, it is true that each person is responsible for his or her own decision. But then, does the local church have the right to draft a position paper that provides guidelines? Many of our friends in the West did not to understand when we formulated the following statement: "Living by faith in

Jesus Christ means for us remaining here in the GDR, in the place God has given us to live, to bear witness, and to serve."

Bearing witness and serving were realities for us during the construction of our place of worship. For three years, our Baptist congregation in Berlin-Oberschöneweide has been in the process of transforming the vision of our fathers into reality, that is, a chapel of our own. That meant frequent work assignments for members of the congregation because we had to do almost all of the labor ourselves. There was no other way that we could build a church structure.

We obtained a building site by tearing down an old wooden house, laid a foundation that in some spots was twelve feet deep, located and hauled in building materials from many places, carried in blocks, and learned how to mix mortar and build the walls. Since we had only 120 members, the construction work demanded considerable amounts of time, labor, and money. We sensed very much how strongly dependent we were on one another.

But when several of the brethren moved to the West, those who remained had the feeling of being abandoned. I'm sure many thought to themselves: "The others are building for themselves a nice life in the West with those things which we often dream about, and now we have to continue building without them." True, we could understand quite well the reasons for leaving. On the other hand, these same reasons caused many of us to face the question: "Why am I still here?"

Those who had left had helped us write our statements of faith and hope and had sung the words in the hymn "God desires to live among us." We had all agreed to step out in faith on the building project. Then, as one after another left us, we were saddened and began to doubt whether God really was giving us a life here in the GDR. Should we instead seek our fulfillment in the West after all?

It was not only sadness, doubt, and the feeling of abandonment that concerned us. Our coworkers were now gone: E. as church treasurer, B. as organist, H. as youth director, E. as missionary worker, K. as one of the few skilled craftsmen, along with S. and P. who were involved in the construction of the chapel, J. from the youth choir, and G. and H. from the adult choir. Nevertheless God allowed the congregation's work to continue.

Then came the fall of 1989, and we experienced perhaps as never before just how much our God is also the Lord of history. The Gospel inspired hundreds of thousands to rise up, stand tall, and use nonviolent methods.

We celebrated the first free and secret elections to the GDR parliament with a worship service of thanksgiving. We thanked God for His faithfulness in these last years, for the opening of the Wall and the beginning of its destruction, and for the democratization, victory over the Stasi, and the free elections.

We continued to work on our church building because we knew the market economy did not have the power to save. Nor would the introduction of the Deutschmark in the East provide fulfillment in life. Our task is to make this known so that the houses of God will remain what they were in the fall of 1989—places of truthfulness and solidarity, places of the Gospel that grants us shalom and nearness to God, places where the country was illuminated by the light of innumerable candles.

We want to remind people of the experiences whenever they talk about the "growing together" of the churches in the once-divided Germany. Will anyone pay attention to our voices?

A Feeling Like Bleeding to Death

For those who wanted to or had to remain in the GDR it was a feeling like bleeding to death. When it was clear that the Hödtke family was going to leave, the emigration wave seemed to have reached the small Baptist congregation in Berlin-Lichtenberg. Thereupon the church council decided to direct a "Spiritual Word" to the congregation. Pastor Uwe Dammann composed it.

At its session on 4 September 1989 the church council took up the emigration problem. This is something that has deeply troubled our fellow citizens, and it has not stopped at the door of our chapel. For this reason, we would like to convey this Spiritual Word to our congregation.

We confess that Jesus Christ is our Lord. He has called us to discipleship and given us forgiveness of sins and a life full of meaning. Christ wants to make us in his image. Through the power of the Holy Spirit we shall become more like him.

The belief in Jesus Christ as our Lord applies to all areas of life and to all questions that concern us. This is true also in regard to the matter of staying or going.

Jesus too resettled once. He left the heavenly world in order to serve us. He was like God, but he viewed this advantage not as something to hold on to. By his own free decision he gave everything up and took upon himself the form of a servant. He came as a human being into the world and lived like a human (Phil. 2:6-7). He became poor for our sake (2 Cor. 8:9). This attitude of Jesus was passed on to us.

We see the danger in wanting to unburden ourselves of this "servanthood" of the believers when we place societal problems, freedom to travel, and the desire for more luxury above God's mission for our country. We are ashamed that the desire to have the abundance of this world's goods determines our lives more than concern for the neighbors he has entrusted to us. We confess our guilt before God and before our brothers and sisters throughout the world who are enduring sorrow, suffering, hunger, terror, injustice, and often a martyr's death for Jesus' sake.

We clearly see abuses in our country and are distressed that the government shows no signs of yielding. All the more, we desire to heed the admonition of Scripture "to pray for the rulers" (1 Tim. 2:1-2).

The living God promises us His peace, which is higher than all reason. When Jesus is the main person in our life and the main purpose for our existence, we have peace and are satisfied.

Only if we possess a clear sense of mission, will courage and hope grow in us so that we may be able to serve the Lord in mission and social work in our land.

We would like to encourage all members of our congregation to view their lives from the standpoint of mission and service to others and to order their lives accordingly. Jesus challenges us to place the Kingdom of God first in our lives. The Kingdom of God will be built, throughout the world and in the GDR. We believe that the desire to leave the mission field of the GDR does not come from the Lord. God expects us to serve Him in this country. We have the confidence that He who has begun a good work will complete it.

The Church Council of the Baptist Congregation in Berlin-Lichtenberg, 10 September 1989.

Prayer
Dietrich Mendt

This was delivered at a prayer service for peace during the time in the summer of 1989 when the mass exodus was taking place through the West German embassies in Hungary, Czechoslovakia, and Poland.

Lord,
All of us here have dared to remain
in this land until today.
　　For this we thank you.
You have preserved us, although we often thought
in these forty years that faith and the church
would soon be at an end.
　　For this we thank you.
You have created for us Christians a new basis of confidence.
Many come to us today, openly or in secret,
who previously did not know you.
　　For this we thank you.
And we have had peace for over forty years,
we have enough to eat,
and we are better off than most people in the world.
　　For this we thank you.
You have now given us new hopes;
provided us with signs of a new openness;
made many things possible, that no longer were possible.
　　For this we thank you.
In spite of disappointment,
you gave us courage
to persevere in this country.
　　For this we thank you.
And you have seen to it that even in our country,
Your coming kingdom is preached and proclaimed
over and over again.
　　For this we thank you.

Now we beseech you:
Help us to hold fast to your Word,

to exercise love, and to remain humble before you!
Help us to build openness and new confidence together,
untiringly and patiently!

Help us to prevent violence and provocation!
Give us courage to remain in the land!
Help us to encourage others to remain in the land!
Look after all those who have left our land
and whose hopes were dashed!

Make those who rule over us be ready to talk
and give them the courage to admit errors and to correct them!
And don't permit us to be arrogant and self-righteous!
Strengthen our hope in your future
and our confidence in your power and in your love and mercy!
    Amen.

Baptist Union of the GDR—Study Group for Peace

Berlin, 14 October 1989

Dear Sisters and Brothers:

In its session on 14 October 1989 the Study Group for Peace discussed the current problems in our country.

We as Christians in the Baptist Church do not stand above the situation. The departure of so many people (even from our own congregations) makes it imperative that we give expression to our deep feelings of concern.

We believe that the reasons for the present difficulties are to be found within the society of the GDR itself. Failures need to be admitted and honestly analyzed so that things can be done to improve the situation.

The most recent statements by representatives of the government give us reason for hope. We expect of the regime that it will open a constructive dialogue with all segments of the population and these will lead to the introduction of the necessary reforms.

We recognize this to be a special hour, given by God, in which the members of our congregations, motivated by the hope in

Christ, are called upon to contribute by prayer and spiritual reflection to the renewal in our land.

Yours most sincerely,
Manfred Sult, Berlin; Christian Wolf, Buckow; Siegfried Schmidtmann, Berlin; Annelies Dietrich, Waren; Andreas Heinrich, Wernigerode; Manfred Lusky, Falkensee; Manfred Preusse, Forst; Siegfried Rosemann, Berlin.

Profiles in Courage: Eyewitness Accounts

The East German Revolution of 1989 cannot be understood properly without paying special attention to the experiences of those who were involved. Accordingly, this chapter will focus on the human dimension of the revolution by utilizing personal accounts by Baptists. Some of these descriptions are drawn from diaries which the participants kept while others were written expressly for the book. In these one can gain a feeling for the mood of the times and how people reacted to what went on. The mixed feelings of uncertainty, anxiety, longing for change, and euphoria are readily seen in them. In accordance with the German custom of protecting the identities of third parties, people mentioned in the diary entries are designated only by the first letter of their names.

Lord, Hold Your Hand over This Country

Regina Sensel, born in 1951 and the mother of two children, was forced to give up her career in teaching for ideological reasons. She and her husband Frank were active members of a Baptist congregation in Forst/Lausitz, a city on the Polish border. In addition, they belonged to the Ecumenical Peace Group in Forst, where Frank devoted himself particularly to environmental matters, and she was constantly beset by the fear that her husband would be arrested. The later discovery that the Stasi had created internment camps for dissidents proved how well founded her anxiety was and why her prayer was: "Lord, hold your hand over this country!" In the following excerpts from her diary she documents her experiences during this troubled time.

25 August 1989. We met with people from the International Peace Pilgrimage, an offshoot of the Christian Peace Conference. The group was on a walk along the "Peace Border" with Poland, the line which the Allies had drawn along the Oder and Neisse Rivers after World War II. The West Germans saw it merely as a temporary boundary, which caused the Poles no end of anxiety, while the GDR regarded it as permanent. For me, this delegation of people from all corners of the globe was something very unique. It was a breath of "the world" in our little town. I experienced my first worship service in the open air. It moved me deeply to hear the Lord's Prayer recited in various languages. In the middle of our circle a little child played. This scene was so meaningful for me that during our time of prayer I looked at the child again and again. This sight made a deep impression upon me. I experienced a feeling of inner solidarity with people of other backgrounds. In the evening a stimulating conversation took place in the parish center of the Protestant church. Unfortunately the entire gathering was much too brief.

26 August 1989. This morning, at a destroyed bridge across the Neisse River we had a devotional service with prayer, songs, and dancing. Our guests were a Polish youth group and some people from the "Mountain Hikers for Peace." Then we walked with our new friends to the train station carrying a banner which read, "Bridges for peace instead of borders." When we noticed that some men who were "inconspicuously" accompanying us through the town did not interfere, we were quite relieved. Of course, we knew that this was only so because the group was an international one.

27 August 1989. In the display case outside the church door, a newspaper that advertised World Peace Day had been posted for a few days. It contained the slogan "Swords into plowshares." Until now the authorities had shown no objection, something which they usually did even with much lesser "offenses." Was it an oversight or a sign of tolerance? We were skeptical but nevertheless glad that it was permitted.

1 September 1989. Today, along with the Ecumenical Peace Group, we participated in an SED meeting devoted to World Peace Day. We carried our banner from the peace pilgrimage. They wanted to know how things were going with the group. We replied that we were exploring all the new possibilities in the GDR. We had hardly arrived when some officials tore down the banner. Also we were told that another placard we were carrying, "For Civilian Alternative Service," had to go. We maintained a calm demeanor and did not yield. Nevertheless, our appearance delayed the beginning of the celebration. The party members stared at us disgustedly, but to avoid causing any further disturbance, they left us alone. The meeting followed the same pattern that it has for years. I gazed into the loyal faces of their "voluntary" guests and students. Somehow it hurt to see the people here looking this way. It was the first time that a group of Christians in our city had made such a public appearance.

As we were returning home, the Stasi pounced on us. It was a brutal attack and our children were distraught. One girl was thrown to the pavement and suffered a head wound. Someone shouted: "Fascist!" I was ashamed that our Polish friends had to witness this. The Stasi confiscated the placard but the group closed ranks and prevented anyone from being whisked away in a police vehicle. Later, an old friend from our youth who was now a teacher came to us and shook our hands: "Too bad. I would liked to have joined you, but you know what my profession is. . . . In any event they have already noticed that I am greeting you."

The Protestant Church held a worship service for peace that evening. Pastor P. read the letter he had composed in the afternoon in which he appealed to the worshippers to work with patience and perseverance for changes in the country. The Peace Group had gained good practical experience in developing group solidarity. My daughter could not understand why the police wanted to say what might be on a placard.

11 September 1989. B. spent eleven hours in custody in Berlin, where he had gone to take part in a demonstration against election fraud. G.'s house was searched, because "leaflets" allegedly were there. G.'s mother shouted at the Stasi officers as they left the house: "Just wait. The tables will be turned." I marveled at her courage. The main topic of conversation, the problem of the mass emigration, still remained unmentioned in the media. Around town, people ignored what was happening. Their attitude was one of waiting to see how the newspapers dealt with it or if there would be any comments on it at all. The tactic of withholding information is the usual way of keeping the people in the dark.

Representing the Peace Group, Frank attended a meeting of environmental activists. Tensions were rising between these groups and the church, for which involvement in societal issues was becoming too controversial. Of course, it is not the church's task to assume the political responsibility of the state, but we all are responsible for democratic renewal. Too, it is a matter of self-respect to do something to counter the existing conditions. The emigration of GDR citizens by way of Hungary has begun, and we hear that 6,000 people are waiting to leave. We don't want to believe it. It is clear that a nasty wave of propaganda will be washing over the country. The figures vary so much that one doesn't know what to believe.

13 September 1989. The refugee problem is really serious. I can't believe that so many people want to go. At an "ecumenical evening" at the church, movie director Konrad Weiss talked about neo-Fascist tendencies in the GDR. His explanations were very well informed and based on solid research. He spoke quietly and gave the impression of being modest. Still, he radiated a strong inner determination. One sensed that he was a person who thinks deeply. The hall was packed. People looked around to see who might be from the Stasi. The security forces certainly don't want to miss out on this. At the conclusion Weiss read an appeal for his audience to join the Democracy Now movement, of which he was a co-founder, and he distributed leaflets containing it. This was a new experience for us, but what he had to say went directly to the heart of the problems facing our country. His courage inspired us, but at the same time we were concerned about him. Everyone knew that this speech could have serious consequences.

15 September 1989. M. came for a visit. He brought a copy of an appeal calling for the formation of a grassroots democratic renewal organization. The authors were anonymous and its readers were requested to send their signatures to a disguised address. The attached outline appeared to be rather immature. We don't like to play games with concealed cards, and don't believe that people who want to remain unknown possess enough courage to stand up for their beliefs. We turned M. down and he was disappointed. Immediately, of course, a sense of mistrust crept in. It is difficult to fight against this sort of thing. I feel distinctly how much harm this mistrust causes, even between brothers and sisters.

16 September 1989. The reports about the refugees are astounding, and I struggled whether to believe them or not. I think it is due to mass hysteria, which after all is relatively easy to trigger. I believe that most are looking for material advantages. Gradually I am coming to understand how much this situation reflects a deep crisis in our society. Most of the refugees interviewed on Western television were unable to articulate their reasons for leaving and simply said they wanted to get out. The general feeling of discontent in our country has intensified so much that people are leaving in droves. Things are approaching the breaking point.

18 September 1989. Several new people have joined the Peace Group. The atmosphere is always rather tense when a new face appears, and mistrust again raises its head. But we have to live with the spies in our midst. Everyone tries not to let their doubts show and just accept each other. B. gave an eyewitness report of the arrests outside the Nikolai Church in Leipzig, and we decided to hold an intercessory prayer service for the detainees on Wednesday.

20 September 1989. A service was held at the church in support of those arrested in Leipzig. Approximately 100 people came but no one else from our Baptist congregation except us. Astonishingly, few Stasi agents were there. Considering that the announcement was posted only yesterday, we were gratified that so many people wanted to participate. We collected 87 signatures on a petition and sent it to the Leipzig District's Department of Internal Affairs. The people even gave their home addresses. We were amazed that the people showed so much confidence in these church-sponsored campaigns. The State Security did not bother those leaving the service.

21 September 1989. We heard about the New Forum, which has already gathered 1,500 signatures on its petition. The group has objectives similar to those of Democracy Now. The feeling that something is "in the air" is getting stronger by the day. As far as I'm concerned, we must offer resistance and become involved somehow, somewhere.

22 September 1989. At 11 o'clock in the morning the Stasi called. Frank was picked up at his workplace and taken in for the "clarification of some facts." I drove immediately to see M., since it was clear to me that this was aimed at the Peace Group. When I arrived, I saw two men hastily leaving the house; they had been asking about G. I learned about more detainments. We decided to inform the church office and to maintain contact with all the families affected. When I got home, I telephoned the factory and found out my husband was not back yet. I was concerned, since I too might be detained. I prepared for the worst and made provisions for someone to care for the children. I am not afraid. It is now clear that I must concentrate all my energy on coping with this situation. I spent a few minutes in meditation and then I was somewhat calmer.

Toward evening Frank was released. We both have the distinct feeling that "it" is going to happen now.

During the course of the day four people came from the Protestant church with Pastor P. to find out we were doing. We hadn't counted on so many taking a personal interest in our situation. It was a great joy to us. We realized that we were more closely aligned with the established Protestant church than our own Baptist congregation, where politics was, for all practical purposes, excluded. In the press we read that the regime officially rejected the New Forum and labeled its members as "counterrevolutionaries" and "enemies of the Constitution."

23 September 1989. Five of us were at M.'s for a birthday celebration. They served Bulgarian onion bread, tomatoes, and red wine. Almost as by prior agreement, we put aside the cares of the day and simply enjoyed the moments together..

24 September 1989. Interrogation followed interrogation. In all, ten people were detained. We couldn't understand what the reason for this was. The only thing in common was that everyone had been with K. the previous evening. We assumed that it concerned him and his appeal for action. For the first time, the current events were mentioned in our congregation, albeit by Pastor M. from the Moravian Church who was filling in as our preacher. He went into detail about the ongoing Stasi investigations. He figured that they were seeking to instill sufficient anxiety to deter us from carrying out any protest actions on the fortieth anniversary of the GDR's founding. However, no one in the congregation spoke to us. The flow of people to Hungary continued and I watched the TV reports in disbelief. The Minister of the Interior once again ordered the New Forum to cease its activities since no "societal need" for these existed. Still, the movement had become so strong that it was now mentioned in the press.

25 September 1989. We are now involved in something every day, and people are in regular contact with one another. This informal information service functioned well, except that the authorities had cut off Pastor M.'s phone service and efforts to get it restored had been fruitless. P. was picked up today, and we sat together anxiously in her apartment until she returned. She reported that the local Stasi knew intimate details about her, although she had lived elsewhere and only moved here recently. We all became very uneasy. They had questioned her about everything—the Peace Group, church activities, even her private life. A woman clergyperson from the Protestant church dropped by to see us, and she said that so far the police had not acted against the local pastors, although at least four of them had taken part in the unauthorized demonstration against neo-Nazis. That, of course, was due to the state-church relationship.

We tried to figure out some pattern as we reconstructed the interrogations but couldn't determine what their objective was. We also learned that the Stasi knew all about our birthday party two days ago. I felt sick to my stomach.

I see it as fortunate that so many young pastors from the Protestant church in our area are open-minded about and active in dealing with the situations we are facing. I thoroughly enjoy being with them. I believe that they are more effective in their service than one might think.

26 September 1989. For several days I have been unable to work; I am psychologically paralyzed. New interrogations took place with five additional detentions. The ones picked up this time were people who did not belong to the Peace Group but ordinary members of the church. One was a man over seventy years old. Our outrage is growing! The questions asked now ranged from the position paper on Democracy Now to the Peace Library and even the local church organizational structure itself. The police pointedly asked about activities planned for 7 October. The fear "up above" seems immense! At the Moravian parish house we began preparations for the annual "Peace Decade." During this time a dispute arose between the pastor and the Peace Group, which demanded that the church register a firm protest against the Stasi methods.

27 September 1989. The refugee problem is worsening by the day and now affected our immediate area. Border controls have been tightened to prevent people from crossing into Poland and going to Warsaw and militia units have been mobilized. We don't know whether they have been given an order to shoot. Every morning abandoned cars were found in the woods. The interviews with refugees on Western television are unconvincing. Not one gave societal-political abuses as a reason for leaving the country. It was some trivial material matter. They are not proud, self-assured people who thought through their actions, but indifferent and resigned individuals.

We heard of many cases of irresponsible behavior regarding children. My daughter told me about two children who sat for an entire morning on a hospital bench because no one knew what to do with them. Their parents had been caught while trying to escape. Many children were simply abandoned at home. This exemplified the moral decay that has occurred in our society. For too long we have not talked about ethical values, either publicly or in the schools. Except for Christian values, what others are there in our country? More and more despair is welling up inside me. This simply can't be the solution. Something has got to happen. I simply cannot accept what I am seeing. The emotional stress is tying up my stomach in knots.

28 September 1989. After today there would be no more detentions. Still, I feel crushed internally. I have slept little in the last days. I have been tired and listless, but now there is relief. The inner tension is easing. I attended a parents' meeting at the school. A.'s teacher was totally depressed and said she was giving up her profession. She addressed the parents even though she had no notes or written agenda. Since she is a warmhearted person, the parents were very receptive and an unusually open discussion took place. At the conclusion of the meeting a party member who was present to keep an eye on the proceedings reprimanded her. The individual declared that not having notes indicated insufficient preparation and she would report this to the principal. This is what resulted from the attempt at an open discussion. I was sad. I invited the teacher to become part of my ceramic group. To some extent this was for therapeutic reasons because she is quite low, but also I didn't want to let her out of my sight. I had the feeling I must help her. The children take only their brains with them to school; so often they must leave their hearts at home.

29 September 1989. I really needed a break, so I decided to take a weekend trip to see my parents in Mecklenburg. I assumed I wouldn't be able to make any visits home in the coming days. Either it is going to be a long and tough process until changes come in this country, or the state will strike a brutal blow to keep its power. The tension in the country seems about to explode. The emigration problem is escalating and chaos reigns in Prague and Warsaw. The emotion-laden television scenes of refugees arriving in the West had an unpleasant effect on me. This type of reporting clearly had a definite purpose, and it struck me that hardly any internment camps for the refugees were shown. For me the important question is what happens after one escapes. Perhaps my bad mood was a natural reaction to the pain over these events that I experienced.

2 October 1989. The news reporting in our papers is becoming worse and worse. Such miserable journalism is nothing new, but in this situation it is like being slapped in the face. It is terribly insulting how they consider the people to be so stupid. My outrage knows no bounds! I can't read a newspaper anymore without becoming upset. How is it possible that they can consistently ignore the facts that are so obvious? I feel helpless, drained of all energy, and I scream out in rage each evening at the TV reports about the refugees. I don't listen to the commentary and I can't see the pictures because of my tears. It is simply terrible.

4 October 1989. The Peace Group met this evening. We discussed the proposals and objectives of the new democratic organizations, of which there were now four. We are full of hope and know that the next days will be very important ones.

5 October 1989. The fortieth anniversary is approaching and the tension heightens. On the street people speak about political matters only with close friends and then with their hands covering their mouths. Time is running out! We are relentlessly followed by police agents. That gets on one's nerves. The uncertainty is so great that people are now openly talking about the existence of opposition groups. We decide not to engage in any political activity on 7 October that would give the local Stasi the opportunity to strike down a "counterrevolution." We just want to lead them around by the nose since they are so feverishly working on security measures. They are convinced the Peace Group is up to something.

Special trains with refugees from Prague arrived in West Germany. The unrest is growing. In Berlin several people occupied the embassies of the U.S. and the Federal Republic. Entire families were arrested.

6 October 1989. The Peace Group met and evaluated the political situation. At the same time, the various protest groups gathered at the Gethsemane Church in Berlin and adopted a resolution calling for calm and careful action in the next days. Unfortunately, being in the countryside, we can only follow what is taking place elsewhere in a fragmentary way and from a distance. But we all know how grave the situation is.

7 October 1989. I awakened early and offered a quick prayer: "Lord, hold your hand over this country today." We set up our little peace literature sales stand in the morning, as we wanted to see how things would develop. Suddenly, trucks with uniformed personnel pulled up behind us and sealed off the side streets leading to the town center. Guards with cameras took positions on the roofs of the high-rise buildings surrounding the area. It was as if we were in a state of siege. An acquaintance from the church took several pictures of us as he stood across the street. When he noticed that we recognized him, he smiled sheepishly and disappeared. A continuous stream of men passed by our stand whom Frank remembered seeing at his interrogation. It was a depressing situation but surveillance didn't bother us anymore. We returned home two hours later quite relieved that no incidents had occurred. A gentle rain set in and the city soon was empty.

Frank drove immediately to the Environmental Forum, where he was slated to give a talk. Since they planned afterwards to march to the nearby open-pit mine, I went home quite uneasy. I was certain that the Stasi would react to any gathering today, that is, to every "riotous mob."

In the afternoon I was alone. The children were away, so I played the piano for a short while in order to relax. Then M. from our congregation came to the door. I was surprised to see him. He asked worriedly how we were doing and whether everything was quiet at our place. He then told me about police actions in the large cities. I was grateful for his sympathetic interest. It had a marvelous effect on me. After he left, I called the Protestant pastor and was relieved to hear no incidents had occurred there. Our police must have concentrated their efforts in the city center.

Later, I saw the reports on TV of the violence in Leipzig. I screamed at the top of my voice. Actions like this caused me to completely lose my self-control. I will never understand how people can beat up their fellow human beings. I was beside myself with despair! If only I could run away somewhere. But I didn't want to go into town since it was already late. Finally, just after midnight Frank came home. I was still in shock at what had happened.

9 October 1989. Tonight 70,000 people took part in the prayer services in Leipzig. We were excited. Now something has burst forth that can't be stopped. The outcome of these events is still uncertain, but something decisive will result. We prayed with all our strength that no second Beijing would occur in the GDR. That would be horrible. We were torn by fear, since we operate on the assumption that a totalitarian power will out of desperation fight for its life and that it will have no concern about casualties. Yet, we hope that our country will be spared great suffering.

10 October 1989. This time there were tears of joy. Father, whose heart did you touch? The first truthful reporting about current events in the GDR appeared in the *Union* newspaper. How thankful I am that these people finally are listening to the voice of their conscience. This the the *Wende,* the turning point! The paper repudiated the earlier false reports and announced a readiness for dialogue. That means no more violence. A stone has rolled from my heart. I raced joyously through the apartment; it was just like in the fairy tale when the spirit of goodness wins.

The church now assumes the role of mediator between the people and the state. I have great confidence in those who stood face to face against the security forces. If they are real Christians, then everything is in good hands. I embraced my children and shouted euphorically that we will soon be able to travel anywhere in the world! We laughed and decided we would first fly to Africa.

Everything Is in Turmoil Inside Me

These are entries in the diary of Ingrid Ebert, aged 43, married and the mother of four children, who also lived in Forst. A professional journalist, she worked for the Märkische Union *newspaper. For many years*

she has been actively engaged in work with youth and young adults in
her Baptist congregation. She is also the author of numerous essays,
poems, and a book.

1 July 1989. I am in complete turmoil. This morning I received a fat letter in the mail from the Baptist Union. Impatiently, I ripped it open and papers cascaded from it. The Union was sending me to a workshop in Rüschlikon, Switzerland! At first I couldn't believe it. I read the letter again and again. There it stood in black and white: "Delegated to be a participant." It is scheduled for the beginning of November. I am excited. But what if permission for the trip isn't granted? No, it will be. The language of the conference will be English. I immediately secured some books to freshen up my grammar school English. There are many forms to fill out. I must write a résumé.

I never thought it possible that I would someday go to Switzerland. I still can't really believe it. I would like to tell everyone, but I decide to keep it to myself. Only the family knows about it. After all, the trip must receive official approval. I am forty years old and haven't seen much of the world: a week in Czechoslovakia, a few days in Poland, and three days in Moscow, a trip I won as a prize. And now this. How many times have I read the letter? Five times? Ten times?

10 August 1989. Hundreds of citizens are leaving the country daily. And the frightening thing is the silence of the media on the matter. The authorities refuse to recognize how rapidly dissatisfaction is growing—that people are giving up their secure lives, nicely furnished apartments, single family houses, and beautiful yards. Preferring the uncertainty, the unknown, that lies before them, they leave friends and country behind. Many applied to emigrate before the election in May, and the numbers have soared since then.

Can't the authorities see the significance of all this?

And then there are the others, those with suitcases in hand or a rucksack on their back hastily and precipitously seeking freedom and protection in the embassies of the Federal Republic in Warsaw, Prague, and Budapest. Fleeing, fleeing, they scamper over the open Austro-Hungarian border or swim across the Danube. They say that we don't shed any tears for them. But it is enough to make me cry. Daily I hear: "He is now gone, and he and she."

Our circle of friends in the church congregation is not large and none of them has left., but I have heard shocking reports from other congregations. Didn't God put us here? Is it good to leave? Is it right to stay? The more people decide to leave, the more I ask these questions. It is though I have to find reasons for staying. The topic "going or staying" is constantly on our minds. We consider the possibilities. These are existential questions. We are seeking answers. The situation in our land is making me uneasy.

The silence of our leaders depresses me. Ought we not to be talking about these things openly? In our news reports, the world is intact. The pages of our newspapers are flooded with success stories. There is no admission of fraud in the recent election. Have we all lost the sense of what reality is? Are we all running about wearing rose-colored glasses? How long will they continue to sweep the dirt under the carpet? What was the slogan at the last SED Central Committee meeting? "The local elections are a clear vote for our policies." What self-deception! And it was just recently that the CDU Chairman Gerald Götting told his party members: "We consider the finest result of the past forty years to be the steadily growing mutual trust among people of different political, ideological, and religious beliefs."

Where are the eyes and ears of our leaders? What do they think are the reasons why so many thousands have left the country? Are all of them adventurers? Criminals? Traitors? People who only see prosperity elsewhere?

Why are they all going, when, according to the official line, the country is becoming stronger year after year, its effectiveness and productivity are growing, people in the cities and towns have an increasing sense of well-being, and everyone has a secure existence? Social security means a great deal, but not everything. What is social security without freedom, social security in a country where nothing moves except those who are fleeing? How many more will leave? What must happen before the leaders finally pay attention and really look and listen?

It isn't well that so many people are leaving the country. It brings grief to families, friendships, and children. The separations cause pain. I often think of the final get-together at S.'s place. He had to wait years and brought everything upon his head, including discrimination and alienation. Finally, the permission to leave came. Then came the hasty packing, decisions about what to take or leave, and the farewell drink with friends sitting on wooden crates in almost empty rooms. The champagne corks were flying, but the mood was terrible. Everyone sat there in silence. "We wish you the best!" "Here's to your health!" "Goodbye!" One last hug.

Where might he be living now? What is he doing? Has he found friends? The pain of parting is bad enough but that of not admitting the pain is even worse. "I Love to Live in My Country" was the theme of a recent children's essay competition. I wanted to write: "It's all a lie!"

> Again and again to be abandoned.
> Again and again to be alone.
> Again and again to have to experience
> that friends are going.
> Again and again to have to live,
> here and today.

11 September 1989. Today I read an article in the newspaper about dreams by a Dr. Tögel:

> One should not be ashamed of one's dreams, but rather should try to catalogue their content. This would help one to gain better access to the inner self. That includes the perception and integration of the dark, problematical areas of our personalities. Every member of the society, even journalists, are challenged to do this. They know, probably best of all, the picture that our press draws of present reality in our society. Reality is much more differentiated and has more shady areas than these pictures. In the same way, it a mechanism of repression. As is the case with the press, many people are concerned only with themselves.

I don't remember anything else of what he said. But I believe the idea about the integration of the dark areas is true. You can only jump over your shadow if you accept that you have one.

But there aren't any shady areas in socialism. They must not exist. We love optimistic colors and superlatives. Socialism lives on slogans—we don't work simply well or better, but rather better and better. Improving quality, greater effectiveness, highest achievements, beautify our cities and communities, my work place a place of struggle for peace—such are the phrases we hear.

We are told to compare everything with the very best; attain the highest! Statistics prove it. We are getting better and better, are consuming more, are living more comfortably, and are happier. We are experts in repressing the shady aspects of life. We don't want to remove our rose-colored glasses because then we would have to see the gray façades of the houses, the crumbling buildings in the cities, the windows with broken panes nailed shut, the falling chimneys, the missing roof tiles, and the moss in the gutters of the houses. Yes, we would discover the trash in the parks, the filthy train stations, the defective toys, and dirty sandboxes. We would notice the dying trees and miss the rich variety of species in the animal world. We would be shocked by the number of broken families, alcoholics, and people who have given up on life. We don't want to see reality. Socialism doesn't have any shady sides. "May the sun live forever!" Here we are all happy. Those who aren't have left the country, voluntarily or involuntarily. We don't shed any tears over them!

We are experts in the art of repression. And yet the shadow grows larger and larger, and the repressing consumes all of our time. Political banners adorn the fronts of stores with empty shelves, slogans the crumbling stucco, flags the leaky roofs. I remember the words of C. G. Jung: "One changes only that which one accepts." Cover-ups, glossing over, boasting, shimmering soap bubbles, economic plans fulfilled with a sharpened pencil—such is life in the GDR.

And I? I didn't learn it this way when I was a journalism student. No one told me: "You have to gloss over the bad and bandy about slick phrases." But I learned from experience in my day to day work as a journalist. With every bump that I acquired, I went more cautiously about my work. After each false step, I avoided them more skillfully. "More tact and sensitivity," my experience taught me. With each interview I sorted out that which was usable and that which wasn't. I jotted down the good information for my articles, and swallowed, forgot, and repressed the bad stuff. Bring on the announcements of successes and highest achievements! The reader wants to be deceived! We needed the lie, for what would remain if it no longer was there?

The truth can hurt; it is like oil poured onto a fire or water on the enemy's millstone. Because of the frustration I constantly have stomach aches. My doctor believes I am in the wrong profession. But in which profession would I be better off?

14 September 1989. Far too long the answer to the wave of refugees has been silence. Now they try to find words, explanations, and someone to assign guilt. Our system, of course, cannot be at fault. No, it is a "militarily organized provocation against the GDR," the "grand coup from the Federal Republic," a "heartless racket with the lives of GDR citizens," and "thirty pieces of silver for the traitor Hungary." In the newspapers we read about the "illegal, cloak-and-dagger operation," and "head money." The Soviet news agency TASS reported: "The mass media and certain political circles in West Germany are carrying on a biased campaign against the GDR."

Everything is just a propagandistic smoke screen. OK, wonderful! The repression still works flawlessly. Like always, there is no lack of scapegoats. Why should we look for mistakes in our own country? I recalled the slogan used by the National Front two weeks ago: "Four decades GDR; forty years of stable and dynamic economic development and of growing effectiveness and quality in all areas of life." The problem couldn't have arisen from internal causes, even though people risk their lives to leave this country. No, the guilty ones are elements in the West "who deal recklessly with the fate of human beings and violate international law," "openly lure away our citizens," and carry on an "unrestrained campaign of slander against the GDR."

We are warned that "after the initial euphoria will come the valley of disappointment." Yet, tens of thousands have left the country. Were they all lured away or deceived? Were they all people who voted overwhelmingly in favor of the country's policies at the last election?

Not only are the contradictions becoming greater, but the silence regarding them more and more frightening. My stomach aches tell me that it can't continue this way much longer. I would like to just drop out, close my eyes and my ears, and scream—scream everything out of my system. Or should I go also and begin afresh? Is it better to flee? Because so many have already fled, remaining behind is becoming increasingly more uncertain. Is flight the only option?

No, there is another way, the one leading onto the streets. Every Tuesday, the West German TV news programs report on the prayer services for peace in Leipzig and the demonstration that followed. People are arrested, but each Monday the number of those increases who undauntingly go *their* way, but not into the West. "We are staying here," they shout.

16 September 1989. Thomas Münzer, the Spartacus of the sixteenth century, was lavishly praised at his monument in Thuringia. We were told how he struggled to attain his dreams and lived fought for his ideals. Where would he stand today? Also, Gorbachev announced he would visit the GDR. Now there is hope.

25 September 1989. What is happening in Leipzig is cause for optimism, but it also makes me anxious. The Monday demonstrators call for renewal of the country. Without violence, they unequivocably demand reforms and changes. And more and more of them take to the streets. But why am I so fearful? I think of China and the brutal measures taken against dissidents. The tanks rolled, yes, they rolled over people. The "Army of the People" went against its own people. What a crime was committed on the Square of Heavenly Peace! And yet not one word of criticism came from our government. In every newsaper we saw in bold headlines: "Counterrevolution successfully put down." I am quite anxious because just recently I read in a newspaper: "We will not tolerate any attack upon the stability of our political order!"

3 October 1989. Yesterday, the CDU county secretary asked how I had gotten the opportunity to take a trip to Switzerland. The Department of the Interior had inquired about me. He assured me that he said only good things. Well, I really ought to have expected this. They don't allow just anyone to go to Switzerland. They weren't satisfied with the umpteen forms I had to fill out. My résumé was not clear enough either. No, Berlin made inquiries in my hometown and asked the functionaries what they thought and knew about me. So, the decision whether I may take a church-related business trip depends on statements by people I don't even know. It makes me angry. I hadn't told any of my friends about the trip, and now I learn that others have been talking about it for a long time. Everyone is under surveillance. Is that the reason why packages constantly come already opened and letters arrive late, and C. from Cologne hasn't written me for a long time? Or perhaps the letters are just lying around somewhere.

But today someone from the Department for Church Questions said: "You have a long trip before you." I replied: "If it is approved." Then she reported: "If the Interior Ministry has given its blessing, what can go wrong?" It bothers me to be dependent on the decisions that others make. But I am happy because she told me, off the record, that the trip would receive approval.

Yesterday evening was our prayer service for peace. I believe it is very important to gather together in prayer for our country and to accompany all demonstrations with prayers. A bloodbath simply must not occur. Often I think that what happened in China can't happen here in the middle of Europe. They wouldn't dare do that. Nevertheless, our leaders are obviously very interested in China. Egon Krenz is heading a delegation that has been there for several days. They laid a wreath at Tiananmen Square which read, "For the heroes of the people." They did not mean those students against whom the most brutal force was used. No, they celebrated the "overthrow of the counterrevolutionary uprising," and Krenz conveyed Honecker's fraternal greetings. It seems to me like a threat. I have fear and hope at the same time. Even as I prayed with the others, the people in Leipzig were chanting: "No violence!" and "We are the people!"

7 October 1989. Forty years GDR, yet tens of thousands have left the country in the last months and tens of thousands more go out onto the streets, Monday after Monday, registering their dissatisfaction and desire for reforms. But Honecker had the young people march as a "powerful testimony." The torchlight parade yesterday evening in Berlin was a unique form of self-deception. Who is kidding whom? Never in my life have I experienced such a strong contradiction.

Fear is in the air. But there is no fear among those Christian activists who had been interrogated hour after hour during the last weeks, no fear among those who were subjected to high fines, no fear among those who were spied upon while taking part in peace activities. No! Rather, fear is manifested by those who are exerting the pressure, who are spying, who are interrogating.

This afternoon we as a family went into town and observed the activities at the *Volksfest*. The merriment with the flea market, wagon rides, games for children, and music was superficial. We ran into F. from the Ecumenical Peace Group and chatted for a few minutes. When we walked away, I noticed two men were following us. From then on we couldn't shake our two "inconspicuous" escorts. I recognized the first one from earlier encounters; I will know the other from now on. We wandered aimlessly among the booths, occasionally stopping to buy a few trinkets. Everytime I looked over my shoulder, both of them were not far from us. But they weren't the only ones standing around seemingly uninvolved and inconspicuous. Such people were everywhere. What a contingent! And I spotted on the roof of a building in the town center two men in green uniforms.

What were they expecting? Why were they so afraid? What did they think would happen on the anniversary of the republic? Hadn't the people professed in such dynamic ways their support for the policies of the party and government? What did they expect after forty years of "successful struggle for socialism"? Are they afraid of a few hooligans, criminals, or antisocial types?

Our "escorts" disappeared only when we went home. If we were being tailed, then who else also? And who isn't being watched? And how many have made themselves available for this kind of work? Perhaps they are even well paid.

The conflict that was in the air in our little town has now exploded in the major cities. Gorbachev, the one who brings us new hope, is in Berlin. The Soviet leader had said: "He who does not go along with the times will be overtaken by them." In Berlin, Leipzig, and Dresden there are serious clashes—the people on one side, the power of violence on the other.

8 October 1989. I just heard from R. that he and some young people had been arrested by the Neisse River this morning. They were on the way to the flea market. Either the boys intended to cause some trouble or more likely they just wanted to relieve themselves under the ruins of the old bridge. Regardless of the reason, uniformed men jumped out of the bushes and seized the three youths. Two of them did not have their identity papers with them and were forced to lie down in the grass with their arms and legs spread apart. R. had to stand in this position. They were accused of the crime of "fleeing from the republic," loaded onto a truck, and carried some disstance to another border town. The police interrogated them for hours and tried to persuade them to confess, telling them that they wouldn't get into much difficulty since so many were escaping anyway. R. told me that when one man frisked him for possible weapons, another one hit him on the backside of each knee. He moved forward to avoid falling over. "Don't try that again," barked the cop. "You'll be shot immediately if you try to escape." "Do you know," R. said to me, "I had never thought about leaving the country, but at that moment, the idea crossed my mind."

How I was dismayed! When I was a girl I used to go swimming with the children in the Neisse. Often we threw a ball at the other side so we could retrieve it and say we had been in Poland. In the fall we collected chestnuts and in the winter rode our sleds down the embankment. As young people we sat in the grass, and sang and laughed. We seldom ever saw a border guard.

But now? For two weeks the border has been sealed off. The regular guardss have been reinforced by militia units. Day and night these armed men hide in the bushes and walk along the embankment. Riot police and the State Security men are also there. Off-limits signs appear on the roads leading to the border towns. While hunting mushrooms in the woods, one is likely to be stopped by uniformed people who demand to see an ID and ask questions. All vehicles are checked. Anyone who cannot identify himself or herself, or who for any other reason is suspected of attempting to flee from the republic, will be interrogated by the police or Stasi. Frequently one can hear shots in the night, and people report that once again somebody has been caught.

Is this still the "peace border"? All I see is barbed wire, barriers, and walls. Can an entire people be locked in? What right do the authoriites have to do this? Wouldn't it be better to ask why people are leaving their homeland? Wouldn't it be more proper to begin a dialogue? I am terribly afraid of war in our country—a second China right here.

My hands have been trembling often and my stomach aches persist. The doctor recommended a sedative but I don't want to take any pills. A coworker said: "Have a drink, then you'll feel better." No! I *want* to get annoyed by those things that are causing me to get upset. I *don't* want to be calmed down when a spirit of restlessness seizes me. I *want* to experience the trembling because it is the fear in me. And the pressure on my stomach tells me more than I can read in the newspapers.

10 October 1989. Today I glanced at the headline in the CDU newspaper *Märkische Union;* "It is possible to talk to one another." I then read the article—honest, sincere words about the events in Dresden. For the first time I saw decent words about demonstrators. I could hardly believe it. I wiped the tears from my eyes, but they kept cascading—liberating, freeing tears. Is this reality? In unbelief I stared at the text. Something new is happening! Truth is making headway! There is hope.

11 October 1989. I see new indications of change. The dialogue has begun in Dresden and hope for an agreement has replaced the fear of violence. And now, even the demands being made are printed in the newspapers—at least in some.

The saving word is dialogue. Our country isn't what it was a few days ago. Those who were in a trance have moved. Those who did not speak are beginning to talk. Indeed, they are shouting the words that they once swallowed. More and more of the blind are beginning to see. But the other factor remains; violence continues to be used to stop those who speak out openly. There it is in the paper. Police units are necessary and the demonstrations are still portrayed as "disturbances of the public order" and "illegal mobs." The papers still talk about "troublemakers who have been incited to violence" and "criminal elements with antigovernment slogans." Will truth or the big lie gain the upper hand?

The despair is deep, but hope remains. A little seed sprouts, takes root, and grows up to be a tree. Does nonviolence have a chance? Can nonviolence defeat violence? Yes, I would like to believe it. An entire people is on its feet, but not everyone is going in the same direction. Far too many see the way out only by fleeing and starting a new life. But increasing numbers believe there is another way out—seeking a new beginning in their own country. For a long time the church doors have been open to facilitate talks. Many say that isn't the task of the church, but all other doors remain closed to those who want dialogue. May a Christian shut himself off from the society?

16 October 1989. People anticipate every Monday with renewed enthusiasm. Today over 100,000 Leipzig citizens demanded freedom of the press and the right to travel freely. Two days ago

Honecker met with the leaders of the bloc parties and asked their advice. Did he really get advice? Or did he simply tell them what is to be done? Does he know what must be done? What does he see and hear? What does he know about what is happening in the country? But if the Stasi sees and hears everything and then doesn't inform those above, then our situation really is desperate. Who is lying to whom and why? Why is Honecker so stubborn? Doesn't he grasp the seriousness of the situation?

24 October 1989. Things are happening fast and furiously! Often I cannot write but just make a few notes. Honecker has resigned, supposedly for reasons of health. And what we feared has come to pass; Egon Krenz assumed his position. Today the parliament elected him head of state. I hope it is only a temporary situation. What have we gained by getting a new man at the helm who has played such an inglorious role? He should comment honestly on the election fraud and his applause for China. I don't believe it was wise to put such an unreliable person in the top leadership position during this tense situation.

A few days ago Krenz met with editors. We journalists have been demanding a new media law and an end to Stasi inference in our work. The latest instructions for us editors were really none at all. There will be no more instructions; each will be personally responsible for his or her work. There are no more taboos; now we can, we must, report the truth. I can hardly believe it. Are changes really taking place in our land? People are speaking more openly, the masks are falling. Is it really true? Or will there be a rude awakening?

26 October 1989. Finally I received the papers for the trip to Switzerland, and buying the train ticket was an exciting experience. I am curious about the week in Rüschlikon, but even more curious about what things will be like in my country when I return.

31 October 1989. While Krenz traveled to Moscow today, I went straight through the Federal Republic. I rode in an Inter-City train for the first time, and as I chatted with several of the other passengers, I found the interest in what was happening in our country to be very great. People admire the new political openness of the citizens of the GDR.

It has been raining since I started my trip. Here I am traveling on this stretch for the first time and it rained incessantly, but suddenly I saw a rainbow, the symbol of reconciliation. All at once I felt very close to my country again.

1 November 1989. I am now at Lake Zurich in Switzerland where I can see the snow-covered mountains in the distance. The experience is unfathomable. Christians from nineteen countries have gathered here to learn how to produce Bible-study materials. As we pray the Lord's Prayer, each in his or her own language, our solidarity is evident. We are children of one Father. Even though we have much to do here, my thoughts are on my home. Others ask me about the situation there. What happens in our country is important not only for the GDR and the German nation, but also Europe as a whole. As we watch the evening TV news, I have the burning feeling that something decisive is happening back in the GDR.

4 November 1989. I have never seen pictures before like the ones which appeared today on television. A half million people, young and old, demonstrated completely nonviolently for freedom of expression, press, and assembly. As we sat spellbound in the clubroom, tears welled up in my eyes. A half million people on the streets, peacefully, in harmony with one another. I wanted to be there, to be part of it all. For some time now it has no longer been a question of reforms, of papering over the problems. A revolution is going on! What will I find when I cross the border again in two days? Is this still the country in which I grew up? Is this still the land of the functioning functionaries?

Many words have come into fashion: dialogue, turning point [*Wende*], yes, even "two-faced" persons. [The word *Wendehals* was a play on words seen during the revolution. It means literally "weathercock" and was applied to the cynical survivor types who suddenly shifted when the winds of change began to blow.] Now it is no longer just freedom to travel and freedom of the press; thousands of feet are carrying the message challenging the claim of the SED bigwigs to leadership. I doubt that they will step down without a struggle, but it is too late to use force to silence the people. Too many have come out of their closets and are learning to stand tall. Not only in Berlin, Leipzig, and Dresden was there an awakening; everywhere, thousands and tens of thousands of people have used their feet to gain their rights.

8 November 1989. I am back home again, but it is not *I* who is doing the talking, as normally is the case after such a trip. No, the others are telling *me* their stories. They have so much news to relate. I have been carefully reading the newspapers of the past days, and every article grabs my attention. Just a few weeks ago, I would merely skim over the headlines. Now I understand why the GDR was always a land of bookworms. The newspapers simply weren't readable. Ten minutes would suffice, but today I need at least an hour to read them. And no longer is everything identical in all the newspapers.

Everyone is excited. Everyone wants to talk. There is only one topic: the revolution sweeping the country. Whether buying bread, riding on the streetcar, at a birthday party, or taking a stroll, people are talking about the changes in society. Everyone is an active participant. It cannot and will not continue as it has up until now. Yesterday the Council of Ministers resigned. A proposed new travel law was immediately rejected as too inadequate. We don't want our freedom doled out in thin slices anymore. Everywhere one hears demands—civilian alternative service, a new education law, and so forth.

And still the people are fleeing to the West. They are leaving their families, work, and unfinished tasks. We miss them. Where will all this lead? It is frightening. In a public appeal Egon Krenz declared: "Have confidence in our policies for renewal! Your place, dear fellow citizens, is here!" But confidence has disappeared and it cannot be restored with words. Enough words have been exchanged. Now is the time for deeds.

In spite of a continuous rain, 100,000 people demonstrated in Dresden last Monday for free elections and against the SED claim to leadership. "Stasi into the work force!" they shouted over and over, as well as "Dismantle the administrative structure!" and "New school curricula!"

I just heard on the radio that the SED elected a new Politburo and confirmed Krenz as general secretary. Names have been changed but will that alone change everything? In mid-October Krenz stated: "We are standing face to face with the people!" He also said: "A party like ours has no other interests than the people," and, "As of today we will bring about a *Wende*."

Face to face with the people? An interest in the people? Such words have lost their credibility and value. No one believes them anymore. *We* will bring about the *Wende*? No, you and your henchmen didn't bring it about. It was the product of those who came together at the prayer services for peace, who, in spite of rubber truncheons and beatings, in spite of interrogations and imprisonments, time and again took to the streets.

10 November 1989. It can't be! That is sheer madness! The borders to the Federal Republic and to West Berlin are now open. An ecstasy of joy has broken forth. The world has turned upside down! Or is it now coming right side up?

12 November 1989. All at once everything has become simple. A personal ID suffices; a rubber stamp is enough. Long lines form outside the police stations. Everyone wants to travel as soon as possible. Who knows whether the borders will remain open? The DM 100 "welcome money" which the West German government offers every GDR citizen is also a reason. The year will soon be over, so get a move on! Don't let this opportunity slip through your fingers! Everyone is excited and shoving one another as they try to be among the first to go over. Everywhere there are tears of joy. People are hugging one another. Champagne corks fly into the air. A *Volksfest* is in full swing in West Berlin. It is unreal, wild, wonderfully crazy. If someone had told me during the summer this would be possible, I would have laughed at him. The Wall has holes in it. Masses of people pour through the openings. Once again, everything is in motion in a westerly direction. There is only one topic of conversation: a trip to the West.

Was this a diversionary tactic? Had the rulers opened a floodgate to release the pressure? After all, whoever is strolling along the Kurfürstendamm in West Berlin can't be demonstrating in the East at the same time. The borders to the West are open, but freedom to travel isn't everything. Do not let the pressure diminish and the shouts grow quieter. So much needs to be changed and so much corruption and misuse of power uncovered. "Don't be hoodwinked," I want to cry out.

26 November 1989. Fortunately, my fears have not materialized. In spite of the wave of travelers to the West, the demonstrations continue and 100,000 were on the streets in Dresden on 20 November. In the government rapid changes in personnel take place; however, not name changes but rather the alteration of structures are required to provide something really new. The country is on the brink of economic ruin. We must move away from centralized planning and control as soon as possible. Factories, schools, and other institutions must no longer be under SED control. No more dictatorship! Democracy!

New groups are forming so quickly that it is difficult to know which way to turn. So much deception is coming to light that emotions are running high. Hatred, often blind hatred, is raging. Violence must be avoided now as well. Can fire be extinguished by fire?

1 December 1989. The last month of the year has begun. How will this year end? Advent? Christmas? I don't have much Christmas spirit. I am out every evening taking part in meetings and demonstrations. The things now being uncovered are absolutely incredible. Those who demanded an ascetic existence from us lived like kings themselves. Until now, I had thought that, although we were poor, we were an honest, public-spirited country, one with ideals. Now it is clear that the rulers were in every way the equals of the feudal princes. Each of them feathered his own little nest. They publicly preached water but secretly drank wine.

A TV camera crew tried to visit the government retreat center at Wandlitz near Berlin, but some things had to be cleaned up before it was permitted to come in. The lie continues! Didn't Krenz promise that everything would be uncovered? Nothing is being uncovered. People only admit what is known. Is this what the radical change looks like? It is a scandal. Now that light is focused on the wheeling and dealing, the blatant hypocrisy has been exposed.

Fancy houses for the families of officials, and how does the average citizen live? With their special hunting preserves and stores stocked with luxury goods at ridiculously low prices, they were worse than the princes. Why? Because they claimed they were sacrificing for the cause, working for the people. They took care of themselves, ripped off the people, ruined the country, and lived at our expense. I am so angry. I can understand the calls for revenge, but we must not allow our emotions to guide us.. The cry for reunification is getting louder. People have had enough of our system of lies and deception. The SED itself destroyed socialism. The leading functionaries gambled it away by their own feudalistic behavior.

6 December 1989. For or against reunification—that is the question. The issue is now a matter of national debate. Socialism, yes or no? What is socialism? What we had certainly was not socialism. It was dictatorship by ruling functionaries. What the hands of the people created never belonged to the people. Hard currency—where did it all go? And for me the most shocking thing: They even sold weapons abroad so that things would go more smoothly here.

I could scream from rage! My workplace—a workplace for peace? Everything was a lie! In which country has there ever been so much hypocrisy? The secret arms deals, a betrayal of all our ideals, weren't uncovered by Egon Krenz but by alert citizens. I was much too naive about my country. What still goes on behind prison walls? Some former leaders have been arrested, but is that enough? Doesn't the old power structure have to be changed so that it can never again produce such crimes? Is everyone covering up for one another?

7 December 1989. Yesterday Krenz resigned as head of state. Another hope has been fulfilled. There will be an amnesty for prisoners. Today, the Round Table meets for the first time.

16 December 1989. No one is thinking about Christmas. Rallies and demonstrations are now part of everyday life. Although here in Forst there are candles in front of the police stations and on the war monument, the complete about-face has yet to be achieved. The call for a united fatherland is getting louder.

I heard that the Stasi doesn't exist any more, but can that be true? Has the agency of fear really been disbanded? No more fear of being watched? No more fear of being denounced? To be able to speak openly without someone listening? To experience confidence again? Perhaps I am again too naive but this is my dream.

24 December 1989. Signs of hope are shining like the candles on the tree. They must not be extinguished again. The most remarkable aspect of our revolution is the nonviolence. What a contrast to Romania! Thousands died there, but freedom can't be suppressed forever and every dictatorship carries within the seeds of its own destruction. I weep for the dead. O God, Timisoara could have been Leipzig, or Dresden, or Berlin! The bloodbath in Romania could have been ours. The police and army forces had been briefed about counterrevolution. The water cannons and tanks were in readiness. The weapons were loaded. O God, only now do I grasp the seriousness of the situation and the miracle that occurred.

The signs of hope aren't lighting a path or showing us where to turn. Maybe there are some will-o'-the-wisps among them. However, the Bible verse for the New Year 1990, Jesus Christ is the Light of the world (John 8:12), gives me courage and calm. We won't walk in darkness when we follow Him, therefore we must continue the prayers for peace. So much remains to be done.

Some Experiences in Berlin

Where is the path? Baptist Edgar Leopold describes the prayer vigil at the Gethsemane Church on 23 October 1989.

I arrived a half-hour early and crowded my way into the church. It was as jammed with people as a rock concert. I found a seat in the balcony where I could observe everything. By the 6:00 p.m. starting time 3,000 must have been there; people were sitting and standing everywhere. I overheard snippets of conversation like "freedom to travel" and "do you have opened letters that. . . ."

When the organ prelude began, an inward calm settled over me and I looked forward to the worship service. Following some comments about activities, it was announced that the 146,389 marks given in the offerings during the last three weeks would be earmarked for fines and legal counsel for those who had been arrests. The audience responded with loud applause.

The pastor stepped into the pulpit and began the service with "The Lord Be With You." Then came a brief prayer and the singing of the "Shalom Hymn" as a canon (round). When we finished singing inside the church, we heard it echoing back from the crowd standing outside: "Shalom, shalom." It was fantastic. If the shalom of God reverberates in such a way, it is a sure sign of the love of God. It was very comforting to know that we are enveloped in his peace.

The pastor's wife delivered a political devotional showing how the path of God is woven into our activities. Unfortunately, she did not tell us about that part of the path of hope that we tread when we are in Jesus. She talked about "not despairing," "struggling," and "not simply putting up with everything." But where is the path that leads us out of our hopelessness and into the freedom that Jesus gives us?

Now we reached the distinctive part of the service—the intercessory prayers. I was eager to fold my hands and pray myself but was disappointed by the liturgical character of the proceedings. There were seven general petitions and requests made to God; between each we sang the line *Kyrie eleison* (Lord have mercy). I was unhappy because there were no words of praise, of thanksgiving, or of worship. Who are we to make demands of God again and again?

To my surprise, the worship service ended here. The leaders went on to read countless letters from opposition groups. I listened to them all, clapped now and then, but after forty minutes decided to leave, as the building was just too stuffy. It took ten minutes to push my way to the exit.

First Pray, Then Demonstrate

The report of Siegfried Holtz, Youth Pastor for the Baptist Union.

After Edgar left somewhat disappointed with the prayer vigil, I took his place, so to say. In front of the Gethsemane Church, a procession formed that planned to deliver a letter to the Council of State. It asked the parliamentary deputies to put forward candidates in opposition to Egon Krenz for the head of state position which Honecker had just resigned, and urged them not to be intimidated to vote a certain way by the SED leadership. Although the proposal was ignored, this demonstration (my first) was an important experience for me.

I joined the procession as it reached Prenzlauer Allee and headed downtown. I heard slogans like "Turn off the TV—Come on out." In general, I had the impression that this "demo," with its specific objectives, was permeated by a high degree of peaceableness. Did the blessing of the bishop given before it set out really have an effect after all? It was certainly not just his prayer. But the fact that people were praying did have positive results.

Again and again the participants shouted "We are the people." There was a grand sense of community. Somehow we all knew that we belonged together, in spite of our diverse opinions and views. The countless numbers of candles made quite an impression on me. In their own way they contributed to the peaceful mood.

A police car drove in front of the procession; another followed. And at every intersection our "friends and helpers" were there to see that we did't have any trouble. They blocked off the side streets and turned off the traffic lights so the procession could move unhindered. My, how times had changed in just two weeks!

At the outset I was a little uneasy, but after a few minutes I had "broken free" of this feeling. After we delivered our letter, the demonstration disbanded peaceably. Everyone went on their way home, all the while discussing these events with one another.

The November Demonstration in Berlin

Martin Swoboda, twelve years old, relates his experiences at the Alexanderplatz demonstration.

On Friday, 3 November, my mother asked me if I wanted to come with her to the demonstration tomorrow morning. Since I wanted to take part in a "demo," I asked my teacher to be excused from school this Saturday, and she agreed to it.

We left our house in Buckow, a few miles east of Berlin, at 8.00 a.m. When we changed at the Ostkreuz station to the elevated train going in the direction of Alexanderplatz, it was already rather full. At the next stations, so many people tried to get on that several were left standing on the platforms. When we arrived at our destination, a large crowd had already gathered, and people were streaming into the area from every direction. It was a strange feeling to stand in the midst of so many people who had the same objective as I did.

It seemed like half of the demonstrators were carrying banners or posters with creative sayings on them, such as, "Democracy without limits," "The freedom to surf in the Baltic," "Sick people belong in bed, not on the throne," and "Long live the November Revolution of 1989!"

My mother and I walked to the Palace of the Republic, the large meeting hall in downtown Berlin, and climbed to the top of the steps so we could see how many people were there. As we watched, two people on the street began to shout "Stasi out!" Within fifteen seconds everyone was shouting along with them. The mood was simply fantastic. It was as if we all had known one another for a long time.

Then we were back down to the street where we saw a couple that had just gotten married join in the celebration in their formal clothes. There were a lot of police officers posted along the streets and several people gave them flowers. After the demonstrators had finally reached Alexanderplatz, a massive rally took place. When the author Christa Wolf and other well-known speakers addressed the crowd, people were jubilant. On the other hand, when the SED bigwigs Schabowski (the Berlin party boss) and Markus Wolf (the head of East Germany's espionage agency) came to the podium, the booing was so loud that they couldn't be heard.

Later, on our way home, a few of the demonstrators told us that they had seen several masked individuals in the crowd. They didn't have any banners nor did they shout along with everyone else. No one knew why they were there. For this reason, no one wanted to have anything to do with them. After a few moments they disappeared as quickly as they had come.

It was a fantastic experience that I will never forget.

Leipzig—City of the Monday Demonstrations

". . .and if it must be, then with weapon in hand!"—Memoir of Raphaela Russ, a nineteen-year old nurse.

"And don't forget if they take you away—there is no one here who can look after you," my brother told me as he drove off. My parents were also not home. What would happen then if I couldn't escape the clutches of the State Security? They not only beat everything that moves near them, but also throw everyone they can grab into their trucks. My memory of the most recent demonstrations—I should say, the conclusion of them—was less than encouraging. Again and again the picture was the same: security officers armed to the teeth and with dogs chasing people through the downtown area. Then came the encirclement—the most brutal use of police violence. Those who were beaten lay on the street, crying. What remained was fear, impotence, and the question: "How will it all end."

The head of the SED in the city of Gera, Wolfgang Heiland, answered the question on 3 October with a public threat: "We will deal with provocateurs and counterrevolutionaries who try to disrupt the fortieth anniversary of the GDR just as it was done in China."

"There will be a second China," many people told me, looking toward 9 October. And everyone who planned to go onto the street had a ominous sense of foreboding. "We are afraid. . . . We are the people! Violence in our midst will leave behind wounds that will bleed forever." These words were found in a flyer distributed that day in Leipzig by three grassroots organizations.

But was this fear well founded? The media fanned the flames under the big stew pot that the Marxist-Leninist leadership had been cooking for forty years. The GDR media, always submissive, was the mouthpiece of the SED leadership since the beginning. What the media was propagating since May 1989 could hardly be exceeded for its militancy, lack of contact with reality, and contempt for the people. No wonder the masses felt betrayed.

The manipulated results of the phony election on 6 May were celebrated in the *Leipziger Volkszeitung* as a "powerful declaration of the people" with "a splendid atmosphere and a festive mood." On the other hand, the newspaper condemned the Monday demonstrations as "insolent, outrageous, and provocative." Regarding the mass exodus through Hungary and Czechoslovakia, the press was completely helpless. The fate of these individuals was depicted in a pitiful fashion. "Cold-blooded, professional slave traders" drugged them with menthol cigarettes and then dragged them into the "headquarters of the counterintelligence." Twenty-four letters from readers adorned page three of the SED's *Neues Deutschland* on 21 September that spoke indignantly about "unscrupulous slave organizations that have long been preparing for this day," and who were attempting to undermine socialism. The news programs of GDR television spoke about the heroic Chinese army which overcame the rabble-rousing and destructive forces in the country. While the press, radio, and TV lauded the forty years of sunny efforts on behalf of human rights, the economy, and social welfare, tensions among the people escalated because of the events that had come tumbling upon them one after another during the year.

Since the police raid a year ago at the Zion Church in Berlin and the exiling of several prominent artists and others, the country hasn't had a moment's rest. The censorship of the church newspapers, the terrible election fraud, the suppression of the movement for freedom in China, the countless arrests of opponents of the regime—again and again caused protests to flare up. Demonstrations and letters of protest, followed by a wave of arrests, fines, and imprisonments, were a never-ending cycle. Members of the outlawed Initiative Peace and Human Rights as well as those in other study groups found themselves alternately in custody, under house arrest, in prison, and then free again. Afterwards would come detainments "for the purpose of clarifying a matter." Activists of various groups were under constant surveillance. On especially "hot" days there might be as many as a dozen State Security agents deployed in front of certain apartment blocks..

By utilizing the most brutal force, the police intimidated the grassroots organizers. A typed document, distributed by hand, stated about one case: "Rainer Müller waved from an open window of the police station on Dimitroffstrasse. Thereupon he was thrown over a table, beaten and kicked, and then dragged to the door. In the entrance hall of the police station he was brutally beaten by four individuals who had been present during his arrest an hour earlier and who identified themselves as members of the criminal investigation department. After his release, Müller found a physician and had his injuries confirmed in writing. When he later attempted to report his mistreatment to the authorities, he was rebuffed. Because the incident took place following a worship service on 29 May, the Saxon Bishop Dr. Hempel filed a formal complaint.

This resulted in the Leipzig District SED leadership receiving a formal reprimand for "poor political activity and the inability to maintain peace and order." The possibility of personnel changes was openly discussed, and the security forces grew increasingly nervous. This showed up in the unjustified detentions of various opposition figures. By mid-June the Leipzig riot police had already used up its gasoline allotment through November, which indicated the constant deployment of its vehicles. The Leipzig protests were a thorn in the flesh of the SED power monopoly because they not only damaged the GDR's international reputation, but also they threatened the structure built of lies that had been so masterfully crafted.

Fearful of the growing protests the regime decided to demonstrate its power through drastic measures. On 11 September 104 individuals were arrested by the use of brutal force as people left the service at the Nikolai Church. Many wee sentenced to pay fines between 1,000 and 5,000 marks, and twenty were held for trial.

But slowly the populace awakened. In the background were the democratic forces such as the New Forum and New Democratic Departure. The old leadership didn't react. While the fortieth anniversary was being celebrated with pomp and circumstance, a virtual civil war raged that evening in Leipzig (and elsewhere). The rulers trampled on every civil right and thereby denied their legitimacy and public responsibility.

The authorities were "ready" for the coming Monday demonstrations and sent out directives. The heart surgery section at Karl Marx University was placed on standby alert. Emergency Medical Service ambulances were only to take patients to the prison hospital. The doctors at surgical and intensive care stations were told to prepare for gunshot wounds. The doctors serving in the downtown area were issued special permits. In nearby counties (such as Oschatz and Bitterfeld) members of the civilian militia groups had to sign documents where they agreed to shoot even at other members in the event of an emergency. Monday drew closer and with it the plans for a Chinese solution. On 6 October the *Leipziger Volkszeitung* declared under the headline, "We will no longer condone hostility toward the state," that: "We are ready and willing, to put an end to these counterrevolutionary actions, once and for all. If it must be, then it will be with weapons in hand."

The security forces stationed units of 100 men each about the city. People in the schools, universities, and factories were told that those who side with the "instigators of the people" will suffer "consequences." Parents were directed to pick up their children early from the kindergartens and daycare centers, before 3:00 p.m. At the outskirts of the city (for example, in Mockau) tanks were in readiness. The downtown area of the city looked like an armed camp. Everything was planned and ready to be carried out. Everyone was waiting for the order to the troops to move. At the blood donor center thousands of units of blood were made ready.

When riot police with plastic masks and tear gas vehicles were seen around 5:45 p.m. at Karl Marx Platz, the St. Thomas Church decided to set up a dispensary for the wounded. After the prayer services the churches in the city would open for refugees seeking protection.

But God had another plan! "God rules," Karl Barth once said to his friend Eduard Thurneysen. God intercedes and dictators go, walls cave in, people awaken, and nations break out of their bondage. And where was our faith?

"The biggest mistake that one can commit is to watch all of this while comfortably seated in an armchair in front of the television," someone said next to me, while I was pushing my way with thousands of others through the middle of Leipzig. In spite of countless warnings and terrible doubts, once again an immense mass of humanity had made its way here to experience it all. Seventy thousand people pitted their own powerlessness and fear against the army with its weapons and cold-bloodedness. They sensed their responsibility for those who were imprisoned for conscience's sake, who believed the lies, and who became silent or perished because of the system.

> Rescue those being led away to death;
>   hold back those staggering toward slaughter.
> If you say, "But we knew nothing about this,"
>   does not he who weighs the heart perceive it?
> Does not he who guards your life know it?
> Will he not repay each person
>   according to what he had done?   (Proverbs 24:11-12)

With impressive calmness the mass of people moved forward, past the onlookers who lined the edges of the streets, past the assembled security forces, past the barking dogs in the courtyards, streets, and bushes, past the heavily fortified Stasi headquarters—and we enjoyed every foot of our nonviolence, by which hope grew for a peaceful end. Over the Leipzig radio station we heard some good news. Six prominent citizens of Leipzig had addressed an open letter to those on the streets. At the beginning of the prayer services the letter composed by the conductor of the

Gewandhaus Orchestra, Kurt Masur; theologian Dr. Peter Zimmermann; the cabaret performer Bernd-Lutz Lange; and three Leipzig District SED secretaries, Dr. Kurt Meyer, Jochen Pommert, and Dr. Roland Wötzel, was read in all the churches:

> Our common concern and responsibility have brought us together today. We are troubled by the developments in our city, and we are searching for a peaceful resolution. We all need a free exchange of opinions about the continuation of socialism in our country. We herewith promise all citizens to do everything in our power to make this dialogue possible, not only in the Leipzig District but also with our government. We ask you earnestly for prudence so that a peaceful dialogue will be possible.

Cheering and jubilation broke forth. Was this the turning point, the *Wende*?

I often asked myself how the Israelites must have felt on their journey through the wilderness. The Egyptians were at their heels and, humanly speaking, they didn't have the slightest chance for a successful resolution of their situation. Since I was there when my fellow citizens took their troubles to the streets, I could empathize with the Israelites. Through my own painful experiences, I learned to bear the burdens of others. "We want to bear every burden with those who are sorely afflicted," are words that many well-fed, contented Christians sing. However, they never had the experience of being tossed to and fro, not knowing a way of escape, and living through a crisis of existence. They had their "ways of avoiding problems." But in so doing they forgot that such hindrances were woven into the fabric of our lives so that we might recognize our own mortality and place everything in God's hands. Then God can use us Christians to share the pain, joys, powerlessness, and hopes of our neighbors. In so doing, we take on a more human countenance. Jesus did not merely notice the sufferings of his fellows; he shared in them and had "compassion" on them (Luke 7:13). What an example!

"Church—we thank you" was a slogan I read on a placard. This meant not only the overall achievement of the churches but also of individual Christians who "on their own" devoted themselves to the political task at hand on 9 October. Besides the pastors who organized prayer services and thereby planted the seeds of calmness and peace in the tumultuous souls of the people, every Christian who was simply there representing Christ was important. I now understand what Karl Barth meant when he said:

> The concept "the Christian in society" becomes a promise. Thus, a new element appears in the midst of all that is old—truth in the midst of error and the lie; a bit of righteousness in the sea of unrighteousness; spirit in the coarseness of materialism; a formative life force amidst the flickering spiritual movements; and unity in the derangement of society, even in our time. The individual committed Christian—but not all Christians per se—represents Christ.

When I look back over the past months I thank God. The bloodless events on the ninth of October rang in a new era. Who would have believed it could have happened that way? Who hindered the intervention by the security forces? For me, God wrote history here.

> His mercy extends to those who fear him,
>   from generation to generation.
> He has performed mighty deeds with his arm;
>   he has scattered those who are proud in their inmost thoughts.
> He has brought down rulers from their thrones
>   but has lifted up the humble.
> He has filled the hungry with good things
>   but has sent the rich away empty.   (Mary's Song, Luke 1:50-53)

Meeting Place Leipzig, Nikolai Church

Monika Müller

I, a Baptist and a forty-eight-year-old mother of four children who never cared for political activity, have just taken part in the first demonstration in my life. Although my heart was filled with fear, my husband and sons encouraged me to become involved. I realized this was a "historic moment," and over the weekend we made our preparations. My sons painted an old bedsheet with the words: "FREEDOM IS INDIVISIBLE." We fastened it to two wooden slats and rolled it up so it would look like window blinds on spring rollers. This way we could take it on the streetcar to the downtown area with no difficulty. That was my job assignment.

On Monday, 23 October, I boarded the streetcar at two o'clock, so I could reach the Nikolai Church on time. My heart was pounding. The prayer service didn't begin until five o'clock, but for weeks one could not find a seat even at 3:30. As I arrived, people were already streaming into the church. My neighbor takes a day off each Monday in order to be there, so great is her personal commitment. During the service, a well-known hymn and the canon "Dona nobis pacem" were sung, and a church grassroots group distributed information about the present situation. From the words of Superintendent Magirius and Pastor Führer we sensed the determination to press for changes and to stand up for justice; we also detected the strain from all that had happened in the last weeks and their concern for nonviolence on both sides. Because of this, the closing prayer for peace had a special meaning and the congregation sang the *Kyrie eleison* at the appropriate times.

Outside, the crowd who could not get into the church surged and began to chant. I had arranged to meet my sons, Karsten and Simon, at the exit to give them the banner. Inside the church I felt secure, but now I was overcome by fear of the police. As I left the church, it struck me that those who came Monday after Monday were quite different from the regular churchgoers. They were people bound together by the longing for truth, justice, and freedom. Very much has to change in our country. I learned in the church that the appointment of Egon Krenz was not an adequate solution, the malicious TV program "The Black Channel" must go, and the demonstrators were not a handful of rowdies or a group wanting to leave the country.

On the street one saw opinions and demands presented massively through a variety of chants and posters. It was a powerful experience to move through the middle of the city with 200,000 others shouting: "We are the people." At first it took a while for the unorganized procession to move, but once we got on the Georgi-Ring, we walked past the main train station and Friedrich Engels Platz and soon reached the Stasi headquarters. Here, people crowded together cut loose with ear-deafening catcalls and shouts like "Stasi into the mines," "We are earning your money," "For shame!" and "You're the worst." Especially important were the shouts we heard repeatedly, "No violence," and these were directed at both sides. In all fairness, I must say that the police kept their distance from the demonstration and limited their activities to directing traffic. Already a kind of cooperation had begun, since in contrast to previous Monday demonstrations no riot police or civilian militia units were to be seen. My fear had dissipated. Because there were so many people of the same mind, I felt secure. Everyone had to realize that he demonstration and our demands had nothing to do with right-wing extremism, although some made these charges against us. We have had enough of communism and socialism, and democracy has been declared. For that reason I am going back again next Monday.

Democracy—Now or Never!

Monika's husband, Dr. Ansgar Müller, was a lay minister in the Baptist congregation on Hans Poeche Strasse in Leipzig. He was employed as a research scientist by the Saxon Academy of Sciences. Following the dictate of the First Commandment, he kept his distance from the ruling ideology, but during the Wende he became involved in the weekly demonstrations and assisted in the takeover of the Stasi headquarters in the city. He also began giving talks to Christian groups on the topic: "Christian Discipleship and Political Activity in a Dictatorship, in the Wende, and during the Time of Democratic Development."

Self-critically he said: "We Baptists got involved in these events only hesitantly and late. That is to be expected given our history—the one-sided understanding of Romans 13:1-7 and other New Testament passages, and the Free Churches' low membership figures." But, he and his wife and their son Simon helped found the Christian Social Party of Germany, which later became part of the Democratic Social Union.

Here are excerpts from two letters in which he described his experiences in Leipzig.

22 November 1989. Since September the events have happened in a topsy-turvy fashion so that every day something new and significant occurred. We were overwhelmed by the emotion of the events and the time necessary to gain correct information. Each day for hours at a time we discussed this within the family circle and with friends, neighbors, and members of the congregation. Through this we worked off the stress and decided together how to act appropriately at the next demonstration and to ratchet up our demands higher. The actions of the people seemed to follow an indwelling logic—without planning or organization. This

nonviolent revolution, spontaneously emanating from the people, was really a miracle from God.

Our own personal participation went like this. Our sons, Karsten and Simon, were involved from the beginning of September when the "Protestants" gathered each Monday following the prayer services in the square in front of the Nikolai Church. At the demonstration on 4 September, our boys watched as the Stasi officers people ripped up the placards and loaded demonstrators into trucks. On 18 September, the cries "We want out" competed with demands for democratization within the country. On this Monday, the police cordons could no longer contain the demonstrators to the church square, and the surging mob spilled on to the adjacent streets. The boys watched someone dump water on the police from a window at the corner of Grimma and Ritter Strassen, and the crowd roared with laughter.

On 25 September our boys were there when the demonstrators at the Nikolai Church broke through the police lines again. They were aided by people standing on the other side of the cordon. The crowd poured over Grimma Strasse all the way to Karl Marx Platz. Traffic was brought to a standstill and, for the first time, the people marched across the Georgi-Ring to the main railway depot where some briefly "occupied" the vast waiting hall in Germany's largest station. This was the first full-blown mass action in Leipzig, and the demonstrators carried bold banners and loudly shouted "we are staying here." This confirmed that they were not a small group of malcontents who wanted to leave the GDR but people who desired genuine reforms in the country.

With renewed courage we returned on 2 October. After the prayer service in which Pastor Christian Führer admonished us to hold firm to the policy of nonviolence, the demonstrators took the same route as the week before. Once again, traffic came to a halt, the marchers broke through the cordons, policemen plunged into the crowd to regain control, and the trucks carrying the militia units waited on the side streets for the signal to move out. There was some anxiety, but the courage of the others pulled us together. We moved forward between the streetcars and parked cars and encountered heavy police resistance at the Tröndlin-Ring. On this day, in spite of police resistance the demonstration pushed all the way to the Dittrich-Ring, where they cut loose with a "catcall concert" in front of the Stasi complex. At the St. Thomas Church, the riot police wearing plastic visors and carrying shields finally "dispersed" the demonstrators. As we walked away from the market square, we came to the place where a large contingent of militiamen were posted, and we tried to persuade the "workers in militia uniform" that they were on the wrong side. They were very embarrassed and afraid because of course they were caught in a bind between their commanders and a crowd composed of simple folk just like them. When we arrived home late in the evening, we found that the family was greatly concerned about our safety.

A non-Monday demonstration occurred on 7 October, the fortieth anniversary date. To prevent the event from being a disgrace, the state agencies knew they had to stop this demonstration. For the first time they utilized a water cannon, and our boys barely escaped being hit by the stream of water and captured by the police.

A decisive situation was shaping up for Monday, 9 October. Once again Karsten and Simon went out alone, since Monika was in West Germany for a family birthday and I was in Wroclaw, Poland to deliver some lectures at the university. That night both their father and mother anxiously telephoned from abroad to find out whether their sons had gotten home unharmed, which proved to be the case. Thanks be to God! This evening police violence was averted at the last minute and the demonstration marched around the entire inner-city ring. They carried many banners and people shouted, "We are staying here" and demanded "Freedom to travel," and "Democracy—now or never!" They called upon "Gorbi" and emphasized "We are the people."

On the following Mondays, we moved around the entire downtown ring, each time escalating the demands. Regardless of the weather, the numbers kept rising until they topped 200,000. Our entire family as well as our relatives marched. Sometimes we met colleagues, neighbors, or friends; sometimes we didn't know a soul in that huge mass of humanity. It was fascinating to observe how the "creativeness of the people" expressed itself in posters and banners, and what imagination the people developed. There were sayings like "Don't forget the seven little goats, when Egon talks of reforms" or "The cart is stuck so deep in the mud—the old coachmen have to leave." How great was the joy and encouragement as success followed success—Honecker's resignation and that of the Politburo members and then the opening of the borders.

Since the churches in the downtown area now overflowed each Monday and solidarity was an absolute necessity, our Baptist congregation on Hans Poeche Strasse held a prayer service for peace as well. At first it was set at a relatively late time in the day to convey the message that we were not going to the demonstration. But a learning process occurred and the time was moved up, "Since perhaps there were those who wanted to take part in the demonstration."

After the opening of the borders a slight drop in participation by the demonstrators took place. A banner made reference to this: "The SED and the Stasi are laughing; the people got drunk on their visas." But soon the numbers increased again.

We were there, not only in the prayer services but also in the demonstrations, and we gave up our traditional Free Church reserve. We joined in the shouting and singing; we painted and carried placards. Our shouts were not merely addressed to those in power, but also they were directed from the swamp that our society had become: "Out of the depths I cry, O Lord, unto you."

I would like to offer thanks for two things: First, that the unceasing prayers for nonviolence on both sides were answered, and second, that not only our demonstrations but also other things contributed to our liberation: the unsettled situation in the Soviet Union which resulted in the inactivity of the Soviet troops stationed here in our country; our own political and economic plight; reform efforts in Poland and Hungary; and the courage shown by the churches and other groups.

29 December 1989. No one would have dreamed that the events would happen as fast and furiously as they have. In Poland, the political turnabout took a decade; in Hungary, several years; in our country, several months; in Czechoslovakia, several weeks; and in Romania it would last only days. But no one thought that the terror in Romania would take on such bloody dimensions, and so our tears of joy upon the overthrow of the dictator were mixed with tears of sadness and compassion. On 24 December I suggested to the congregation that the Christmas offering be designated for Romania. It amounted to more than ten thousand marks, and showed how much we all were moved by the events.

But let me return to my report. First, my family made a visit to West Berlin on the weekend the borders were opened, and the joy was so enormous that another essay would be needed to describe it. Then the demonstrations on the Mondays of 20 and 27 November became more intense and the political demands were more broadly diversified but also contradictory. Two main things came into the foreground: On the one hand, the cries grew louder for "Germany, united fatherland" (a quote from the GDR's national anthem), while placards calling for reunification and the flags with the GDR emblem torn out of the middle were increasingly evident. The opposing voices of a minority emphasized two sovereign German states. The other major topic was the Stasi. Pandemonium broke out each time the marchers reached the Stasi headquarters. Everyone wanted to stay there longer, and this resulted in considerable pushing and shoving. Also there was a deafening concert of catcalls followed by a symphony of boo's and shouts of "For shame!" and "Stasi, out of our demo!" Burning candles completely surrounded the building. Self-appointed "law-keepers," however, kept the demonstrators away the entrance.

Then, on Monday, 4 December, my wife got a call from the New Forum: "Have your husband come to the Stasi headquarters; the building is going to be occupied." Right after it came a second call: "Immediately!" Monika and the two boys met me at the exit of the Nikolai Church where I was at the prayer service. We went to the Stasi building not knowing what awaited us. The procession had not yet arrived, but several people from the New Forum had gathered there. Five members were engaged in heated negotiations with General Hummitzsch, the headquarters commander. They made it clear that the people would storm the Stasi complex if an orderly occupation by a citizens' group were not permitted. They said the people were greatly aroused because they had learned that in other Stasi buildings there were only smoking remains, empty folders, and masses of shredded paper. Such a destruction of documents must be prevented here.

Reason prevailed, and I entered the complex with about thirty other people. At first, we stood on the balcony over the main entrance to show ourselves to the demonstrators and to assure them that the building was in the hands of the people, thus averting violence. It was an unreal, indescribable feeling standing here as a civilian looking down upon the procession.

Then we went to work. We demanded keys, plans of the building, seals, and attorneys form both sides. Under the guidance of Dr. Wolfgang Schnur, a prominent lawyer and political activist in the revolution, we reached an agreement whereby we would divide up into groups to inspect all the rooms and then affix seals on the most important file cabinets, data banks, and even entire rooms. After we fended off a group of television and newspaper reporters, I was dispatched to an area called the "auditorium building." A senior official accompanied us, and we sealed everything that seemed worth protecting and gave the seal to the attorney when we finished.

The mood was mixed. The anger about this institution with its immense expenditures for personnel, facilities, equipment, and its web of lies and deception gradually gave way to the rather routine tasks we had. We even sought words and gestures of solidarity or any other common ground we could find with the Stasi officials who slowly found their way to their work rooms. I would excuse myself ("Unfortunately we have to disturb you in order to seal your safe.") or try to find some polite phrase ("a long evening today, isn't it?"). Others of our number proved to be tougher, more confrontational, and better suited for such an endeavor.

After concluding our "work," we gathered in the conference room. The reports revealed that many documents had already been destroyed, several rooms were not accessible, and the number of subbasements was uncertain. Our work probably had more symbolic value than anything else.

Towards one o'clock in the morning I stepped onto the balcony once again and looked down at the now empty street below and raised my heart in thanksgiving to the Lord God, who guides the affairs of people on this earth, so often in such astonishing ways. Since I had an important appointment in the morning, I eventually had to leave my "fellow citizens," who were in the process of setting up the Citizens' Committee and organizing round-the-clock supervision of the entire building complex.

Christians Speak Out

One of the distinctive features of the *Wende* were the many courageous statements, open letters, appeals, and sermons that came
from concerned Christians. These individuals knew that such out-
spokenness would cause them no end of difficulties with a regime
that did not look lightly upon criticism from its citizens. Three
examples are included in this chapter. The first is a letter sent by
the Baptist congregation in Plauen, a textile manufacturing town,
to the head of the state. The next is a sermon preached on the
weekend when revolutionary tension in the GDR reached its most
critical point by Dr. Theo Lehmann, who, as mentioned above, was
a popular youth evangelist. The last is a sermon delivered by Baptist pastor Lutz Reichardt on the weekend that the borders were
opened. All of these reflect the deep concern which they had for
the spiritual problems that afflicted the people of East Germany
and their desire for change in their country.

Dismay and Uneasiness

*Letter from the Baptist Congregation in Plauen to the chair of the State
Council, 5 October 1989.*

Dear Mr. Honecker:

The developments in our country have aroused so much dismay and uneasiness that we feel compelled to inform you as
honestly as we can about how we view of the situation. Through
offering this constructive criticism, we as a Baptist congregation
would like to contribute to the well-being and future of our land.

We know many people who have a profound sense of hopelessness and see no future for themselves in our country. The fact
that tens of thousands of our citizens are giving up everything and
leaving fills us with deep sorrow. We are even more dismayed be-

cause most of them are young people, that is, citizens who were born and grew up under socialism. That the youth are fleeing from their country in such numbers cannot simply be attributed to seductive propaganda from West Germany, as our media constantly asserts. The point is, if I live in a place where I am finding personal fulfillment, I will not casually give up that which I love. Certainly if propaganda could have had such a decisive impact on people, then a stream of refugees in our direction should have begun a long time ago.

Thus the present situation must arise from deeper causes. The educational policies of forty years obviously have not succeeded in inculcating much love for our state. Accordingly, we would like to point out what we believe are mistakes that have contributed to our problems. At the same time, we urgently plead that you be open to our constructive criticism. Please do not look upon this as an accusation.

Educational Policies. Many in our congregation have gone through the ten-year course of study in our public schools, and for this opportunity we are very thankful. Although the schools place great importance on developing the "socialist personality," we now recognize that this educational policy has borne negative fruit. What might be the reasons for this?

The children are taught from the beginning not to think independently but rather in stereotypes. For example, a first grade teacher is likely to write in her evaluation of a pupil at the end of the school year: "Felix asks too many questions: 'Why am I supposed to do this or that?' and 'Why do we do such and such a thing?' If he doesn't stop this, he could get into difficulties later on." This teacher was brought up just like everyone else, and therefore she cannot express herself in any other fashion. She is a product of her own experiences.

During the public discussion sessions held in the schools and in the factories where apprentices are being trained, the topics are almost always predetermined by the teacher. The long term effect of this educational policy has been to produce "yes-men" (who, however, secretly say "No"). The ones who are doing the teaching deliberately manipulate this "Yes" to foster their own careers, even though such actions stand in fundamental opposition to socialist educational objectives. An education journal from the Soviet Union declares:

> A person who has never taken any significant steps on the basis of his own convictions cannot be a self-aware, creative communist. Such a one is, at best, a disciplined automaton doing somebody else's bidding. But that will not suffice for the people of tomorrow.

This quotation, from a communist, speaks for itself.

The unhealthy path that our education policies have followed is painfully obvious when we look at the development of our youth organizations—the Free German Youth and the Young Pioneers. Sadly, these are really only mass organizations in which priority is given to the outward appearance of conformity, as exemplified by full attendance at their functions. No meaning at all is given to one's inner thoughts. Importance is placed on the spoken confession, but not on how one actually lives. This policy is bearing fruit nowadays that leaves much to be desired.

We ask you, therefore, to insist on a policy of educating children to become people who say what they really think about their existence and the country in which they live. Only in this way will they come to identify personally with our country and learn to love it. Let us abandon the long-established, deeply ingrained practice of saying that which is *allowed* and what others expect to hear. The basis for such behavior has been laid in the elementary school, yes, even in kindergarten.

News Reporting. Everything we have said about education applies to media policy as well. We find the information policy to be very unrealistic and one-sided. Everyone sees the contradictions between news reporting and reality. It is a mistake to report only positive things and avoid difficulties and problems. One gains the impression from our news programs that the GDR is a paradise, but what we experience from day to day is actually quite different. It is precisely the most recent events that have made this one-sidedness so obvious. Why do our citizens have to find out about the statistics and circumstances of the refugee situation from the media of the Federal Republic? Why is our reporting so slanted that our citizens feel "compelled" to turn to foreign sources to find out what really is happening in the world?

We urgently need open and frank public discussion (not pre-arranged themes) about the realities in our country, one that allows dissenting views to be expressed. We can learn from the openness now occurring in news reporting in the Soviet Union. We request that our government permit the third part of the GDR slogan, "Plan along with us; work along with us; rule along with us," to be put into effect.

Please do not let open and public discussions be halted, even when they might lead to demonstrations (as in Leipzig). They are, after all, the visible, tangible embodiment of these discussions. We are convinced that most people in our land desire what is best for the country, including those who utilize demonstrations to voice their opinions about the problems and errors of socialism. Please take the initiative with the media to encourage citizens to express themselves freely. Convey to them the hope that our country can change, and that the involvement of every citizen is needed in this endeavor. We are deeply distressed that the government's current rigid attitude has given us no signs of hope for change.

Travel Opportunities. We are grateful for the changes in recent years that have permitted more travel to the West. Unfortunately, these provisions have not gone far enough and have caused great dissatisfaction among the populace. Only those who "have the good fortune" to have close relatives in the West can enjoy the limited travel opportunities, and this automatically leads to some being treated as second-class citizens.

Capricious decisions by local officials in approving travel requests degrade people and give the impression that GDR citizens cannot manage their own lives. Surely, your government does not want to see its people treated that way. Many of them simply will not put up with this denial of freedom anymore.

This great dissatisfaction among the populace can only be eliminated by granting all citizens the immediate right to travel abroad. At the same time, a currency reform must take place that allows people to freely exchange money in the West so they won't have to feel like beggars. The inadequate opportunities for travel are a fundamental reason for the current situation. Also, the current refugee situation in the West German consulates in other countries raises many questions about the ability of our government to provide its citizens abroad proper legal protection.

Is it not one of the most elementary human rights, that citizens of a country may travel where they wish and live where they want to? People may be encouraged to live here in our country, but they can never be "compelled" to do so. Compulsion is a weapon of an old world and it can never engender fraternal relations. Little that is happening in our society today contributes to the growth of public spiritedness, and reintroducing the requirement for an exit visa to travel to our socialist neighbor Czechoslovakia is a regrettable step in the wrong direction.

Government Subsidies. For many years we have faced creeping inflation and the situation is worsening, even though no one talks about it openly. The value of goods corresponds increasingly less to the prices we pay. On the one hand, more and more items are being sold in the luxury specialty shops where prices have no relationship to their real value. Often products are taken from the regular stores and marketed under the label *Delikat* at higher prices, such as sausage and other meat products. On the other hand, the prices of many staple food items remain at ridiculously low levels.

This automatically results in the populace being "educated" in wastefulness. The whole policy of subsidies must be reformed. This would free up financial resources that could be devoted to dealing with other problems in the economic sector. We feel that the shortcomings in our economic policies are an additional reasons for the continuing dissatisfaction.

Mr. Honecker. We Christians of the Baptist Congregation in Plauen are deeply concerned about the future of our country. We would like to contribute to helping to make our country a better place so that no more citizens will leave for good. Our land needs everyone. Therefore, in the name of God, we ask our government, not only to pay attention to the problems enumerated above, which we believe have led to our present situation, but also to enter into a truly fruitful dialogue with all segments of the population. This will enable the maintenance of peace in our country.

In a democracy, the government cannot make policies without the consent of the people; in the long run, a dictatorship cannot do this either. Let us fill the name of our republic with new life by translating the word "democratic" into deeds. May God's blessing be on this.

Johannes Rosemann, Pastor   W. Spranger, Moderator

A People Builds a Wall

A sermon delivered by Pastor Dr. Theo Lehmann at a young people's worship service in Karl Marx Stadt (Chemnitz) on 8 October 1989. The text is Nehemiah 9.

Dear friends, once upon a time a people built a wall in the capital city of their land. At first it was the vision of a single man. Initially he kept his idea absolutely secret. He didn't even tell the city council about it. Then, as the construction of the wall began, it was a very curious sight. One-half of the people worked on the project, while the other half stood ready with weapons and armor.

So it is written in the Bible: "Half of my men did the work, while the other half were equipped with spears, shields, bows, and armor" (Neh. 4:15). [The word for armor, *Panzer*, also means an army tank. The hearers would have undoubtedly noted the play on words.]

The people about whom I am speaking are the Jewish people. The city is Jerusalem, and the time of the building of the wall is 445 B.C. This story is found in the Bible, in the Book of Nehemiah.

We'll not concern ourselves with the building of the wall, but rather with the time following it. There was a massive assembly of the people, and something took place that usually does not happen at such a gathering: They read from the Bible. This was unusual enough, but even more unusual was the length of time; they read from sunrise until noontime.

A wooden pulpit was set up so the masses could see and hear the ones who were reading. This is the first time such a thing is mentioned in Scripture. It was the primitive form of the present pulpit and about the size of our podium here. Then Ezra stood on it, with his coworkers on his left and right, and he read and read, and the people listened and listened, from sunrise until lunchtime. These Bible reading sessions continued on the following days, and there was a genuine enthusiasm for the Word of God. The people couldn't get enough of it.

I don't know whether you occasionally read your Bible, or if you do, it is any longer than five minutes. What about reading it for a few hours or even days in succession? I know that everyone who does this makes new discoveries, gains new understanding. Whenever people become intensively involved with the Bible, it always has concrete results.

The reason is that the Bible is not like any other book. It is the Word of God, and God has said that His Word will not return unto Him void. His Word always produces results, and at the time about which I am speaking the consequence of Bible reading was a movement of repentance.

The Bible is like a mirror. If you just glance at a mirror, you don't see all the details. But if you look at it intensely, you see the crow's feet, pimples, and hairs that are out of place. The same is true with the Bible. If you merely look quickly into it, you won't get too much from it, and usually it will have no significance or impact on your life.

But the longer you read, the more clearly you see yourself in its light. All of a sudden you discover things in your life that you have previously overlooked, things that you didn't believe were possible, things that you would regard as a stain, a disgrace, a cause for shame.

Now, to come straight to the point, whenever you read the Bible, you recognize your sin and see clearly what has gone wrong in your life. However, in that very same place you find there is forgiveness for your guilt, regardless of how great your sins may be.

That is the great thing about the Bible. It doesn't show you your guilt in order to finish you off, but rather to prepare you for repentance. It not only mercilessly reveals your sin, but in a merciful way it also reveals the way of escape from your guilt. It is the way to God and this Way is Jesus, for He said of himself: "I am the Way that leads to the Father."

The way out of the dead-end street of sin is the reversing of one's steps, the turning to Jesus. Accept Jesus, and the burden of sin that you carry is no longer your concern. It has become His concern; He will struggle with it himself.

The burden of sin that lay upon the children of Israel was immense. God had freed His people from slavery in Egypt, led them through the Red Sea, spoke to them, gave them his good commandments, and provided them with bread to eat and water from the rock. As we read in Nehemiah 9:21, "For forty years you provided for them in the wilderness." Their life in the desert was not an easy one, but God had cared for them.

But the people were unthankful, disobedient, and impudent. They turned away from God and toward mere materialism. They made themselves a golden calf and said this was the god who had led them out of Egypt. They blasphemed God, transgressed His commandments, and killed His prophets, those godly men who again and again admonished the people to return to God.

But the word return or *conversion* was like waving a red flag at them. They didn't want to hear this, because conversion in the biblical sense meant a turning back, reform, a change of heart, new thinking. They didn't want to know anything about this. And when the prophets pricked their consciences, they regained their peace by simply doing away with the prophets.

But eliminating the critical voices didn't really get rid of the problem, but rather created more of them. Strangely, however, every time the Israelites had trouble with the neighboring tribes, they came running to God for help, and strangely, He did come to their aid. Repeatedly, God heard them when they were in need and called upon Him.

But when everything was once more all right, they didn't give God another thought. And so it went back and forth, and God in His incredible mercy forgave them again and again.

Verse 29: "You warned them to return to your law, but they became arrogant and disobeyed your commandments. They sinned against your ordinances, by which a man will live if he obeys them. Stubbornly they their turned backs on you, became stiff-necked, and refused to obey."

This description of God's people 2,500 years ago applies equally to human beings in all eras. The Bible provides a mirror image in front of our eyes; we are proud, stubborn, disobedient. It is the same story today, the same misery as then. Humans are too proud to subject themselves to God's authority, too stubborn to admit their errors, too disobedient to follow God's commandments. In a word—they have turned their backs on God.

God? That's a fairy tale from the childhood of humanity that we have put behind us. Commandments? These are outrageous restrictions of our freedom. We've had enough of that. Preachers who warn us about God's judgment are poor, confused individuals. We don't need them.

God puts up with a lot from us, but He will not prevent individuals from rejecting him. God will not strike out with His fists in rage against those who choose to live without Him. Rather, He withdraws His outstretched hands out of sadness because His love has been spurned. God does not use an iron fist to compel someone to remain with Him. Whoever wants to go, may do so. Whoever does not wish to be led by God's hand, can try it on his own. Yes, God lets such people go. As we read in the letter to the Romans, God has given up on those who rebel against Him.

And here in Nehemiah 9:30 it is the same: "Therefore you handed them over to the neighboring peoples." Behind this short sentence was the long history of the humiliation of the people of Israel: deportation to Babylon, life in captivity, always under the control of victorious powers, no national sovereignty, no freedom.

But we didn't hear the usual criticism: "God, how could you have allowed that?" Instead, after an intensive study of the Bible and hearing of God's goodness throughout history, they came to a great realization. As Ezra held the mirror of God's Word in front of their eyes day after day, they recognized: "In all that has happened to us, you have been just; you have acted faithfully, while we did wrong" (v. 33).

It is a catastrophe when someone is so arrogant that he says: "I never make a mistake. I am always right. It is only the others who are wrong." But if someone says to his critics, "I admit, I made a mistake," that is a sign of progress. But the greatest thing that a person can do is to say to God: "Yes, Lord, you are right and I am wrong." Such a one ceases resisting, complaining, and criticizing, and acknowledges: "I have gotten in my life what I deserved."

If you have come this far, you are ready to receive forgiveness. That is the goal toward which God is working. God doesn't want you to stop with a confession of guilt and remain burdened by remorse. He desires that you throw yourself into His arms and accept His forgiveness.

There are some people who believe they are O.K., that they are not sinful and don't need forgiveness. Others suffer so intensely under the burden of their sin that they think: "What I have done is so bad, there can be no forgiveness for me." Both of these are wrong!

There is no one without sin, and there is no sin that cannot be forgiven. The only sin which will not be forgiven is the sin you do not confess. Therefore, I urge you to read the Bible, measure your life against the standard there, and confess every sin that you are aware of. You can do that by talking to God alone, without any witnesses present.

It is also possible to confess guilt before God in the presence of someone else. To be sure, that is difficult, but it has the advantage that you then have someone to promise you forgiveness in God's name. Whichever way you choose is up to you. The main thing is that you get forgiveness. That is the most important thing about the Christian faith. God wants to forgive you so that you will have peace and eternal life.

I urge you to give up the arrogance which leads you to think you don't need forgiveness. I beseech you to give up the scruples which tell you forgiveness isn't possible. With outstretched arms, Christ is waiting for you on the cross. There He paid for your guilt, took upon Himself the penalty for your sins, and died for the ungodly, according to the Scriptures (Rom. 5:6).

We have been ungodly—that is the confession of these Jewish people and modern-day Christians alike. That is absolutely incredible, for those who say it are in fact the ones we regard as godly, as the believers. They insist they have been ungodly, not merely that the others are. No, "We are!"

Those "others" are then specified in verse 34: "Our kings, our leaders, our priests, and our fathers did not follow your law; they did not pay attention to your commands or the warnings you gave them. Even while they were in their kingdom, enjoying your great goodness to them in the spacious and fertile land you gave them, they did not serve you or turn from their evil ways."

The Scripture speaks here of a "prosperous" land. That was our country one time, rich and beautiful. Now, the forests through which I wandered as a boy are sick or dead. The rivers in which I swam as a young person stink and are full of poison. I don't want to list all those things that are *kaputt* [ruined or destroyed] in our land, from the road system to the crumbling cities, to the many people who are so shattered that they can't cope any more, down to the newspapers that are the worst of all, for they will not admit these things and in fact deny them all.

I do not intend to assign guilt to individual people or institutions for these failures. Rather, I want us to recognize that in some way we are all guilty. We have prayed too little for those who occupy responsible positions, or we simply remained silent regarding our situation. Yes, we too are among the ungodly, and we cannot make a new beginning without this confession of sin. But it is just that, a new beginning, that we need, so that still more things do not go *kaputt*. We are not so far gone that salvation is no longer possible.

There is a Savior, whose name is Jesus. I refuse to accept that Jesus is a "God of the West" who travels without a visa and has nothing to say to us. I believe Jesus is also relevant for those of us in the GDR, and that is the reason why I am staying here. For me it is exemplary, how the people of Israel made a new beginning by an all-encompassing prayer of repentance. At the same time, turning to God doesn't mean that we may turn a blind eye to the problems of our society.

The lament over the terrible social conditions was part of their confession. These poor souls bowed before God, while at the same time they called on Him for help against those who were exploiting them. They knew that God's righteousness is all-encompassing and He intervenes on behalf of the poor against their oppressors. To be sure, Israel was once a free people, but now in the year 445 they could only live in their homeland and in Jerusalem as a satellite state under Persian bondage.

As we read in verses 36 and 37: "But see, we are slaves today, slaves in the land you gave our forefathers so they could eat its fruit and the other good things it produces. Because of our sins, its abundant harvest goes to the kings you have placed over us. They rule over our bodies and our cattle as they please. We are in great distress."

Of my fifty-five years, I have lived forty in the GDR, but I have never in that time experienced such distress as today. We are in great need, because the people are fleeing the country—no longer by the dozens, or by the hundreds, or by the thousands, but by the ten thousands. In this year already more than one hundred thousand have left. And one can't meet anyone who does not ask the question: "What is going to happen next?" We are in great need because the tears stream down our faces whenever we sit in front of the television and see the refugee trains, the clashes on our streets, and the water cannons in action.

We weep for our country and ask ourselves how we ever got into in such a situation where dialogue is denied and water cannons are deployed. We are in great need because the anxiety in our land is becoming worse all the time and fears are increasingly being expressed that yet more violence and possibly bloodshed will take place. How did we get to such a place that we must even fear bloodshed?

We have reached a point in our history, where everyone, or almost everyone, sees that things cannot continue this way any longer. We need a new beginning, and the Bible shows us that the way to the new start in life begins with confessing our sins and our guilt. Only in this way can we experience change and new life. Where no change occurs, only death is to be found.

In the church's confession we affirm: "After death and darkness the light was victorious." Therefore, whoever believes in the Risen One has nothing to fear.

A People between Jubilation and Misery

Baptist pastor Lutz Reichardt delivered this sermon on 11 November 1989 at St. Anne's Church, the main Protestant church in Annaberg in the Erzgebirge region of Saxony. Approximately 3,000 people filled the church and another 5,000 to 7,000 heard the worship service over loudspeakers in front of the church. This was part of a series on the theme "Prayer for our country." Following each service a peaceful demonstration took place.

On Monday I spoke in the town auditorium as a representative of the New Forum; today I am speaking to you as a pastor. Christians have a little booklet which contains a Bible verse and the "word for the day" for each day of the year. Today's verse comes from Psalm 130, which is entitled: "A people between jubilation and misery!"

The heading on this psalm is "a song of ascents," or better, "a pilgrimage song." The word pilgrimage conveys the image of something extremely joyous. From all directions the people thronged to the temple in Jerusalem to rejoice in all the good things that God had given them, His people. The closer they came, the greater and louder the jubilation became.

Many things have happened in the last week to cause jubilation among our people. God, the true Lord of history, did not let history pass our country by. Several of our illicit leaders have finally stepped down, new democratic groups are now to be permitted, and yesterday the people at the borders sang: "Such a day, as wonderful as today. . . ." People made a pilgrimage to the border crossings, a pilgrimage to the district police headquarters, and today a pilgrimage to St. Anne's Church. All this is reason enough to give thanks—to our God, to the people, and to those in positions of responsibility in Berlin. And for many among us that is cause for a great flight of fancy or at least a day's outing to nearby Bavaria.

But wait! The psalm brings us quickly back to reality. "Out of the depths I cry to you, O Lord!" In the midst of all of these joyous events, we are suspended over depths that scarcely can be fathomed. Our country is bleeding to death, and I ask myself how will we ever be able to recover from the loss of so many people. Our unrealistic planned economy has systematically brought economic ruin. To be sure, the Stasi has been silenced for the time being, but that by itself is no great success. It had always worked quietly in order to be able to hear better. True, the SED flagship, the Politburo, has been reoutfitted, but the SED submarine, the Stasi, hasn't even surfaced. And submarines are dangerous as long as they can still get air.

"Out of the depths I cry to you, O Lord!" According to the psalm, these depths are not our fate but rather the result of sin. We were led into them by those who claimed for themselves the role of leadership. This must cease. But a certain share of the blame falls upon our shoulders as well. There were some individuals who did not permit themselves to be led around by the nose, but the majority of us marched to the wrong drummer. This was out of fear of losing some personal advantages or suffering undesirable consequences if we didn't.

For too long each of us said to him or herself: "I will do that which is important to me, but I will stick my head in the sand and come to terms with the system." And so this disastrous system became more and more entrenched. Some took their fears into account and worked as well as they could, while others allowed themselves to be paralyzed by their anxieties and were driven to resignation. But many, including many non-Christians, poured out their fears before God during the prayer services for peace. I see it as an answer to prayer that the anxiety that was so rampant in the society was removed from us. Likewise, we can today express concern for our land and our future, and where we recognize our own personal guilt, we can also plead for forgiveness.

But not only are the guilty parties those individuals who have been replaced. The basic cause of our worst problems are faulty structures—the political system, the economy, and the State (In)Security Ministry (I will not permit the use of the fine Christian term "service" for this agency!). The psalm also points out that with God there is salvation and he makes His people free. Liberation in the Bible never means the superficial removal of symptoms. What good is it if the rust spots on a car are merely covered over with paint?

It is the same in society as in our personal lives. Let me say something about each of them. The offer is valid for both. With God there is liberation, the power to make a complete change, the courage to undergo radical treatment. Anything less than this will be of no help to us. We don't just want an improved GDR social-ism based on the old pattern in which a few loose stitches have been tightened up. We desire another socialism (in fact, now we don't want any socialism at all, a thing that would have been un-speakable before today) that is radically different from that which has been forced upon us. It must be a new pattern which the people themselves shall choose. In the Bible, "salvation" means not just freedom from individual failures but also from wrong struc-tures. Therefore we must cry out unto God from the depths until the unalterable legal foundations for these new structures have been laid. God also hears the thousandfold cries of the people on the street, and these must not cease.

In the stores in the West are the so-called special offers: "Buy five items at a time, and the unit cost is cheaper." We must learn how to cope with our new situation. Up until now we never had such offers in our stores; but we did have them during our elections—several parties linked together in a bloc but they received only one vote In the future our vote will be too valuable to squander on such "special offers." We are praying for elections in which all the old parties will be placed individually on the scales, and that the new parties and societal groups will be allowed to compete as well. We will never again have to choose "between one party." We want to "rise up out of the ruins" [a phrase from the GDR national anthem] again but this time in a democratic way. We will not allow ourselves to convinced that we have to be spied on for our own safety.

Not only do we need renewal in the society, but also in the general populace and on an individual basis as well. Marxism teaches that new relationships in the society will produce a new type of "man." The GDR is one of the best arguments against that. In fact, Jesus Christ has been saying the opposite for two thousand years: "Only new people can create better relationships." A person becomes new by confessing his or her sin. Whoever is in Christ is a new person. Old things have passed away; the new has come into existence.

With all the problems afflicting our society at present, perhaps our personal problems will for a period of time fade into the background—broken marriages, dependence on material possessions, lack of concern for others, character deficiencies, lack of self-control, and failed attempts to find meaning in our lives. All of these things will catch up with us again, sooner or later. Thus, this psalm has such a fascinating message for us: "With God there is forgiveness; He will release our people from their bonds and all their sin."

We used to be happy when we had "connections" with the right people. Hopefully this will not be necessary any more! But there is one that we will need—the connection with the God who forgives sins and heals the innermost wounds, both in our personal lives and in our society. Many people in our country have suffered wounds These injuries must be healed, so that we don't come apart because of hatred, bitterness, and the desire for revenge.

Forgiveness from God, however, does not preclude punishment by the society. For the little people there will be the summary court proceedings; for the more important ones investigative commissions will be needed. Action must begin at once. The people have not granted amnesty to those responsible. Therefore, we need independent courts that will call the big wheels to account and not just use the small fry as scapegoats. Something must be done to see that the past is never repeated again.

We call to God from out of the depths. Our God is credible. He chose to leave his heavenly realm and came down into our human depths through Jesus Christ. Therefore He can understand us and help us to practice restraint. Jesus gave up the privilege of being with God in order to effect changes in us. He even gave His life and went to the cross, and in so doing He turned the world upside down.

We can travel now, but we must not leave the country. Each individual who departs from the land leaves the place a little darker. As each one goes, two hands, two feet, one head, and one voice are lost, and that diminishes the great opportunity we now have in this country. Therefore I close with a challenge to you all: Keep on hoping, remain here, and don't be absent when we vote!

Those Who Were Arrested

Many hair-raising stories circulated in the GDR during the month of October 1989 about police brutality. A large number of those arrested in the three main cities—Berlin, Leipzig, and Dresden—gave sworn statements for use by investigating committees or told their stories to various oppositional groups which duplicated and distributed them widely through the dissident networks. Often these were read in churches or posted on bulletin boards there where people attending the prayer vigils could read them. Several of them were later published in collections such as *Schnauze! Gedächtnisprotokolle 7. und 8. Oktober 1989* (Berlin: Berliner Verlags-Anstalt Union, 1990). Reproduced here are an interview with a young man who had been arrested in a demonstration in Karl-Marx-Stadt, the report of a pastor in Berlin picked up for questioning, and a moving poem about the power of Jesus.

" . . . as if the air were trembling."

Jörg Swoboda

As I arrived for a youth evangelistic campaign with my associate Dr. Theo Lehmann at Lampertswalde near Meissen on Monday, 9 October 1989, I found our coworkers there in a state of utter confusion and dismay. One of them, Friedhelm Dietzel, whom we affectionately nicknamed "Friedchen," had been taken into custody two days earlier during a demonstration in Karl-Marx-Stadt (Chemnitz). They could not understand how the police could make such a mistake like that, as Friedchen was peaceableness personified. His friend Henoch Mischke told us that the last thing he saw was Friedhelm's arm raised in the air. His parents tried to find out about their son but were denied any information. They were told that in four weeks they would learn where he was and why. As our team celebrated the Lord's Supper before the opening of the six-day campaign, we prayed for Friedhelm and all those who had been arrested.

Something was sure to happen on 9 October! There was a dreadful atmosphere of tension hanging over the entire country that day. It was as if the air were trembling. The cry heard more and more frequently at the demonstrations, "We are the people!" signaled that the citizens of the GDR were in the process of finding their own identity. In the showcases outside the entrances to churches one could see posted the founding appeal of the New Forum or revealing quotations from leading lights in the "ideological leadership of the SED in the struggle against capitalism." One was from Carl von Ossietzky: "Democracy loses its meaning when the 'representatives,' the party leadership and elected legislators, remain out of touch with their 'patrons,' the people, and thus form their own clique." After the brutal police actions of the past weekend, everyone was wondering how the "state authorities" would react to the traditional Monday demonstration in Leipzig that evening.

In spite of, or because of, the tense political situation, attendance on the first evening of the evangelistic campaign was quite good. The band that provided the music interrupted its planned program after one song. One band member stepped to the microphone, lit a candle, and dedicated it to a young person who had been arrested at the demonstration in Dresden. He placed it on a loudspeaker. Another musician took a candle and did the same. The 250 attendees in the small village church were spellbound as they watched these actions so laden with symbolism.

Following the sermon by Dr. Lehmann, I offered a prayer, sang a song, and urged the young people to turn their lives over to Jesus Christ. On this evening no one publicly responded to the challenge, but we had some good conversations with people after the meeting and later learned that one young person turned his life over to Christ. As soon as we got back to our rooms, we immediately turned on the radio and were relieved to hear that no bloody confrontations with the security forces had occurred at the Leipzig demonstration.

On Tuesday evening, the local pastor, Rev. Müller, told us that his daughter telephoned from Plauen. She worked as a nurse in the local hospital's intensive care unit. On 7 October, a demonstration had occurred and a helicopter flying at a height of 100 feet harassed the 3,000 people milling around below. At the main square, Otto Grotewohl Platz, the authorities utilized a fire truck to spray water on the crowd. People began throwing paving stones, and one hit the fire department captain, who was now hospitalized in her unit where no one had any sympathy for him. Some of the civilian militia personnel refused to go into action because they would have had to shoot at their own neighbors and friends, and yes, even at other members of their own unit. She also said that SED members were resigning from the party in droves. For example, in one Plauen factory, only two out of the original twenty-two members still retained their cards.

Shortly before the service was to began, Superintendent Krellner, the Saxon church's area executive minister, arrived with two guests from Tanzania who had said they wanted to attend. After I sang a few songs with the young people, I suggested that everyone greet those around them since the sermon that evening was entitled "A Festival for Friends." Rev. Krellner turned to the girl sitting behind him and introduced himself: "I am Friedrich from Grossenhain [a town about five miles away]." She responded likewise and then asked: "Are you [*du*] here for the first time?"

Before the sermon I interviewed the two Africans. They reported that the Lutheran Church in Tanzania had been established in 1885 by Saxon missionaries and then encouraged the hearers to follow Jesus. They talked so enthusiastically about their faith in the risen Christ that everyone listened attentively, and their comments fit perfectly with the subject matter of the sermon. At the end of their remarks they sang in Swahili the familiar chorus, "I have decided to follow Jesus, no turning back, no turning back!" The three hundred people in attendance joined in with them, some humming the tune and the others singing the words in German, and this made a powerful impression. Dr. Lehmann preached his usual Bible-centered sermon that was clear and to the point, and two young people responded to the invitation to begin a new life with Jesus Christ.

The offering bought in 800 marks, and the money was earmarked to help with the legal defense costs of Friedhelm Dietzel and others who had been arrested at the demonstrations. Just as we left the church at 10:30 p.m. we heard the good news that Dietzel had been released. Three days later he was in the service, where he gave a clear testimony about Jesus how is there with us when we are in distress. Ten young people responded with a decision to follow Jesus. On the next morning I formally interviewed "Friedchen" and made a transcript of his remarks for the record:

Jorg S. Friedhelm Dietzel, you live in the village of Linz in Grossenhain county, you are twenty-one years old, and you were "detained," as our police so innocently label it. Please describe the circumstances of your arrest.

Friedhelm D. By chance I happened to be in Karl-Marx-Stadt. I was on my way to Czechoslovakia with three friends, and while passing through the city we learned that the GDR had closed the border to prevent people from fleeing, either by going to Prague and taking refuge in the West German embassy or traveling on to use the Hungarian escape route to the West. Then we heard that a forum on democracy was going to take place at 10:00 a.m. at a theater called the Luxor-Palast. Having nothing else to do, we decided to attend. When we arrived we saw a huge crowd, comprised of people of all ages. I was certain that many Stasi officers were present.

Jörg S. How could you recognize them in the crowd?

Friedhelm D. All of them had a red triangle on the zipper of their jackets; this caught our eye. The theater manager then informed us that the building had to be cleared because it was overcrowded. We got in anyway and were surprised that plenty of seats were still available. It was hardly overcrowded. The people were annoyed because they realized they had been given a raw deal.

Then a man in a front seat stood up and pleaded with the highly agitated crowd in the theater to keep a calm and compassionate demeanor. He declared that the event had been forbidden yesterday evening; no forum on democracy was to take place in this hall. After a short discussion, he suggested that the event could take place next week at a church in Karl-Marx-Stadt, the name of which I have forgotten. We left the theater but no one was in a mood to go home. Small groups gathered on the street to discuss the situation, and suddenly a spontaneous demonstration, a silent march, began to move out.

Jörg S. How many do you estimate were there?

Friedhelm D. Later I read in the paper a figure of about 600, but at its height the demonstration certainly attracted 3,000 to 4,000 people.

Jörg S. You talk about a silent march. Did the people really not speak at all?

Friedhelm D. The people talked with one another. Then they clapped in rhythm from time to time which helped to create community and give mutual encouragement. We soon reached the central streetcar boarding point, and found the police had cordoned off the area. Except for the people in civilian clothes in front of the theater we hadn't seen any police until now. As we faced the police a helicopter circled overhead. We really didn't know how it would go from this point, but I did take some photos with my camera.

Then, some militia units wearing white helmets moved on us from behind, but they halted at some distance from us. Several demonstrators began shouting "Shame on you, shame on you!" I regarded this action as unfair and of no use in trying to establish a dialogue. Using loudspeakers the police ordered us to disband the demonstration and we obeyed. But as we talked with the onlookers standing in groups at the edge of the street, we learned how many people really desired reforms. Others said that if we were to stay there, the whole thing would escalate out of control.

We proceeded to climb over the traffic barrier and mix with the onlookers. I continued to take a few pictures. That's when the police action began. Perhaps 100 people who had not yet dispersed were still standing in the street . The militia units moved up and began shoving the demonstrators and beating them with rubber truncheons. I saw no demonstrators engage in any acts of acts of violence. We were starting to leave but I stopped to snap a few more pictures. Suddenly three men surrounded and grabbed me and demanded that I come with them.

Jörg S. Did you identify yourself?

Friedhelm D. No.

Jörg S. Did you ask them to?

Friedhelm D. No. At that moment I was too taken back. I shouted something to my friend Henoch, but he was shoved away. He also had a camera, but he wisely had taken out the film and exposed it. Then they dragged me into a bus. They rewound the film in my camera and took it out. I asked for a receipt because it is my personal property, but all I received was some rude answers. They flung me into a seat, told me to watch out or I would be sorry, and said that I should keep my trap shut. About ten others were taken away in the bus with me. Since seven or eight had cameras I assumed that was the reason for our detainment. Through the window I could see the crowd being sprayed with fire hoses.

Jörg S. Against this group of 100?

Friedhelm D. I had never experienced anything like this. It was deeply moving. One felt so powerless. It was really stupid. The militia forced the people back in rows and they stood there soaking wet. The police units then took over. The Stasi people in the bus clapped and shouted: "Give it to 'em! Finish 'em off!" That really shocked me. They seemed to be itching to go into action and to unleash their aggression on us. The bus took us to an open area in front of the Centrum Department Store. (It was closed for the national holiday.) Henoch and my friends saw me in the bus going by and I flashed the victory sign to them. The beautiful thing of this was that as the bus traveled down the street, people on the sidewalks waved to us in support.

At the department store we were ordered to get out. One rather heavy man did not move as quickly as the Stasi men wanted, and a senior official shouted: "If he doesn't do what he is told to, hit him in the face!" Then the person in front of me said: "You can't be serious." The older man repeated the statement once again but in a harsher tone. Everything was done to intimidate us. Frequently I heard: "If you don't do as we tell you, you had better watch out. . . . "

Then we had to climb into a truck. A wooden box lay on the floor which was divided into two parts and covered with a steel grate, and we were ordered to empty our pockets into it. Next we were handcuffed to each another in pairs. Now it was just before one o'clock in the afternoon. The trip out of the city lasted approximately ten minutes, and we arrived at a barracks which had been hastily outfitted for use as an interrogation place. We were forced to stand against a wall with our hands behind our backs, and I was kept in that position for an hour. I saw many riot police who were my own age there, and the noise was terrible because everyone was shouting constantly.

Each of us was then removed to another room where the criminal investigation people worked. I found them to be fair. They asked for our personal information: name, address, profession, and so forth. They also fingerprinted us, took three pictures, and insisted that we empty our pockets of absolutely anything else that we might have. We even had to give up our shoe laces. We also had to identify what we had already given them, and everything was properly entered in the books.

I was then returned to the room with which I was already familiar and had to stand there for an additional one and a half hours. Standing for such a long time caused me to develop back pains. I was interrogated from 4:10 p.m. until 5:45 p.m. The individual was quite fair. Basically, it wasn't an interrogation but more like a conversation. I gained the impression that the captain was in favor of reforms in the GDR.

After this, I was brought back to the large room. Then I was taken two more times to be interrogated, and finally they told me: "Come with us. We are going to take down your statement. You are under arrest." The magistrate, a woman, sat at the desk. By this time I couldn't stand up straight any longer. I was allowed to lean forward slightly. Whenever my knees began to buckle and I almost fell over, they yelled at me. Around 11:45 p.m. the formal order for my arrest was issued. When I returned to the waiting room we were finally permitted to sit on little stools, but not to sleep. Soon we were taken away in a police van. In this were small plywood crates in which we, still handcuffed, were forced to kneel and then the top was closed.

Jörg S. How large were they?

Friedhelm D. They were two feet by two feet by four feet. There were no bars; they were simply locked.

Jörg S. And how did you get air in these "coffins"?

Friedhelm D. Probably through the cracks. Whether there were disguised air slits in them, I didn't notice. After arriving at the detention facility in Karl-Marx-Stadt we were brought to the fourth floor. I had to go to the shower room first, where I had to undress completely and even turn my socks inside out. The official ran his fingers through my hair and watched me from all sides while he forced me to do a kneebend to make sure that I wasn't smuggling anything in. Then I was allowed to take a shower and placed in detention room 427. Finally I could go to sleep.

At 5:30 a.m. we were awakened by a siren. We had to make our beds and at 6:00 a.m. had breakfast—bread, margarine, and sausage. There was enough to eat. This was followed by roll call in the main detention room. Around 11:30 we had a normal factory kitchen meal and it was quite satisfactory. During the course of the first day I was taken to interrogations and to the doctor in the clinic. We were given supper at about 3:00 p.m. and at 5 o'clock were locked up. When the siren sounded at 7:00 p.m., we washed up, and 8 o'clock was lights out. Our cell was eleven feet square and contained five beds, a toilet, a wash basin, two clothes lockers, a folding table, and some stools.

A day later I was moved to a neighboring cell. In the entire time I was there, I met two genuine criminals. The rest were there because they had attempted to flee the country or were demonstrators. The sense of community in the group was really great. What little we had, we shared with one another. The fear we had of what might await us in the detention center quickly dissipated. For a long time, though, I had inwardly prepared myself for going to jail because I was a total conscientious objector to military service, and I had informed myself about prisoners' rights.

So I demanded that I be given a list of lawyers in the entire GDR. They supplied me with the names of only those in Karl-Marx-Stadt. I insisted I didn't know any of these thirty or forty lawyers and thus was not informed as to their philosophical approach was and how they worked. Once again I demanded a list covering the whole country. They claimed they didn't have one. Then I asked to have my parents contact a lawyer, but I wasn't allowed to speak to them. Although I requested from the prosecuting attorney permission to write a letter, this too was denied.

Jörg S. Your parents had tried to make contact with you. They were told that it could be as long as four weeks?

Friedhelm D. Yes, one had the feeling of being totally cut off in that place. True, it was possible to buy a newspaper, but otherwise during the entire period of my detention nothing from the outside world came in or went out. It was a total roadblock.

Jörg S. Many newspapers wrote rather openly about the political changes starting to take place. What effect did that have on you?

Friedhelm D. We talked about these. After I was moved to the other cell, where I was housed with a criminal, two individuals who had been caught trying to flee the country, and another demonstrator, you can well imagine what kind of conversations went on. I was very pleased that the local newspaper admitted on 9 October that much in our land needed improvement and that errors had been made. For me it was a great feeling not to have been in prison in vain and that we had gained a hearing from the state authorities.

The recaptured fugitives, however, did not see that as a ray of hope. They dismissed it out of hand, saying that in our country a lot of things are written. But the news report in the Tuesday *Freie Presse* was really absurd. It asserted that at the demonstration on Saturday twenty-six "ring leaders" had been arrested.

Jörg S. You belonged to that group?

Friedhelm D. Yes, I belonged. In fact, the provocation had been well prepared. The proof of this was that the ringleaders came from other places in the GDR. I myself was from the Dresden District. I was in effect criminalized by the newspaper headline "unscrupulous provocation."

I asked to see a copy of the law. There I read that ringleaders may receive a prison sentence ranging between one and eight years. Inwardly, this went right past me and I felt quite secure. I knew I was not alone; Jesus was with me. I was very calm during the interrogations and told the truth at all times. I prayed a lot during this time which gave me strength, and I quietly sang to myself as well. I also sensed that many people outside were praying for me.

Sometime after Tuesday I received an inner sense of assurance that on Friday morning I would be released. Then I carefully studied the provisions of the law and wrote a juicy complaint about the concept of the "formation of a mob." Given the ambiguous wording of the law, they could have convicted me on every count. For example, I left the demonstration, but they could charge that I didn't go far enough away. But what is "far enough"? Then they could have accused me of hindering the work of the security forces, but that didn't apply to me either. Finally, we were accused of disturbing a *Volksfest* and blocking traffic. Strictly speaking this was true, but it was completely exaggerated and blown out of proportion in the newspaper.

Jörg S. That took a good deal of civil courage.

Friedhelm D. During the interrogations, I never told them what they wanted to hear but always gave them my own viewpoint. I also said that I intended to take part again in peaceful demonstrations on behalf of democratization in our country. To be sure, one had to be very careful how one stated such things. These people are veritable artists with words and can twist what you say right in your mouth.

About 6:00 p.m. on Thursday evening, after we had been locked in, an alarm sounded in the hallway. People scurried back and forth and cell doors slammed. We heard the order, "Pack your things," and we thought that maybe we would be leaving. A half-hour later the jailer came to our cell, opened the door, and said, "Dietzel, pack your things!" I went with him down a flight of stairs. I had to get undressed again. My things were searched so that I wouldn't take anything outside. I got my personal belongings back and I signed that I had received them.

Next we were brought to the prosecuting attorney who demanded that I sign a statement that basically said: "I have been instructed to avoid taking part in mob actions. I will obey the laws of the GDR in the future. I was treated properly while detained and do not intend to press any charges against the state agencies." With a tape recorder running I was instructed about the provisions in paragraphs 214, 217, and 218 once again. I had to agree that I relinquished any claim for damages from wrongful imprisonment and that I would not bring any charges against the agencies involved. I refused to do so, as I wanted to leave that option open. My six days of detention were at an end. I was quite happy to be outside again.

Jörg S. Friedhelm, I thank you for this interview.

Report of My Imprisonment

Andreas von Essen

On 8 October 1989 I decided that I would, in my position as a pastor in the Berlin-Brandenburg Church, take part in the vigil and memorial service at the Gethsemane Church in Berlin for those who had been arrested for political reasons. I parked my car around 9:45 p.m. on Stargarder Strasse close to Lychener Strasse and headed out for the church. Just down from the corner at Pappelallee I observed scattered groups of people holding candles and singing. It was obviously not an organized gathering, but rather individuals who could not get into the church. A formation of security personnel hindered access to Pappelallee. A man whom I did not know was passing out sheets of paper containing the platform and an appeal from the Social Democratic Party. I only gave it a cursory reading, as the situation did not permit a more careful perusal.

I went to the officer-in-charge of the city police unit who formed this human barricade, identified myself as a pastor, and in a business-like manner asked him if I could enter the church. He used his radio telephone to check out the information I had given him and then allowed me to do so. After the service I spoke with several people, among them a number of church workers, most of whom I did not know. Toward 11 o'clock I left the church carrying a lighted candle. Since the cordon had advanced from Pappelallee toward Lychener Strasse, I found myself behind the formation. A police officer knocked the candle out of my hand and growled at me: "Beat it!" Meanwhile they drove the people into a narrow opening formed by the security forces, who then attacked them indiscriminately. It was clear that the police had provoked this action. They randomly grabbed retreating demonstrators and arrested them. Because the people were surrounded, it was hardly possible to escape these pointless arrests. An acquaintance of mine shouted to me that the police were using electroshock truncheons.

I fled around the block, crossed over Pappelallee, and ran in the direction of Lychener Strasse, when six security personnel spotted me and immediately seized me. It was now 11:15 p.m. They bound my hands and beat me with rubber truncheons. I mentioned my car parked on Stargarder Strasse, but they paid no attention. They forced me into one of the waiting buses by beating me again. Some of the State Security officials had alcohol on their breaths, and they hurled coarse insults at us. From the window of the bus I could see the police breaking up the peaceful demonstration with nightsticks and chains attached to wooden handles and people were being arrested in droves. The forces were drawn from the city police, security police, army, and the civilian militia groups, although the latter were remarkably restrained in their actions.

Within fifteen minutes a group of about thirty to forty of us were brought to the prison in Rummelsburg where our identity papers were taken from us. The bus sat for a half-hour on the square in front of the prison, and we were not allowed to go the toilet. Finally, we were driven into the inner courtyard of the prison, where a massive contingent of police guarded us as we got out of the vehicles. We had to stand outside facing a wall with our hands raised.

After around three-and-a-half hours of standing in the courtyard area in the same position—anyone who stepped out of line in any way was immediately beaten—we responded in a peaceable manner. Then our names were called out and each person had to step forward individually. The police had formed two lines about three feet apart and we were forced more or less plainly to run the gauntlet from one police official to another who shoved us along and beat us with wooden rods. I was then locked in a twenty-five-foot square cell with forty-five other people for about twenty-two hours. We had to stand as there no room to sit down. After an interrogation I was put in an adjacent cell where eighteen people were herded together in half the space of the previous one. In neither of these cells was there fresh air. During this time each of us received two "sandwiches" (one piece of sausage and one pat of butter), and were allowed to drink four swallows of tea and one swallow of water, all from the same cup. After eleven hours the first ones were allowed to go to the toilet, but only because we had demanded so strongly to be allowed to do so, and even then it was only one time.

Several in the cells had suffered injuries, mainly cuts and abrasions, and two had lost consciousness. A medic was summoned through a loudspeaker, but she provided only the most minimal aid. Several prisoners whose children were left home alone wanted to telephone relatives or friends and ask for help, but their requests were denied. The reason given was that they should have thought about this beforehand. In spite of the physical and emotional strain, a feeling of solidarity developed among the prisoners. I even held a devotional service for the ones in my cell.

I wish to describe in more detail the situation of a young woman in a cell next to ours. Her husband had been arrested as well, and their three-year-old child was left at home alone. The woman tried every way imaginable to get help for her child, but her pleas were rejected. She cried and screamed and stretched her hands pleadingly through the bars. Blows from truncheons silenced her only for a brief time. When she started screaming again, two jailers beat her so brutally that she was left lying unconscious on the floor of the cell. She was among the last to be released.

Around 9:30 p.m. on 9 October the police started getting personal information from us and the formal interrogations began immediately afterward. I was questioned three different times. First I was asked to describe the details of my arrest, and the questions were phrased in such a way as to try to criminalize my behavior. I flatly refused to be led into this trap. Additional accusations were read to me that were based on the provisions of a police law that was unknown to me.

The main thrusts of the interrogations were to determine the origin of the materials from the Social Democratic Party of the GDR and to gain information about internal church problems. They even tried to tell me that the candle had no symbolic Christian value. I was able to deflect most of their accusations, or so at least I thought. I would not sign the report of the interrogations until I had made some corrections. A fourth and final questioning took place at 4:00 a.m., and then we were supposed to be released.

I was given a stern warning and threatened with fines. They demanded that I sign a confession of guilt, but once again I refused. Likewise, I would not accept the obligation that I comply with all the demands of the security forces. I was also ordered to testify that I received good treatment in the prison, but this too I declined to do, and they returned me to my cell. However, a few minutes later an order for me to leave was issued. At 5:00 a.m. I passed through the gate once again a free man.

Jesus, My Joy
Gerhard Schöne, 1989

Jesus, my joy, the pasture of my heart,
Jesus, very God.
Who desires to listen to You anyway?
Your words disrupt our daily routine.
You endanger our security,
You are sand in the machinery of this world,
You do this with your love.

You were imprisoned, You have survived
prison camps expulsion, and jail.
They could not kill You;
No one can defeat the power of Your love.
Whoever tortures and kills You,
is counting on Your death in vain.
You are the very seed grain of life.

Jesus, friend of the poor,
great is Your mercy toward this sick world.
Rulers pass away, dreamers become cheerful,
who are enlightened by Your Word.
And when I am in the valley of deep despair,
I know that You are at my side,
Jesus, my joy.

Reflections on the Wende

The revolution of 1989 deeply affected the thoughts and actions of East German Christians. An outpouring of books and articles in 1990 and thereafter reflected their feelings about what appeared to be a miracle and their deep compassion and concern for their fellow believers as they entered into an uncertain new era of German unification. Included here are commentaries from a Baptist parish minister, the senior member of the faculty at the Baptist theological school in Buckow, and Jörg Swoboda. All of them breathe of the emotions and apprehensions of the time.

Aspects, Possibilities, Challenges

Pastor Gottfried Zimmermann, January 1990

Astonishing Things Have Happened. First we held our breaths. Will blood be shed? Then we uttered a sigh of relief. The weapons were not utilized. Although events moved at a breakneck pace, now much of what happened has become like "yesterday's snow." Still, we should go back and recall what transpired.

The GDR citizen became a responsible adult. No longer did he have to wait until he was sixty-five to make up his mind where he wanted to travel. Now he can do so at any age. The Berlin Wall is open. People are now treated humanely at the border crossings. Those in power have been removed. Caught in a network of lies that was fabricated over many years, they must answer to charges of "misuse of public office." The sovereign SED divinity has fallen from the socialist heaven. It claimed to be eternal, omniscient, and omnipotent. Its (in)justice was carried out by its omnipresent informers. The people occupied the dreaded buildings of the State Security. Journalists, whose vocabulary had been limited to a few official slogans, can now write in a free-flowing and interesting manner.

Skepticism on the Rise. Fears are noised abroad as to whether the process is irreversible? Yes, a start has been made, but the path to the final goal is uncertain. Really, it is very difficult to make a democracy out of a dictatorship. This requires using democratic means where none of the parties have ever known what democracy actually is.

We Are the People! So rang the cry of thousands. The slogan contributed persuasively and morally to the disarming of those who were supposed to defend the "achievements of the people" by the use of armed force. The so-called "representatives of the people" were disqualified. Their political, economic, ideological, and human mistakes had caused multitudes to leave the country or to take to the streets.

The People of God—also "das Volk"? During the height of the demonstrations, the majority of evangelicals belonged to the "silent ones in the land," that is, people who remained on the sidelines, uninvolved. However, many leaders in the established Protestant churches understood how to channel the restructuring process in a courageous and prudent way, and I shared their outlook. When people asked me for advice about active involvement in the demonstrations, I said: "Go for it, but introduce the message of the Gospel." Merely to "turn away from the weak GDR-Marx to the stable D-Mark(s)," as we often saw painted on parade banners, is not the kind of decisive help our people needed. Obviously, other Christians shared this concern, as some carried banners with such colorful catch phrases [that rhymed in German] as:

> "Instead of so many ND's [the initials of the SED newspaper *Neues Deutschland*]—more NT's [New Testaments]."
> "Without a turning to God our people will once again be bankrupt."
> "The root of our misery is that God wasn't given the glory."

Our Life—Appearance or Reality. In my opinion, the behavior of evangelical Christians has been ambiguous. Many tried to justify their opportunistic restraint when they had been subjected to overt pressure or more subtle coercion by appealing to Romans 13. Recognizing this fact prevents us from becoming boastful and arrogant and provides an occasion for repentance. On the other hand, the Word of God enabled those obedient to it to achieve unity in thought, speech, and actions. They could not avoid conflicts with those functionaries who acted like marionettes, because individuality is the enemy of forced conformity. However, the public trust in Christian believers grew because of their transparent life style. Acts 2:47 applies to these: "They enjoyed the favor of all the people." It was apparent that one who had a "heart conversion" to God would not be a two-faced *Wendehals* who always watched to see which way the political winds were blowing and moved accordingly.

New Freedoms. We have always had the freedom to assemble for worship services. Our work with children and young people was never forbidden. We were allowed to offer Bible studies for all age groups and could place announcements in newspapers inviting people to our evangelistic campaigns. We had the most favorable conditions in comparison with other Eastern Bloc countries. But any person who was a consistent believer was disadvantaged. Young people who rejected taking part in the atheistic youth dedication service and membership in the Free German Youth rarely could study at a university. They experienced discrimination like blacks in the apartheid system. Of course, these setbacks can be helpful in one's spiritual growth.

Although they are still not appreciated, the Pioneer magazine now encourages Christian children to talk openly about their faith. Old barriers are falling and new opportunities for preaching the Gospel are popping up all over the place. Streets, squares, and public buildings are no longer taboo for evangelistic efforts, and youth groups are now free to sing in pedestrian zones, engage passersby in conversation, and distribute tracts. Tent meetings are now allowed; before, services could only be held in a church building. It even appears possible that a Christian printing firm will be licensed and the GDR radio will make time available daily for a Gospel program. We are now considering things and actions that before were only fond dreams.

Challenges. The country is hemorrhaging. In all areas workers are lacking, particularly in the health care fields. Young Christians are helping to alleviate the problem by serving in hospitals and senior citizens' homes. They have many possibilities for bearing testimony in work and song. Can the exodus to the West be halted? The family of God could help by providing a positive example of security and happy home life.

People are looking for scapegoats and many are calling for revenge. Calmer persons remind us of the need for law and justice. The community of Jesus can offer to all the love and forgiveness found in the Lamb of God.

One can understand that the population wants to make up for all that has been denied them in the past. Even the little Trabant cars that we drive on the freeways in the Federal Republic ride more comfortably there than on the GDR roads. The weekend wanderlust leaves large gaps in our congregations, and the youth rallies, church meetings, and Bible conferences in the West have a greater attraction. We need to consider what consequences will result from all this.

New religions and political extremist groups from the Federal Republic are descending upon us, flooding the country with litera-ture that defames "inferior" people (some of this is even antisemit-ic) and offers quick, easy solutions for the country, economy, and spiritual emptiness.

Up until now ideological discussions were unambiguous, open and shut matters. The alleged solutions to the fundamental ques-tions of life were packaged in slogans and proclaimed as scientific ideology. Now the Gospel, which has nothing to fear from intellec-tual discussions, shows itself as the source of strength for daily living. Seeing it as an alternative to the official state ideology, even non-Christians have come to view it in positive terms. As the soci-ety becomes increasingly pluralistic, the absolute claims of the message of the Cross will once again be an offense to many.

Where Do Our Priorities Lie? They are not in the possibilities or obligations now coming to the fore. These could lead us into an all-consuming activism that would divert our attention to goals of secondary importance. The first priority for the church of the Lord is the Lord of the church. Our attention must center on that which pleases Him. Pursuing challenges that deviate from this lead to temptations that produce a loss in spiritual quality. Mind you, our calling to be apart from the world is always linked to our mission within it. Whoever has received the salvation of the Lord and experienced its benefits will also be concerned about the salvation and welfare of his fellow human beings. We should always save time for personal contacts with them, whatever these might be.

My desire and prayer is that we will discern the new possibilities and make the best use of them but not get sidetracked by matters of secondary importance.

Seek the Peace of the City—Now More Than Ever
Christian Wolf, Buckow, 28 February 1990

In August 1984 the European Baptist Congress met in Hamburg, and its scriptural theme was "Seek the peace of the city." I was invited to deliver the keynote address based on this text found in Jeremiah 29:7. The mixed reactions it received left me rather confused. On the one hand, many from West Germany and elsewhere in Western Europe applauded it enthusiastically and told me afterwards how much they agreed with me. The GDR delegates also expressed their approval. The moderator of the assembly, who was from a different socialist country, asked with concern in his voice whether I could dare to go home again after what I had said. The interpreter for a delegation from yet another socialist land was even forbidden to translate certain passages of the speech. On the other hand, some well-meaning brethren from the Federal Republic took me aside and suggested I had spoken a little too much from the socialist perspective. It took considerable effort to persuade them that no church or state body had prescribed or censored anything in this biblical exposition and that I was entirely responsible for everything I said, from beginning to end.

From this experience I learned that such a Bible text will always evoke differing reactions from its listeners, because they simply can't detach themselves from the material and spiritual conditions of their lives. Jeremiah's letter as well met with various responses in Babylon and Jerusalem, among the exiles and those who were allowed to remain in the land. So, I am sure that a contemporary reading of Jeremiah 29 in our situation, which has changed so suddenly, will also bring forth a diversity of opinions. It can't be any other way.

Jeremiah's statement doesn't give any political-ethical rules of behavior because it is a pastoral letter. He is speaking to people who have just experienced a catastrophe and who, nervous and uncertain, are lost in the present and paralyzed by the abundance of strange, new impressions. Thus the comforting words of verse 11 assure those living in uncertainty that the Lord intends to give them "hope and a future." On this basis, they are capable of realistic actions, even though their dark situation will last for a considerable time (v. 10). What I said then was that Christians in the GDR were experiencing in quite a different historical setting what the Israelite exiles had, that is, the tensions involved in balancing political matters with those of a spiritual nature.

Churches, the only nonsocialist organizations in the GDR, made their space available to those who initiated the peaceful revolution. Christians are serving as moderators of the Round Tables at all levels throughout our country, because they are the ones best suited to guarantee that democratic rules will be followed. Pastors frequently have assumed leading positions in the new democratic organizations because they possess the confidence of many people. While Jeremiah's letter had to urge the exile "congregations" to promote the *shalom* of the city (this Hebrew word encompasses the ideas of well-being and prosperity), the GDR congregations at the moment are positively overwhelmed by the political tasks involved in a new beginning for their society. They often find themselves unintentionally involved in the practical political business of seeking "the peace of the city." Their advice and cooperation are so much in demand because in the past they hadn't been taken in and corrupted. But, many are asking worriedly, is that becoming the case now? Are we possibly neglecting our pastoral task in favor of political efforts? The question is justified.

In Jeremiah's letter, praying and working stand shoulder to shoulder as equals. Achieving the *shalom*, that is, the peace and well-being of the state, requires effort in the sociopolitical realm as well as pastoral concern for individual persons. Under the SED regime we emphasized the latter. Whoever tried to be politically active encountered insurmountable obstacles. The few Christians who did so rapidly degenerated into mere "yes-men." Neither free church or mainline Protestants dared to seek "the peace of the city" in opposition to the all-powerful state. Thus, in retrospect, the requests to pray for the government seem like an escape from responsibility. We thought that intercession for the rulers would exclude opposition activities against their misdeeds.

However, those in the opposition groups had God's Word on their side when, following the prayer services for peace, they demanded righteous activities on the part of the state. This is how we see it today. "Praying and performing righteous deeds" (Bonhoeffer) must exist together in a proper relationship. We made it too easy for ourselves when we said, "Only prayer can help." To be sure, I am not speaking on behalf of a superficial balance between prayer and action. An "equalizing of the burden" or a quota arrangement between those who pray and those who take action doesn't help. But a congregation, or even an association of congregations, must see to it whether "caring for the peace of the city . . . and praying for it" exist in a lively relationship of tension that enables the expenditure of energy in both directions.

At the present time we are excited about freedom, a government based on law, and democracy, all of which have suddenly come upon us. Many individuals have become involved in this awakening who really are reluctant to follow the democratic path, one which will be full of sweat, thorns, and thistles. Honest, industrious Christians are needed in politics. Bringing to bear an outlook on life that is shaped by the Gospel, they must participate in the political parties, citizens' movements, trade unions, sports' clubs, and special interest groups. Their involvement in these groups provides a brand new opportunity to bear witness to Christ in our society.

But there are also limits. A pastor must decide whether he will remain as a pastor or become a politician. The church of Jesus Christ in the GDR has for forty-five years tenaciously withstood that "ism" called "real, existing socialism" that wanted to get rid of religion. This resistance was, in my opinion, more courageous and more effective than the resistance to National Socialism. Now, new isms are vying for our attention, ones that have the lure of novelty. They will probably find their way into political life, but the community of Jesus must not be seduced from its actual task by these. The church was able to withstand the political demands of the past forty-five years because it dedicated itself to people. Instead of the "real, existing socialism," it served real, existing people, and that must continue. Slogans can be switched terribly quickly, and often no change occurs in the ones who chanted the old ones and today shout the new ones.

But there are also people who are left with nothing. They truly believed in socialism and brought their offerings to the party which claimed it was always right. And like good children, they wanted praise for this. They were starry-eyed idealists, romantic and religious, who gave themselves over to the party rituals—initiation rites and other ceremonies with godparents or guarantors when some "holy" document was given out and the pictures of their "gods" were decorated with flags and flowers. Blessed was the man who stood face to face with one of these gods and had a medal pinned on his chest. Only now have they come to realize that every ism basically ruins its followers.

The church is sent to aid those whose faith in an ism has been shattered. Such individuals abound in the countries of the Eastern Bloc. But can't they be found elsewhere as well?

It will be of no help to them whatsoever, if we merely paste a few new slogans onto a Gospel that has demonstrated its power even in the winter of socialism. People need the deep, caring love of Christians. I don't believe we can lead men and women to Christ who have been shaken to the core and have just awakened out of their stupor just by using a few Christian slogans and rituals in mass evangelism meetings. They need our total, personal loving concern.

At the moment, Christians in the GDR are being asked in an extraordinary way to help put "everything" right again. As Jeremiah 29 shows us, we have to build and plant and we must rescue our industry, agriculture, commerce, and distribution systems from chaos. We cannot minimize the deep concerns that people have about the value of their money, salary or pension, life savings, and housing costs. Whoever is looking for a spiritual awakening must not ignore this opportunity. The nineteenth-century churches made a great mistake by passing over the needs of the working population in the name of "higher values." But at the same time, a renewed, united Germany needs more than the Deutschmark and a flourishing economy. Many people in our country are now experiencing a spiritual and moral breakdown. We are seeing the bitter fruits of an upbringing grounded in self-centered materialism which in reality was cleverly used for the purpose of mutual surveillance and denunciation.

We as individuals whom Christ has set free for freedom (Gal. 5:1) have been given the grand opportunity to go to these manipulated people. We who are free may turn to any other person, whoever that might be, even if his name is Erich Honecker. We are surrounded by those who have been shamelessly used—broken people who subscribed to a "cause" with every fiber of their being. In so doing, they gave up their own self, family, colleagues, and neighbors. We Christians, as authentic human beings, can help them to avoid ever again attaching their faith to a "cause," to an ism of some kind. They need the Lord whom we freely follow. No course of political action, as necessary as this may be, can replace the pastoral task of the local church.

In addition to the tension between the political and pastoral dimension, Jeremiah calls attention to another area of tension, namely, that between the oppressive present and the promising future. Israel, which was a united kingdom under David and Solomon, had been divided. Afterwards one of the halves disappeared and the other is in its last gasps. The prophet promises a new beginning, but it will require time. He counsels his people in exile in a pragmatic, practical way. Roll up your sleeves and get to work, even though the promised future still has not taken on any definite form.

The people surely have their doubts. They debate and speculate, both those still in a Jerusalem that is bleeding to death and those now in a Babylon that is exuding vitality. The opinions vary widely, from working for the restoration of the old kingdom to revenge against their enemies, to acceptance of and accommodation to a permanent existence in opulent Babylon, or to even the hope for something completely new. To understand better the background of this situation, one needs to look at the writings of Jeremiah's contemporary, the prophet Ezekiel.

Now, we must not carry these historical comparisons too far. To be sure, the Preacher is correct when he says: "There is nothing new under the sun" (Eccl. 1:9). The basic patterns of human actions haven't changed through the ages and that can make us very pessimistic. But it is also true that history doesn't repeat itself exactly. God can always be counted on for surprises, a fact we have experienced so impressively in the last months. For years we thought history was creeping like a snail and that nothing would ever change. Then suddenly history leaps forward like a kangaroo, and our minds and souls can't keep up. We realize that God determines the tempo, the "day and hour" (Matt. 24:36). Whoever is familiar with the biblical story can move within a framework of God's saving grace and not lose track of oneself.

Believers today are being challenged from various quarters to trust in their feelings, or to cite the great poet Goethe: "Feeling is everything; a name is sound and smoke." The existing Christian congregations seem to have lost their heads. Many in the GDR have become panicky in the face of such rapid change, but I don't see salvation for them in an emotion-laden gospel. God tells the exiles in Babylon, where feelings are surging, that he has "thoughts of peace" for them: "I know the thoughts that I think toward you" (v. 11, AV). The Hebrew word here is often translated as *thoughts* or *thinking*, and it conveys the ideas of calculating and planning. Reflective thinking is now "in" during the Babylonian exile, and Jeremiah turns his pastor's heart in this direction. It is not that God disregards our feelings, but rather He utilizes them in such a way as to focus our reflections upon His *shalom* and consideration of its future.

Now we must go beyond Jeremiah 29 and fit the relationship of tension between the present and the future into a framework involving the entire Bible. To do this, we will use the keyword *seeking*. To seek the welfare of the society involves seeking the righteousness of God's reign (Matt. 6:33), and acknowledging that we have no continuing city here, but rather we seek the one that is to come (Heb. 13:14). This is a harmonic triad, not a dissonance where the one excludes the other. For those disciples of Jesus who want to do what is best for this world, a knowledge of the coming kingdom of God is indispensable. Only if we are assured of justice for ourselves and of a future and a hope for the world will we have the strength to contend for justice and peace now. In Matthew 6:25-34 Jesus uses the birds and flowers as a comparison. He argues from the worlds of creation and experience, which is the methodology of biblical wisdom teaching. But at the climax of his speech he moves experience and reason into the light of God's coming kingdom. In this light things turn out to be unreasonable that we presently consider reasonable.

In other words, we constantly must keep our actions open to God's correction. Whenever we become too comfortable and self-satisfied in our earthly ways, our spiritual lungs no longer function and we die from "a fatty degeneration of the heart." In our pastoral dealings with people in this present age, a time where everything is pressing in on us, we must remember that no city or country is a "continuing one" for us. This does not remove us from existing situations; Christians live in the midst of them just as all other citizens do. But the future God has promised bestows on us the position of being a "city on a hill" (Matt 5:14). Here, people torn by conflicting feelings of concern and hope, panic and indifference, can see the total picture.

Time plays an important role in the political-pastoral demands presently being made upon the community of Jesus in the GDR. "We need time and we don't have it," is a comment we often hear. Our strained nerves are focused simultaneously on the past, present, and future. It may have been the same for the exiles of Judah in Babylon. How then does the prophet help them in their state of spiritual emergency? He provides a message that "doesn't suit the times." He tells them, they have time.

God's Word often fits into our thoughts and plans so well that it picks them up along the way. But then things don't continue in the same direction. Instead, God brings about a change of direction so that we are going along the way He wants us to. In this age of hectic activity and paralyzing inactivity, well-founded concern and unfounded panicmongering, we need the message that "doesn't suit the times" Our time is God's time; it is in His hands. We have time.

Looking at the past, we must deal with sin. For many Germans today this seems to be the most needless task and greatest hindrance to getting on with life. Still, it must be tackled along with structuring the present and planning for the future. The ones who remained in Jerusalem and those who had already "emigrated" to Babylon so long ago weren't spared this either: "The sin of the house of Israel and Judah is exceedingly great; the land is full of bloodshed and the city is full of injustice" (Ezek. 9:9).

I refer to the guilt of the people in the GDR, both Christians and non-Christians. Whether people in the other German state should engage in similar sorrow and repentance for sin is not up to a citizen of the GDR to judge. We have enough to do with our own problem of guilt. Not only do we have the last forty-five years to deal with, but also the twelve years prior to that. It was drilled into us that history in the "Workers and Farmers State" began in the Year Zero (1945), free from Nazi defilement. The most convenient way to get rid of the past is to push responsibility off onto a few key individuals. Naturally, the members of the Politburo and Central Committee of the party that ruled over all were the ones mainly at fault.

However, when Gregor Gysi, the current chairman of the former SED, suddenly declared that guilt is always an individual matter, then he covered up the fact that his party claimed it was always right. Another SED slogan was "The party is the truth." This collective claim to the truth must therefore stand up to the accusation of collective guilt. Individuals who submitted to the party's discipline and cheered those who drummed the slogans into their heads share in this collective responsibility. This same is for the members of the so-called block parties who marched in step with the SED. Of course, there are gradations in the extent of guilt according to the level of peoples' positions in the government, institutions, factories, and schools. Some were more active participants than others.

Party doctrine trained people to think in black and white, friend and foe categories. A citizen had to love the GDR and hate the evil enemy of the working class. There were no shades of gray. Now this unrealistic system has been turned upside down. Hatred is directed at a handful of corrupt criminals, while the "people" are good, pure, and beautiful. There is nothing worthwhile at all to be found in the old GDR; our salvation comes from the West. Overcome by shame, the true heroes of the people are withdrawing from the fray. Still others deal with the tension by shifting the blame and excusing themselves, something which we Germans are masters at doing. To deal with our guilt would mean learning how to differentiate, to see the shades of gray, and not just always to condemn others.

Do churches and Christians also have guilt to confess? Certainly we can thank God that the community of Christians and the testimony of the churches emerged from the collapse of "real socialism" in better shape than after the end of National Socialism in 1945. This time, the church was the stronghold of the opposition and the cradle of the revolution. It accepted responsibility for people oppressed by the system and opened its doors to the groups that would not conform. This was especially apparent in the ecumenical gatherings of the later 1980s where virtually all Christian churches openly declared themselves against the state built on oppression.

But, concealed under the cloak of the biblical admonition to "seek the peace of the city" were some unsavory developments. There were Christians, members of a political party which called itself Christian, who not only accepted the Marxist-Leninist party's claim to absolute leadership but also propagated its philosophy and encouraged believers to become involved with its subordinate organizations. But they were a small minority and most church members soon saw through this attitude. Today it is clear that these "court preachers" for the state party really were nothing more than false prophets.

The majority of believers sought the welfare of the city by performing good works for the community and endured their hardships in silence. Not only did they suffer from the oppressive relationships that everyone experienced here, but also under the special disadvantages reserved for Christians. Their children were among the most gifted and industrious pupils in the Marxist-Leninist schools, but higher education for them was out of the question. This disadvantage was carried over into the world of work. Entire professional and occupational areas like teaching, the bar, and law enforcement were off-limits to anyone who did not pass the ideological litmus test.

Often, Christians from the Western democracies asked us why we did not stand up more openly against this system of injustice. Well, we bore a portion of the judgment of God upon the German people after 1945, and this affected German Christianity as well. Our part of the burden was suffering under the policy of the atheistic victors who thought they could eradicate the Christian faith. Since that didn't succeed, the unbelieving rulers tried to come to terms with the powerless Christians by also using the slogan: "Seek the peace of the city." A certain amount of historical distance is needed before we can say how high the percentage of those who fought against the all-powerful state were genuine Christians and how extensive their guilt was.

One example will serve to show how deeply into the dimension of "secret sin" the church reached in its dealings with the state. Christians and churches in the GDR received millions of marks worth of aid from their Western brothers and sisters, some of which was channeled through Genex, a purchasing firm operated as a front by the SED. Foreigners would pay in D-Marks for items imported from the West, like cars and electronic goods, which would then be given to GDR citizens. Without knowing it, the Christian donors and those receiving such aid were strengthening the position of this atheistic party. What Christian, even if he lives in the freest of countries, can remain untouched by sin when functioning in the realm of politics? We have to depend on the forgiveness of God even in the new democratic Germany now approaching.

Also, relevant to present concerns is the untimely sound that rang forth from Jeremiah 29, namely, patience. Neither the Israelites in Babylon nor those still in Jerusalem had any sympathy for this word. They preferred to hear loud slogans and prophecies about the speedy restoration of the old relationships, the bringing back of the temple vessels, and the return to their homeland. They are lies, says Jeremiah, and those who pronounce them are false prophets. Get accustomed to the idea that it is going to take time.

The process of rethinking in the eastern part of Germany, if it actually does occur, will take time, regardless of whether one Germany is simply grafted onto the other one or both grow together. The wounds of the spirit do not heal under the bandaid of a fast economic cure. For example, how quickly will a new generation of teachers emerge to replace the present one that is so spiritually warped? Or how can the legal system of a state built upon injustice pass judgment on its own crimes? Wouldn't that be the same as if Roland Freisler (the judge who condemned those involved in the July 20, 1944 assassination plot) were to sit in judgment against Hitler? After 1945 we learned that no *Persilschein* (a letter of recommendation that a person facing denazification proceedings obtained to show he was "clean" of Nazi crimes) could spare us from the spiritual-moral processes needed for a real change of heart. These take a little longer.

Do not misunderstand. Patience in the biblical sense is not a passive waiting for something to happen, but rather it is actively bearing up under one's load. If God called Christians to help carry the burden of our people during the last forty-five years, then this call is still in effect after the *Wende*. Both we and those in the West must keep working together to seek "the peace of the city."

Real patience also requires guarding against precipitous radicalism. What happened on New Year's Eve at the Brandenburg Gate in Berlin is a case in point. During that joyful night people celebrated enthusiastically the new freedom which they had gained through peaceful struggle. But then some got carried away with the occasion and climbed on the scaffolding surrounding the monument which was under renovation. It collapsed under the weight of the mob, injuring several. What happened occurs whenever radicalism is involved. The scaffolding, from which the people wanted everything and at once, simply did not hold up.

Through radicalism the scaffolding of freedom collapses, and the tender plant of democracy is buried under the resulting chaos, death and destruction. Even the writer Stefan Heym, actually an atheist, referred to these events as "a sign from God."

Christians need not be incapacitated by the pressure of time. Their actions can be objective and patient since their future stands under the sign of "grace." I am using the outmoded word *Huld* for grace. When someone tells me that he is fond (*hold*) of me, he considers me at best to be fantastic, O.K., great. But this old German word "graciousness" conveys well the meaning of what "a future and a hope" God wants to give us. The steadfast love of God for his people includes an about-face and a return home, a new Jerusalem, prayers that are heard, and thoughts of peace. And this "future" will come, but after "70 years have been accomplished in Babylon" (Jer. 29:10 AV). Until that day arrives, God's people are to keep on working right where they are now, in unloved Babylon, advancing the *shalom* of the heathen land where they are "strangers and foreigners."

In the Bible "future" has two meanings. On the one hand is the "grammatical future," that which proceeds from the present through human planning and organizing. The other is the Advent of God, which will take place not as a result of our planning. We do not have any control over it, but we can open ourselves to it in active anticipation.

God has come to us in a surprising way and given us a new Germany. We can work together in shaping its future, but it still will not be the "new Jerusalem." As I said in 1984:

> Babylon, the place you have experienced that is so proud and self-confident; Babylon, where your faith and service have to prove themselves under great trials; Babylon, is not the final end The tensions and testings in an abnormal world aren't God's ultimate purpose for you. The place where you now live is neither paradise nor hell. It is the superpower Babylon which some day come to an end.

This end has come more quickly than we thought. It came upon us as a harbinger of God's gracious (*huldvoll*) future. Let us not squander this experience as we take part in the planting and building of a new order in Germany, in Europe, and in the whole world. Who else then, if not we Christians, could tackle this? We do not need to wait until all of our guilt has been taken care of. We can begin with patience, because God's graciousness long ago provided for our future.

Christmas Letter
Jörg Swoboda

During a visit in the Federal Republic in December 1989, people complained to me repeatedly that letters from the GDR so seldom talked about the joy surrounding the fall of the Berlin Wall. This was, after all, the long-awaited collapse of the old system. Of course, the Wall was really the most important symbol of the SED rule, as well as the inner helplessness of the old leaders. The "antifascist protective wall," as they called it, actually was intended to keep our own people from running away, for the old system was something you wanted to run away from.

The Wall, however, was only the most visible symbol of the oppression that was part and parcel of our daily existence. When the Wall finally fell, it was not certain what else would crumble along with it. Daily we rubbed ourselves raw on the state apparatus that still continued to exist. People were still being spied on and denounced. Highhanded functionaries continued to rule as though there had been no

Wende. The privileges of the SED had to be wrested from their hands by bitter struggle. For a long time, it was not clear whether we would win the struggle. For this reason, many could not really experience the joy that others did.

And so, this Christmas letter from our Baptist theological school did not mention the fall of the Wall. Still, it was marked by joy and thankfulness, but also by fear.

Dear Sisters and Brothers:

In the last few weeks many of you have let us know that we can count on your prayers. These indications of solidarity have encouraged us. We want to let you know how things are going. "And when the time was fulfilled. . . . " The word *Kairos* (time) describes perfectly what God has done for us so impressively during these days. Countless factors are suddenly at work, taking shape, coming together, and displaying the power that in these days has shaken our country to its very foundations and is forming it into something new.

It is dizzying when one considers the rapid tempo at which changes in our society are taking place. We are still poised right on the edge and the abyss of violence stares at us. Once again, the German people are experiencing how human gods plunge out of their self-made heavens. The leaders of yesterday were expelled from their parties and some will soon be placed on trial. The former head of our state, Erich Honecker, a few weeks ago poked fun at false Western news reports of his demise with the choice line: "Those who are declared dead live for a long time." Now he has been overthrown, is bedridden, and in serious condition. He doesn't know what he needs to fear more—the angel of death or a court trial.

One high party functionary told me: "You have it made! You knew, or at least suspected, all along what was going on. I believed it. We were lied to and deceived. I am facing the worst identity crisis of my life." The old leaders asserted that they had Marx in their bones, but they had Engels on their tongues and their businesses activities foremost. Those who believed and followed them are outraged at how the heroes of the antifascist resistance could turn out to be such scoundrels. All that we learn about the wheeling and dealing of these people arouses in many a desire for revenge. However, one of the new political groups, the

New Forum, admonishes us that we need "justice instead of revenge." The role reversal is hard to comprehend. Representatives of this people's movement which helped to get the ball rolling, have together with ministers and pastors used their own bodies to protect frightened officials of the former State Security Service, that once all-powerful agency of fear. This has been especially a challenge to us who are children of the heavenly Prince of Peace.

For the first time in its history, the GDR—the country born from Stalinism by forceps delivery and one which designates in its own name the people as the real political force—now has the chance to do justice to its name. The first attempt to do so in 1953 was quelled by tanks, but God preserved us from this on 9 October 1989. The bloodbath was already prepared. The State Security Service head, Erich Mielke, had said: "Finish them off, the swine!" The people of Leipzig went to the demonstration that day as if to their own funeral.

Four weeks later, when nearly one million men, women, and children took part in the most massive demonstration in the history of the GDR in East Berlin, it was absolutely clear that this people had overcome the spirit that kept them silent for so long. Once again, history books are being rewritten. All those things are wrong which people, either in good faith or under the threat of punishment, had formerly considered to be right. Now, many have embarked on a spiritual search.

To be permitted at this Advent and Christmas time to proclaim the message that "Jesus Christ is the same yesterday, today, and forever" has proven to be God's special encouragement in the face of the momentous collapse and the radical changes accompanying it. We ask you to thank God together with us for all that He has done, and to pray that we will recognize what we must do new and differently in our transformed circumstances. God challenges us with this new freedom. We need to know what direction to take.

We greet you in the name of Him who came as a helpless infant, became our salvation on the Cross, is sitting at the right hand of God, and will return again as Lord,

J. Swoboda, along with the faculty and entire seminary community

Bridge over Troubled Wall
Jörg Swoboda, January 1990

We Christians in the GDR will be forever grateful to the tireless bridge-builders in the Federal Republic because they spanned the gap during these years of separation with their prayers, visits, and gifts of money and goods. We thank God for everyone who did not take the separation for granted and would not accept it as final. For years many took the demeaning procedures at the border in stride and refused to be deterred by them. What the Wall was meant to do but could not was prevent the contacts between us and you. Every attempt you made to bridge this gap was a blow at the Wall, which has now fallen and is being torn down.

In the political as well as the personal level, East-West contacts were, and still are, a sensitive issue. An American whom I had met was completely stunned when I repeated back to him precisely the same promise that he had just made to me. I will relate the incident because it fits in so well with the topic. He assured me that he would pray for us Christians in the GDR. I answered that I would also pray for the Christians in the USA. He hadn't counted on that, and he dumbfoundedly asked why Americans would need intercessory prayers "Made in the GDR."

In my answer I gave him something to chew on. In the United States the temptation to become an atheist perhaps wears the face of dollar-religion; here in the GDR it is the face of an atheistic ideology. But behind these two and thousands of other faces lies the same tempter. The greatest joy for a human being is not to live in the West, but rather to be a child of God. For us the most marvelous thing we experience is that God is in our country. He doesn't put us on the shelf because of either the practical atheism of mammon in the West or the theoretically based atheism of communism in the East.

False compassion never was the right medicine for us anyway, because our self-pity and whining stank to high heaven. In recent years this attitude paralyzed large segments of the church here. We looked to the West, compared ourselves point for point with it, and decided all those things weren't possible for us here, instead of taking advantage of the limited opportunities we did have. We reacted as did Jesus' disciples before the feeding of the five thousand: "But what are they among so many?" (John 6:9 AV). Not very many brought their "bread" and "fishes" to Jesus and had them blessed by God. We had, in fact, many more opportunities in the area of missionary activity than we actually used. We were kidding ourselves when we explained the mass exodus from the churches as solely the result of our atheistic environment. Just looking at the Federal Republic could have told us that this was due more to internal than external factors. Now with our newly gained freedom we have even more opportunities than before.

God gives us our freedom and takes away our excuses. We desire to learn how God is challenging us in this new situation.

Whoever builds bridges is familiar with both the obstacles to contacts between the two Germanies and the communication traps. At one time or another almost everyone has fallen into one. For example, a Westerner came to visit a friend in the East. Since they haven't seen each other for a long time, they have a lot to say. Well, then, where shall we begin? Whether it is due to embarrassment following the enthusiastic greeting at the door or to a lapse in thought caused by the long car trip, after first assuring each another that everything is fine they begin talking about the most inappropriate topics. These include: all the things that one can't get in the East but still can get in the West and in ever greater quantities; what isn't working here but of course does there; and how everything perhaps will turn out all right now that the border is open. Now the fun begins.

Both of them feel their ears getting hot and their lips dry. The economy of the GDR is in shambles; that is clear. Communist mismanagement is at fault, just as the enemies of the working class had always and aptly insisted! The Easterner says this loudly and with obvious enjoyment so that the entire house hears it. With their newly won freedom people can now laugh out loud without coming under suspicion because the Stasi doesn't exist anymore. Or does it?

Where did the Westerner spend his last vacation? Was he at an island resort in the North Sea or in Israel with his own wife? Yes, in fact, he has been to Israel twice. Man! Oh, well. He keeps on asking questions, still in unbelief: Did you pay a reasonable price for the new Toyota? It's unbelievable! The Easterner swallows and can hardly control himself any more. For his new Trabant he had to wait five years longer than the twelve he expected to wait, and let's not even talk about the price. But perhaps everything will be different now. He is completely astonished and complains bitterly. "Yes,' he says pensively. "With you people it's all different." But that isn't the end of it. The Westerner rambles on.

The face of the Easterner grows sad as he realizes he can rejoice no longer. He becomes uneasy as his friend keeps on enumerating Western freedoms. Confronted with all the glitzy products and state-of-the-art technology, he feels himself getting smaller and smaller and terribly inferior. His heart grows heavy within him. The conversation gets more and more strained. Finally, he says nothing at all. He stares at his stomach so that the Westerner can't see his eyes and sighs deeply. The conversation continues haltingly. The visitor feels ill at ease. Instinctively he sizes up the situation. "But look," he tries to console the Easterner, "the price of bread and the rents are so much lower here." And since his host won't respond anymore, the Westerner groans in a whining fashion, with a touch of reproach in his voice: "In the Federal Republic all of this isn't really so simple as the Easterners imagine it to be." The latter motions for him to stop.

We will let the scene fade out here.   In the final analysis, what really counts in life is certainly not how much money we earn. For this reason, I have learned from such awkward conversations to rank the topics I will discuss. My basic principle is that people are more important than things. First we learn about one another and then we go on to more specific matters. Caring for other people causes the heart to take notice and is the key to building a long-lasting relationship.

From the experience of the Christian community at Corinth we can draw a clear lesson. Paul repeatedly told these believers that they must put aside all distractions and turn back to Jesus. The only thing that could tie together the conglomeration of people that comprised this church, one that was the mirror image of a socially fragmented society, was the blood of Christ. The highly diverse congregation at Corinth found that community was possible only when it allowed Jesus to remain the central focus. If the main concern had been their standard of living, the community would have come apart.

I have experienced the deepest sense of community with Christians from the Federal Republic when Jesus was our main concern, over and beyond other matters, regardless of how important they might seem. But I cannot conceal the fact that I was eager to see what a guest brought as a gift, especially if he or she came from the West. Often it was like a little Christmas celebration. In our family all eyes would light up. Sometimes it would be tasty yogurt in a brightly colored container, something that was quite an improvement over the socialist standard yogurt produced in one of the "people's own factories," whose label "temporary packaging" clumsily excused the entire miserable situation.

But it surely is more than an aesthetic problem. Only the person who knows how we in the countryside would look helplessly and angrily at empty stores for weeks and months, sometimes even in the middle of summer, even though in these shops fruit and vegetables were pictured, can understand the joy that bananas and oranges, or even grapes brought us. During such a time when gifts are presented, both of us experienced a brief moment of awkwardness. I amused my friends by calling this the "Santa Claus Syndrome."

On the other hand, I have seen how really necessary things were given to us with a patronizing gesture. At such times I was very uneasy, but actually I don't want to attach too much importance to this. Some rather strange scenarios result when people feel uncertain or, on occasions, superior. But I am very frustrated when a guest pointedly declines our hospitality because he claims he doesn't want to be a financial burden to us. That is stupid. We haven't gone hungry, except maybe in the 1950s. Perhaps what I am offering him isn't quite up to his usual level. But when someone is a guest, that is precisely what he is, a guest.

Likewise, it hurts us when a gift we bring along from the GDR to someone in the West is at first turned down. "You really didn't have to bring us anything. We don't need that." That's true. Almost everything can be found in the shops and boutiques of the Federal Republic and of much better quality. It is a fundamental principle that the symbolic value of most gifts is far greater than their actual value anyway. Many times a present is given as a cheerful gesture, although its material worth is trivial. Only the message that a gift conveys is a measure of its true value. So it is with our presents as well.

It is surely not out of order to say that material help given us in the GDR by faithful friends even proved to be a factor in stabilizing family life. Through these gifts many a mother could stay at home in spite of the father's low salary and thereby devote herself to the upbringing of the children. How many marriages fell apart because both husband and wife hade to work.

Let me give a personal example. From my salary alone we would not have been able to clothe our four children. Our friends in the West provided us faithfully with (for the most part) used children's clothing. Occasionally they asked us if we felt offended. Not at all, I said, because everything was useable and clean. They assured us diplomatically that several families in their own congregations helped one another as well by exchanging used children's clothing. On the other hand, we have experienced quite the opposite with other people we know. Many things were said or done that were not very wise. But I am tactless from time to time as well.

A good basis for all giving and receiving among Christians is the biblical concept of stewardship. Every Christian is the steward of the time, possessions, and talents which God has entrusted to him. To each person he provides what is necessary. When someone gives to another out of his or her own supply, the recipient can rely on the fact that all good gifts come from above. When I had inhibitions about accepting a gift, it always comforted me when a friend said: "God gave this to me; I am passing it on to you."

I have found the following to be helpful: Whenever offers of help are made, it should be clearly stated what is, and what is not, intended. If someone is allowed to express specific wishes about what he or she would like to have, the financial parameters for its fulfillment should be discussed. Should a particular relationship develop at some time that is designed for the purpose of arranging for aid or delivering to someone, this should also be made clear. Anything else will lead to embarrassment and misunderstanding.

Our family enjoyed a special blessing when friends invited us to make our first trip together into the Federal Republic. Because the pastor there was being given a festive farewell, we found ourselves in the midst of a grand, warmhearted time of fellowship. Of course, we spent three hours shopping as well. Our children's eyes were popping out of their sockets, since a shopping center bedecked with Christmas decorations is a veritable dream castle. We made many comparisons and observations. As one child put it: "Everything is possible here." But as the main emphasis of our trip was so firmly fixed on family and community, we were able to get everything back into perspective again.

Such visits with families have been very helpful. During these many misunderstandings have been straightened out. We saw, for example, that even the people in the Federal Republic could not buy everything. And we knew some, thank God, who did not buy everything that they in fact could.

If there is one thing that typifies West Germans, it is their fascinating independence. There is a fantastic certainty in their manner. When we see them on our streets we will more likely recognize them by this characteristic than by their clothing or the healthy color of their skin. To be sure, most of their faces reveal their vitamin-rich nutrition.

With many of these individuals, this independence is more the result of not having any concerns about material want than an expression of mature character. "Having" and "Being," however, are horses of a different color. A high salary does not guarantee a meaningful life; in fact, it doesn't really even provide one with security. This type of independence inevitably comes back to haunt such individuals, since the basis for interpersonal relationships lies in material things. Because such people have no physical needs, they hardly have any need for other people either. In the final analysis one is sufficient unto himself, and the result is the atomization of society. Probably this is a reason for the lack of warmth and closeness in the society of the Federal Republic. Even in many congregations one can feel a cold chill running up and down the spine. But this problem is no stranger to us either.

As long as I can remember, West German guests visiting in the GDR said something when they were about to leave which on the surface seemed like a polite gesture. Later I came to view it in a much different light. They commented that although they couldn't explain why, they felt especially good during their stay with us and would take this feeling home as a gift. Further, they would like to come back again, which they often did.

Here is the reason why. The external pressure was so great here, but God kept the socialist damage to us in check. He made a virtue out of our necessity. In our congregations we were compelled to stick together and found ourselves much more dependent upon one another. So at the interpersonal level there was probably a lot more interaction than in the West. Our guests strongly sensed this closeness and warmth. At the same time, they were surprised they could speak openly in a setting free of ideology that lay in the midst of an environment dominated by oppressive forces which prevented any calm and open discussion of problems.

These encounters repeatedly helped us to evaluate our own self-worth. We too suffered from the consumerist urge, but at a rather different level. Honecker and his ideological, scatterbrained cronies pounded into our heads the idea that socialism was concerned with satisfying ever-growing needs. What he didn't mention was that he was referring to his own needs. One only needed to look beyond the edge of the newspaper to see how things really were. More problematic was the constant comparison we made between Western television ads and our day-to-day existence. It only stands to reason that when little fulfillment results from big dreams, a great sense of frustration results. For four decades we have internalized this. We too have our complexes regarding our brethren in the West, and we are gradually working these off.

The fact that we Christians in the East had intrinsic value to our guests and that they expressed this to us, meant a great deal to us. It loosened the knots in our stomachs caused by thinking we had to offer them something that we really couldn't offer anyway. In fact, we didn't need to offer them anything, because they hadn't come to eat and drink. This corrected a misunderstanding, and our growing self-esteem made us more sure of ourselves, relaxed, and happy.

Now the Wall is gone. Many possibilities stand before us, but many unanswered questions remain open. For example, we have to determine how we can do together for Jesus what we had previously done separately, and do it better.

To be sure, this really never was a question. The worldwide body of Christ is indivisible. The Christians in both parts of

Germany belong together. What God has joined together, let no man put asunder.

The Meaning of the Revolution

Richard V. Pierard

East Germany is no more. The first workers' and farmers' state on German soil proved to be the last one, and after reunification it was absorbed into the Federal Republic. All the old state-owned business enterprises and collective farms were sold off or privatized, and people (or their heirs) who had lost property during the Communist era were allowed to reclaim these lands and buildings and oust the current occupants. New people from the West replaced the functionaries, public officials, teachers, and almost anybody else associated with the old system. Most of them either retired, found different positions in the new order, or simply faded into the woodwork. Vast infusions of Western capital and diligent labor on the part of Easterners resulted in a building boom not unlike that in West Germany after World War II. Old factories were razed and run-down buildings and houses refurbished, and cranes dotted the urban landscapes like trees as new structures sprang up everywhere.

It is amazing how quickly the signs of the GDR disappeared. The ubiquitous statues of Lenin and Ernst Thälmann (leader of the Communist Party in the last years of the Weimar Republic and a secular saint) have largely vanished. Most of the streets and squares that had been renamed for Karl Marx, Friedrich Engels, an assortment of German and other Communists, and events in the GDR's history have their old names back or received new ones. The Berlin Wall and the border fortifications have been totally removed. All that remains to remind people of the ugly structures that marked the cleavage of Germany are a few sections in a museum setting, the pieces chipped off by thousands of *Mauerspechte* ("wall woodpeckers") kept by private collectors around the world, and a few signs warning strollers along the old demarcation line about the danger of unexploded landmines. The Russian troops have departed, but they left behind horrendously polluted areas where their bases once were.

Also there is a legacy of bitterness. The opening of the State Security Service files revealed how friends betrayed friends and neighbors spied upon neighbors, and the churches were just as seriously affected as other segments of society. Those who were discovered to have been compromised by their Stasi connections found it difficult if not impossible to find a place in the new regime. The victims of the previous order (and there were many) harbored deep resentments against their former oppressors. On the other hand, those who believed in the socialist system were dismayed by the total collapse of what they had worked to build. Unemployment rates soared in a society where one full employment (albeit at a low level of compensation) had once existed. The feelings of dissatisfaction were reflected in the rise of ultraright extremism of the skinhead and neo-Nazi movements, violence against foreign residents, and the resurgence of the left in the form of the revitalized Party of Democratic Socialism (the former SED). Its voting strength in the working class areas of East Berlin and elsewhere in the East was sufficient to guarantee it several seats in the Bundestag, now the all-German parliament.

Lessons of the East-German Revolution

Although East Germany was only a brief episode in the 2,000 year history of Germany and its details have been relegated to the history books, Christians today can draw inspiration from the courage of the people who went from prayer services to the streets with nothing in their hands but lighted candles. That demonstrators in Berlin, Leipzig, Dresden, and hundreds of other cities and towns across the German Democratic Republic could march week after week without evoking violent confrontations with the police would be understood as a miracle.

Christians would say that the way events came together reflected the power of God in the world. For instance, who could expected the rise to power of Michael Gorbachev and his program of *glastnost* in the Soviet Union? Because of the deteriorating East German economy, Honecker needed Soviet support more than ever if his regime were to survive the social and economic crises tearing at the fiber of his country. But Gorbachev's decision to promote reform at home stimulated demands for reforms elsewhere in the Soviet bloc and it meant that Honecker was doomed.

Another noteworthy thing about the fall of 1989 was the remarkable weather. Day after day of sunny and mild conditions facilitated the demonstrations. The cold, foggy, and rainy weather that so often marks the autumn in this part of Germany for the most part held off until the middle of November, and by then the regime had come apart.

Another miraculous happening was that no order to shoot at the Leipzig demonstrators was given on 9 October, although most people fully expected it. The actions of the border guards, both on the Berlin Wall and at the fences separating the two Germanies, which resulted in the loss of hundreds of lives over the past three decades, left no doubt that a tyrannical government which shot at its own citizens would do the same with demonstrators. The brutal police actions against protesters in Dresden and Berlin during the previous few days were further indication that the regime was ready to crack down. However, the "Chinese solution" was not implemented; Tiananmen Square was not replicated in Berlin.

The opening of the borders on the evening of 9 November was yet another unexpected event. Obviously some relaxation of travel restrictions was going to have take place, because the regime could not allow the hemorrhage of its people to continue indefinitely. But the suddenness of the decision and the willingness of the authorities to accommodate the vast numbers who wanted to cross over into West Berlin by opening up new crossings were stunning surprises. Such a reversal of policy escapes human explanation. It is no wonder that so many Christians regarded this too as a manifestation of supernatural power.

The second lesson of the *Wende* is that evil will not always prevail. The contributors to this book are virtually of one mind that the GDR regime was an evil one. But they also recognized that God does permit bad governments to exist and that Christians must bear witness in these contexts even though they suffer discrimination, persecution, and worse. We are called to serve God in wicked systems as well as in those more compatible with our way of thinking, that is, the ones which respect our freedoms and may even render allegiance to the Almighty.

Of course we focus our attention on the Eschaton, God's coming kingdom, the blessed hope of Christ's return to rule on earth, and this hope gives us strength for living in these trouble times. However, the events of 1989 demonstrate that God may step into the historical process at any time of His own choosing and strike down some wicked enterprise of humankind. God is here and he is not always silent. He does hear the prayers of His people and will move to cut off evildoers. This is surely the hope of the future, but God does not have to wait until then to take action in His world. He may act at any moment.

At the same time, He expects us to be involved in the struggle. He gives us the spiritual utensils to withstand the Evil One and to resist temptations. Many Christians in the GDR learned how God could enable them to develop community and to help one another in the common struggle to remain faithful to the divine calling. To these Christians he also gave the power of hope in a time of deep distress, when for their faith they were excluded from good jobs and denied promotions, and their children were not allowed to study at the universities. They knew that God had not forgotten His people.

The third lesson is that of the power of nonviolence. The strength which thousands of people armed with nothing more than prayers and lighted candles could manifest defies the imagination. As Martin Luther King, Jr. had shown in the civil rights movement in the United States, a government which knows only violence is rendered impotent by the forces of nonviolence. In the long run, the weapons of the spirit are more powerful than the water cannons, tear gas, guns, and tanks of a wicked system.

Individual men and women manifested "civil courage" in the face of this morally decrepit regime and simply but forcefully said "no" to its demands. Following the biblical examples of Deborah and Esther, of Nathan and Amos, and of Jeremiah and Daniel, these East German citizens spoke truth to power. They risked their jobs, incomes, reputations, and above all their lives in the cause of justice. They in turn can be held up as role models for people elsewhere, now and in the future, who engage in such struggles.

The final lesson is that we must heed God's call to ministry in whatever circumstances he has placed us. The Christians of East Germany, albeit hesitantly and uncertain, eventually rose to the challenge placed before them. Instead of fleeing to the West where they would have enjoyed a comfortable and probably fulfilling life, so many of them chose to stay in their homeland and contend for righteousness. It was not easy for those who for decades had been oppressed and marginalized to stand up and assume positions of leadership in the revolution and in shaping the new order in their country.

What Lies Ahead?

Although considerable time has elapsed since 1989 and Germany is now again one country, Christians still have problems to deal with. The struggle to come to terms with the Communist past will occupy people for many years. The compromises of many prominent church figures with the GDR regime are well known, and the government could count on the loyalty of the "church in socialism." On the other hand, the state had been in existence for forty years, and as a member of the UN, a signatory of the Helsinki Agreement, and recognized by the United States, it was a legitimate member of the international community. It was the client of one of the world's two superpowers, and there was no good reason to believe that the GDR might not endure for decades.

People in the West probably ought not to be too critical of the Protestant church's ties with the state, given their own records of accommodation and commitment to religious establishments. In fact, the Baptists as free church people actually stood to benefit from the Communist regime's disestablishment of the Protestant church, since they would no longer be disadvantaged simply because they belonged to a minority faith. However, the heavy hand of dictatorship fell equally upon all Christians, and so the Baptists were fully justified in taking an active role in the revolution of 1989.

The most difficult aspect of overcoming the Communist past will be that of the secret police, the Ministry for State Security. As mentioned above, the churches as well were honeycombed with informers and so many people were caught in the all-pervasive web of complicity and intrigue that the security service had spun. Continuing revelations from the Stasi files made it clear how serious the problem was. Were the compromises made with the security forces necessary or justifiable for the survival of the church under such a dictatorship? Were people coerced into going along with the demands of the police out of fear, blackmail, or intense pressure? Can those who compromised or spied on others repent of their sins and be received back into their congregations? Should the Protestant church as a body issue a confession of guilt for the mistakes it made in the GDR era?

The bottom line is that in a totalistic order like that of East Germany the citizens were both victims and accomplices. They were watched and persecuted, but at the same time they had to cooperate on some level if they were to lead a normal life. Each step they took, whether in be filling out forms, participating in a mass organization, giving into bureaucratic demands, or joining a political party, made it easier to function within their society. At the same time, these moves made it more difficult than ever to resist its total demands.

The Revolution of the Candles is one of the truly remarkable events of our time. The courageous populace challenged and defeated a brutal dictatorship with the weapons of the spirit. A regime that was morally and spiritually bankrupt was brought before the bar of divine justice and condemned to destruction. Christians who belonged to various confessional and denominational groupings joined hands with the other democratic forces in the GDR and played key roles in the movement for freedom, dismantling of the old order, and reconstruction of the state on a more just and equitable basis.

God has shown that He is alive and in charge. To be sure, His ways are not our ways, and we do not always understand His actions in the historical process. But we can rest assured that even in the darkest hours, all things will work out to our good. The lights of ten thousand candles remind us that God will triumph over evil, even as the resurrection of His Son insures that we will triumph over death. The light of Jesus Christ shines in the darkness, and the darkness will not overcome it (John 1:5). He who is the light of the world has promised us victory over the forces of evil. The ruins of Communism bear testimony to this truth.

Bibliography

Besier, Gerhard. *Der SED-Staat und die Kirche: Der Weg in die Anpassung.* München: C. Bertelsmann, 1993.

_____, and Stephan Wolf, eds. *"Pfarrer, Christen und Katholiken": Das Ministerium für Staatssicherheit der ehemaligen DDR und die Kirchen.* Neukirchen-Vluyn: Neukirchner Verlag, 1992.

Conway, John S. "The 'Stasi' and the Churches: Between Coercion and Compromise in East German Protestantism, 1949–1989," *Journal of Church and State* 36 (Autumn 1994): 725-45.

Dick, Rainer, and Jörg Swoboda, eds. *Bei rot über die Kreuzung: Theo Lehmann auf der Spur.* Neukirchen-Vluyn: Aussaat Verlag, 1994.

Ehring, Klaus and Martin Dallwitz. *Schwerter zu Pflugscharen: Friedensbewegung in der DDR.* Reinbek: Rowohlt, 1982.

Gauck, Joachim. *Die Stasi-Akten: Das unheimliche Erbe der DDR.* Reinbek: Rowohlt, 1991.

Gill, David and Ulrich Schröter. *Das Ministerium für Staatssicherheit: Anatomie des Mielke-Imperiums.* Berlin: Rowohlt, 1991.

Goeckel, Robert F. *The Lutheran Church and the East German State: Political Conflict and Change under Ulbricht and Honecker.* Ithaca NY: Cornell University Press, 1990.

Hahn, Annegret, et al., eds. *4 November '89: Der Protest, die Menschen, die Reden.* Berlin: Propyläen Verlag, 1990.

Hamel, Johannes. *A Christian in East Germany.* New York: Association Press, 1960.

Hanisch, Günter. *Dona nobis pacem: Fürbitten und Friedensgebete: Herbst '89 in Leipzig.* Berlin: Evangelische Verlagsanstalt, 1990.

Henke, Klaus-Dietmar. *Wann bricht schon mal ein Staat zusammen!* München: Deutscher Taschenbuch Verlag, 1993.

Herles, Helmut and Ewald Rose. *Vom Runden Tisch zum Parlament.* Bonn: Bouvier, 1990.

Hugler, Klaus. *Missbrauchtes Vertrauen: Christliche Jugendarbeit unter den Augen der Stasi.* Neukirchen-Vluyn: Aussaat Verlag, 1994.

Israel, Jürgen. *Zur Freiheit berufen: Die Kirche in der DDR als Schutzraum der Opposition 1981–1989.* Berlin: Aufbau Verlag, 1991.

Jarausch, Konrad H. *The Rush to German Unity*. New York: Oxford University Press, 1994.

Joppke, Christian. *East German Dissidents and the Revolution of 1989: Social Movement in a Leninist Regime*. New York: New York University Press, 1995.

Koch, Hans-Gerhard. *Staat und Kirche in der DDR*. Stuttgart: Quell Verlag, 1975.

Lang, Ewald, ed. *Wendehals und Stasi-Laus: Demo-Sprüche aus der DDR*. München: Wilhelm Heyne Verlag, 1990.

Latk, Klaus-Reiner. *Stasi-Kirche*. Uhldingen: Stephanus-Edition, 1992.

Leich, Werner. *Wechselnde Horizonte: Mein Leben in vier politischen Systemen*. Wuppertal: R. Brockhaus, 1992.

Links, Christoph and Hannes Bahrmann. *Wir sind das Volk: Die DDR im Aufbruch, eine Chronik*. Berlin: Aufbau Verlag, 1990.

Maleck, Bernhard. *Wolfgang Ullmann: "Ich werde nicht schweigen."* Berlin: Dietz Verlag, 1991.

Materne, Ulrich, and Günter Balders. *Erlebt in der DDR: Berichte aus dem Bund Evangelisch-Freikirchlicher Gemeinden*. Wuppertal and Kassel: Oncken Verlag, 1995.

Maser, Peter. *Glauben im Sozialismus*. Berlin: Verlag Gebr. Holzapfel, 1989.

_____. *Kirchen und Religionsgemeinschaften in der DDR 1949–1989*. Konstanz: Christliche Verlagsanstalt, 1992.

Neubert, Ehrhart. *Vergebung oder Weisswäscherei: Zur Aufarbeitung des Stasiproblems in den Kirchen*. Freiburg i.B.: Herder, 1993.

Ökumensiche Versammlung für Gerechtigkeit, Frieden und Bewahrung der Schöpfung: Eine Dokumentation. Berlin: Aktion Sühnezeichen/Friedensdienste, 1990.

Oktober 1989: Wider den Schlaf der Vernunft. Berlin: Elefanten Press, 1989.

Philipsen, Dirk. *We Were the People: Voices from East Germany's Revolutionary Autumn of 1989*. Durham NC: Duke University Press, 1993.

Pierard, Richard V. "The Church and the Revolution in East Germany," *Covenant Quarterly* 48 (November 1990): 43-52.

_____. "Civil Religiosity in a Marxist-Leninist Country: The Example of East Germany," *Christian Scholar's Review* 22 (December 1992): 116-30.

_____. "Informers or Resisters? The East German Secret Police and the Church," *Christian Scholar's Review*, forthcoming.

_____. "Religion and the East German Revolution," *Journal of Church and State* 32 (Summer 1990): 501-509.

Rein, Gerhard, ed.. *Die protestantische Revolution 1987–1990: Ein deutsches Lesebuch*. Berlin: Wichern-Verlag, 1990.

_____. *Die Opposition in der DDR: Entwürfe für einen anderen Sozialismus.* Berlin: Wichern-Verlag, 1989.

Schnauze! Gedächtnisprotokolle 7. und 8. Oktober 1989: Berlin, Leipzig, Dresden. Berlin: Berliner Verlags-Anstalt Union, 1990.

Schönherr, Albrecht. *. . . aber die Zeit war nicht verloren.* Berlin: Aufbau Verlag, 1993.

Schorlemmer, Friedrich. *Bis alle Mauern fallen: Texte aus einem verschwundenen Land.* Berlin: Verlag der Nation, 1991.

_____. *Träume und Alpträume: Einmischungen 1982–1990.* Berlin: Verlag der Nation, 1990.

Schultz, Rudolf. *Nach der Wende: Wandlungen in Kirche und Gesellschaft.* Berlin: Wichern-Verlag, 1990.

Schumann, Frank, ed. *100 Tage, die die DDR erschütterten.* Berlin: Elefanten Press, 1990.

Siegele-Wenschkewitz, Leonore. *Die evangelischen Kirchen und der SED-Staat—ein Thema kirchlicher Zeitgeschichte.* Frankfurt/M.: Haag & Herchen, 1993.

Sievers, Hans-Jürgen. *Stundenbuch einer deutschen Revolution: Die Leipziger Kirchen im Oktober 1989.* Göttingen: Vandenhoeck & Ruprecht, 1990.

Solberg, Richard W. *God and Caesar in East Germany: The Conflicts of Church and State in East Germany since 1945.* New York: Macmillan, 1961.

Stolpe, Manfred. *Die Menschen Hoffnung geben.* Berlin: Wichern-Verlag, 1991.

Teztner, Reiner. *Leipziger Ring: Aufzeichnungen eines Montagsdemonstranten Oktober 1989 bis 1. Mai 1990.* Frankfurt/M.: Luchterhand Literaturverlag, 1990.

Turner, Henry Ashby. *The Two Germanies since 1945.* New Haven: Yale University Press, 1987.

Ullmann, Wolfgang. *Demokratie—jetzt oder nie! Perspektiven der Gerechtigkeit.* München: Kyrill & Method Verlag, 1990.

Weber, Christian. *Alltag einer friedlichen Revolution: Notizen aus der DDR.* Stuttgart: Quell Verlag, 1990.

Wolfe, Nancy Travis. *Policing a Socialist Society: The German Democratic Republic.* Westport CT: Greenwood Press, 1992.

The Revolution of the Candles.
Christians in the Revolution of the German Democratic Republic.

ISBN 0-86554-481-6. Catalog and warehouse pick number MUP/P125.
Mercer University Press, 6316 Peake Road, Macon, Georgia 31210-3960.
Text, interior, titles, and cover designs, composition and layout
    by Edd Rowell.
Camera-ready pages composed on a Gateway 2000 via WordPerfect
    dos 5.1 and wpwin 5.1/52, and printed on a Lasermaster 1000.
Text font: Palatino. Display and titles font: Shamrock.
Printed and bound by McNaughton & Gunn, Inc., Saline, Michigan 48176.
Printed via offset lithography on 50# Natural Offset (500 ppi)
    and perfect bound in 10-pt. c1s printed PMS 144 (yellow-red)
        and black with lay-flat film lamination.
Individually shrinkwrapped and bulk packed in cartons on skids.

[First printing June 1996]